UTILIZATION-FOCUSED EVALUATION

UTILIZATION–FOCUSED EVALUATION

Michael Quinn Patton

SAGE PUBLICATIONS   Beverly Hills/London

For information address:

SAGE PUBLICATIONS, INC.
275 South Beverly Drive
Beverly Hills, California 90212

SAGE PUBLICATIONS LTD
28 Banner Street
London EC1Y 8QE

Printed in the United States of America

Library of Congress Cataloging in Publication Data

Patton, Michael Quinn.
    Utilization focused evaluation.

    Bibliography: p. 292
    1. Evaluation research (Social action programs)—
United States. I. Title.
H62.P322   300'.1'8   78-2220
ISBN 0-8039-0982-9
ISBN 0-8039-0981-0 pbk.

SIXTH PRINTING

CONTENTS

TO VITO PERRONE

PREFACE

Sufi stories are tales used to pass on ancient wisdom. One such story is about a noted Sufi teacher, Mulla Nasrudin. Nasrudin was once asked to return to his home village to share his wisdom with the people there. He mounted a platform in the village square and asked rhetorically, "O my people, do you know what I am about to tell you?"

Some local rowdies, deciding to amuse themselves, shouted rhythmically, "NO. . . ! NO. . . ! NO. . . ! NO. . . !"

"In that case," said Mulla Nasrudin with dignity, "I shall abstain from trying to instruct such an ignorant community," and he stepped down from the platform.

The following week, having obtained an assurance from the hooligans that they would not repeat their harassment, the elders of the village again prevailed upon Nasrudin to address them. "O my people," he began again, "do you know what I am about to say to you?"

Some of the people, uncertain as to how to react, for he was gazing at them fiercely, muttered, "Yes."

"In that case," retorted Nasrudin, "there is no need for me to say more." He then left the village square.

On the third occasion, after a deputation of elders had again visited him and implored him to make one further effort, he stood before the people: "O my people! Do you know what I am about to say?"

Since he seemed to demand a reply, the villagers shouted, "Some of us do, and some of us do not."

"In that case," said Nasrudin as he withdrew, "let those who know teach those who do not." (adapted from Shah, 1964: 80-81).

This book records the things that I have learned about doing useful evaluation research from those who know. The pages which follow represent an accumulation of wisdom from many sources: from interviews with 40 federal decisionmakers and evaluators who participated in a study of the utilization of federal health evaluation research; from conversations with local program staffs about their evaluation experiences; from colleagues who are professional evaluators; and from participants in my evaluation workshops and university classes who are struggling to conduct useful evaluations. In particular, I have learned from postdoctoral and predoctoral trainees in the NIMH evaluation methodology training program at the University of Minnesota and from staff members of the Minnesota Center for Social Research with whom I have worked in conducting evaluations during the last several years.

The support of colleagues in the Department of Sociology and in the Hubert H. Humphrey Institute of Public Affairs at the University of Minnesota has also been important to the evaluation activities and research ideas from which UTILIZATION-FOCUSED EVALUATION has emerged; John Clark, Don McTavish, Tom Dewar, and John Brandl have been especially supportive and helpful. Jerald Hage has been particularly important to the development of the approach presented here. His personal encouragement and intellectual stimulation have been a major factor in my work since I studied under him at the University of Wisconsin. The influence of Marvin Alkin, Center for the Study of Evaluation, UCLA, is also strongly reflected throughout the book. In addition, I am most grateful to Marv for his careful and painstaking review of an earlier draft of this manuscript. His incisive comments saved the reader from many unnecessary diversions that would otherwise have appeared in what folllows.

There are also those very special people who have made this book possible through both their friendship and colleagueship. Ron Geizer essentially directed the Minnesota Center for Social Research during the summer and fall of 1977, so that I had time to work on the book. His enthusiasm, commitment, and humor have made working together on evaluations both useful *and* fun. Chris Haupert came back from Mexico to run the day-to-day operations of MCSR. She kept things running smoothly so that I could concentrate on writing. Sharon Studer, as friend and critic, undertook a very careful review of the book that led to substantial revisions in the final manuscript. Neala Yount, more than anyone else, literally labored over the manuscript page-by-page, sentence-by-sentence. She edited every chapter, making both stylistic and substantive suggestions. Nothing escaped her scrutiny as she prepared the final draft. On more than one occasion her subtle critique carried the day: after I had resisted suggested changes from others, Neala would sigh and say, "Well, it's your book, I guess you can decide if you want to put in a lot of crap!" Along the way, I learned that not only evaluators, but also authors, need thick skin. I suspect editors do too. Jeanne Campbell has been editor, critic, collaborator, and consultant. Most of all, she has been a source of power through her unwavering belief that the book would happen. That it did happen owes much to her caring, belief, and support.

This book records the things I have learned about doing useful evaluation research from those with whom I have shared evaluation ideas and experiences. The person from whom I have learned most is Vito Perrone, to whom this work is dedicated. Vito is a person who spends time in a place and leaves it different by his having been there. He touches programs by touching the people in programs. He listens, he hears, he shares, and he cares. Vito treats each person and each program as a unique entity. Thus he dislikes constructing models that, by their abstraction, lose sight of individual differences. He would, therefore, not be at all comfortable knowing that his approach to programs has been the model for what I call the "active-reactive-adaptive" process of program-evaluator interaction in UTILIZATION-FOCUSED EVALUATION. Vito Perrone is a person who knows how to do useful evaluation research and program development.

UTILIZATION-FOCUSED EVALUATION has emerged from many sources: studies of utilization; experiences conducting evaluation; current theories of formal organization and organizational dynamics; recent developments in decision-making theory and policy analysis; work in the diffusion of innovations and utilization of knowledge; and many sources in the rapidly growing evaluation research literature. But most of all, the book records what I have learned from the people with whom I have worked in doing evaluation research, the people mentioned above.

This book is both practical and theoretical. It tells readers how to conduct evaluation research and why to conduct it in the manner prescribed. Each chapter contains both a review of the relevant literature and actual case examples to illustrate major points. Finally, the book is written in an advocacy style; a definite point of view is offered. The approach presented here is derived from the observation that much of what passes for evaluation research is not very useful; *that evaluation research ought to be useful*; and therefore that something different must be done if such research *is* to be useful. This book tries to suggest what it is that should be done differently.

Minneapolis, Minnesota   *Michael Quinn Patton*
December, 1977

Chapter 1

THE EMERGENCE OF EVALUATION RESEARCH

A Setting

It is early morning on a cold November day in Minnesota. Some 15 people in various states of wakefulness have gathered to discuss a county evaluation program. They constitute the Evaluation Advisory Board for a county human service agency. The internal evaluation staff is there; the citizen evaluation advisory board representatives are present; the county board and state representatives have arrived; and I represent the academic community. We are assembled at this early hour to review the past year's evaluation efforts.

The evaluator explains what her staff has done during the year, the problems with getting started (fuzzy program goals, uncertain funding); the data collection problems (lack of staff, little program cooperation, inconsistent state and county data processing systems); the management problems (unclear decisionmaking hierarchies, political undercurrents, trying to do too much); and the findings despite it all ("tentative to be sure but more than we knew a year ago and some solid recommendations").

Then the advisory board explains its frustration with the disappointing results of the evaluation ("data just aren't solid enough"). The county board representatives explain why their decisions are contrary to evaluation recommendations ("we didn't really get the information we needed when we wanted it and it wasn't what we wanted when we got it"). The room is filled with disappointment, frustration, defensiveness, cynicism, and more than a little anger. There are charges, countercharges, budget threats, moments of planning, and longer moments of explaining away problems. Then the advisory board chairperson turns to me in exasperation and asks: "Tell us, what do we have to do to produce good evaluation research that actually gets used?"

The Issue of Utilization

This book is an outgrowth of that question. If the scene I have pictured were unique, it would represent a professional problem for the people involved and would be a largely personal trouble in a local milieu. But if that scene were repeated over and over on many mornings, with many advisory boards, and if that question of how to produce good evaluation research that is used were asked by many people in many milieux, then the question of utilization of evaluation research would be what C. Wright Mills (1959: 8-9) called a public issue:

> *Issues* have to do with matters that transcend these local environments of the individual and the range of his inner life. They have to do with the organization of many such milieux into the institutions of an historical society as a whole. . . . An issue, in fact, often involves a crisis in institutional arrangements.

In my judgment, the utilization of evaluation research represents such a crisis in institutional arrangements. This issue of utilization has emerged at the interface between science and government. It has to do with our fundamental assumptions about human rationality, progress, and science applied to the creation of a better world. The utilization of research crisis concerns the spending of billions of dollars in private and public funds to fight problems of poverty, disease, joblessness, mental anguish, crime, hunger and inequality. How are programs to combat these societal ills to be judged? How does one distinguish effective from ineffective programs?

To understand a public issue or crisis, C. Wright Mills advised us to begin with the historical context out of which the issue emerged. To establish a context for understanding the utilization crisis in evaluation research, it may be helpful to briefly review the historical emergence of evaluation research and to contrast it to two alternative and competing models of program assessment. The emergence of evaluation research is quite recent. Until the 1960s, evaluation of human service programs was based largely on one of two models: the charity model or the pork barrel model.

The Charity Model

The charity model has dominated the private and semiprivate delivery of health, education, and welfare programs. Under the charity model, the criterion for evaluation of programs is the sincerity of funders and program staff; the measure of program worth is that program organizers care enough to try their best to help the less fortunate. The charities are modern manifestations and adaptations of the Good Samaritan example; and as God mandated helping the less fortunate, so God alone will judge the outcomes and effectiveness of these charity efforts. God clearly needs no assistance from the likes of social scientists with their impersonal statistics and objective analyses of human suffering.

The charity model is still the dominant operations approach to evaluation of most philanthropic, privately funded human service programs, e.g., United Way efforts, foundation-supported programs, and church-related welfare activities. As a director of a local service agency explained to me after a recent two day evaluation workshop,

> This scientific evaluation stuff is all very interesting, and I suppose it's something we're going to have to do for funders. But when it comes right down to it, my program is evaluated every night when I get down on my knees and ask God to look into my heart and judge what I do by His criteria. And, by God, so long as His evaluation is positive we'll keep on serving and helping people.

Or as another agency director told me after a measurement session, "All I want to know is whether or not my staff are trying their best. When you've got a valid and reliable and all-that-other-stuff measuring instrument for love and sincerity, you can come back and see me."

Social scientists as evaluators have little to offer those who are fully ensconced in the charity model. Others, however (and their numbers are increasing), have come to believe that, even for the sincere, there are program options and alternative courses of action. Scientific evaluation, then, is not a test of a staff's faith, hope, and charity. Rather, it is a mechanism for determining whether or not staff energies and charitable resources are being expended effectively. Negative findings should not be construed as an attack on staff motivations, but rather as a means of focusing on the fruitfulness of the specific actions that spring from these motivations.

The Pork Barrel Approach

The second major model of evaluating programs has been the pork barrel approach, which takes as its outcome criteria for program evaluation the strength and leverage of the program's constituency. The issue in this case is not one of program effectiveness, but rather one of political efficacy. If powerful constituents want the program, or if more is to be gained politically by support for rather than opposition to the program, then the program is judged worthwhile; no other evidence of program effectiveness is relevant. This is the reason it is so difficult to terminate programs and agencies once they are created by government bodies. Programs rapidly develop constituencies whose vested interests lie in program continuation. The rationale is to give out money where it counts politically, not where it will be used most effectively.

The pork barrel approach is not unique to elected politicians and governmental bodies. The funding boards of philanthropic foundations and service agencies have their own constituencies to please. There are political debts to be paid and political debts to be incurred. The inter-locking directorates of philanthropic funding bodies make for some interesting politics. Under these conditions, program effectiveness is not judged in terms of demonstrable attainment of stated objectives; on the contrary, the issue is whether or not parochial and partisan interests will be served by funding certain programs. Those programs are effective which enhance and serve vested interests.

The Emergence of Evaluation Research

The idea of scientifically evaluating government programs for decision-making is relatively new. When the federal government began to take a major role in human service programs during the Depression and the New Deal, the closest thing to evaluation was the employment of a few jobless academics to write program histories. It was not until the massive federal expenditures on an awesome assortment of programs during the 1960s and 1970s that accountability began to mean more than assessing staff sincerity or political headcounts of opponents and proponents. A number of events converged to create a demand for systematic evaluation of the effectiveness of government programs.

First, in education, there was a growing critique of American schools after the Soviets launched Sputnik in 1957, a critique born of fear that the education gap was even larger than the "missile gap"; there was the growing realization that ten years after the 1954 Brown decision "separate and unequal" was still the norm rather than the exception; and there was enormous pressure on schools as the focus of parents' upward mobility dreams for their children. As sociologists Blau and Duncan (1967) explained, education has become the major mechanism for social mobility in modern society. Parents wanted effective schools. The critiques of schools gave rise to a massive influx of federal money aimed at desegregation, innovation, compensatory education, greater equality of opportunity, teacher training, and higher student achievement. Evaluation research was needed to provide data on how the many programmatic changes inflicted on the nation's children really made an educational difference.

But education was only one arena in the War on Poverty. Great Society programs from the Office of Economic Opportunity were aimed at nothing less than the elimination of poverty, if not before man landed on the moon then certainly shortly thereafter. The nation's health delivery systems were found to be highly effective at ignoring the needs of the poor and elderly; the only real health debate was over which had been most ignored— physical health needs or mental health needs. The creation of large-scale federal health programs, including community mental health centers, was coupled with a mandate for evaluation, often one percent to three percent of total budgets.

Other major programs were created in housing, manpower, services integration, community planning, urban renewal, welfare, and so on, the whole of which came to be referred to as "butter" (as opposed to "guns") expenditures. These Great Society programs collided head-on with the Vietnam War, rising inflation, increasing taxes, and the fall from glory of Keynesian economics. All in all, it was what sociologists and social historians, with a penchant for understatement, would characterize as "a period of rapid social and economic change."

From all the turmoil of that period, something called "evaluation research" emerged as an alternative to the charity and pork barrel approaches to assessing program effectiveness. By the early 1970s, evaluations were being regularly required of health, education, and welfare programs. Although the requirement for evaluation research was a political response to the perceived demand for increased governmental accountability, the evaluation research approach to accountability is quite different from the pork barrel approach to program assessment.

Evaluation research as an alternative approach to judging programs was born of two lessons from this period of large-scale social experimentation and government intervention: first, the fact that there is not enough money to do all the things that need doing; and secondly, the realization that even if there were enough money, it takes more than money to solve complex human and social problems.

While there is still debate about whether or not Great Society programs were ever really sufficiently funded and implemented to test their effectiveness, there is considerably more humility among experienced social activists in the late 1970s about our ability to quickly eliminate long-standing social and economic injustices. The demands for government programs far outstrip the ability of even the most liberal Congress to respond across the board. Expectations and human wants have an uncanny ability to stay well ahead of institutional response capacities. Even if we manage to provide minimum levels of support to all families so as to eliminate poverty in an absolute sense, we can be assured that feelings of relative deprivation will keep the need for new social programs alive and well in the foreseeable future. Since not everything can be done, there must be a basis for deciding which things will be done. Evaluation research (and policy research in general) is not about to replace politics in that decisionmaking process, but applied social science research is one mechanism for facilitating the making of difficult decisions *in an attempt to get as much as possible from the money that is spent.* Evaluation research can not only take the heat off decisionmakers by providing data (reasons) for making unpopular decisions in a world where everything you do makes someone unhappy; but evaluation research is also good politics in its own right: if we do not have enough money to do everything and please everyone, we can at least increase the odds of doing something and pleasing someone by funding demonstrably effective programs.

Secondly, the Great Society programs clearly demonstrated that money is not enough even when it is abundant. The failures of the War on Poverty cannot all be attributed to inadequate funds. Some of those failures were due to too much funding too quickly. There were management problems, cultural issues, and enormously complex psychological dimensions to poverty programs. Wanting to help is not the same as knowing how to help; likewise, having the money to help is not the same as knowing how to spend money in a helpful way. Poverty programs turned out to be patronizing, controlling, dependency-generating, insulting, inadequate, over-promised, mismanaged, misguided and missionary. If money alone is not the answer (and, again, there is still argument on this point), then some mechanism must be found for identifying what combination of factors will work in a specific situation. Some poverty programs were enormously effective; others were awesome disasters. How do we know which ones were which—and how do we find out what made the difference? Evaluation research offers at least a partial solution.

Faith, hope, and charity tell us to do something, but do not tell us what to do. The pork barrel approach to evaluation works best when program constituents are easily identified as more or less important. But in a world where every group is highly politicized, funds are limited, and every decision to do something means a corresponding decision not to do something else, legislators, government officials, and foundation trustees are becoming more willing to at least consider the implications of data about differential program effectiveness before making their decisions.

Using Scientific Data for Decisionmaking: The Emergent Crisis

Concomitant with the optimism of the early 1960s that we would eliminate poverty was a new optimism about the role scientists could play in efforts to improve society. Edward Suchman (1967: 1) began his seminal textbook on evaluation research by quoting Hans Zetterberg to the effect that "one of the most appealing ideas of our century is the notion that science can be put to work to provide solutions to social problems." Social and behavioral science embodied the hope of finally applying human rationality to the improvement of society. By the early 1960s, Zetterberg's "appealing idea" was becoming a reality. Scientists were welcomed to the White House by President Kennedy. Scientific perspectives were taken into account in the writing of new social legislation. Economists, historians, psychologists, political scientists, and sociologists were all welcomed into the public arena to share in the reshaping of modern postindustrial society. Thus, concurrent with the elimination of poverty, the Great Society foretold a new order of rationality in government—a rationality undergirded by social scientists who, if not philosopher-kings themselves, were at least ministers to philosopher-kings. Carol Weiss (1977: 4) recalls the optimism of that period:

> There was much hoopla about the rationality that social science would bring to the untidy world of government. It would provide hard data for planning, evidence of need and of resources. It would give cause-and-effect theories for policy making, so that statesmen would know which variables

to alter in order to effect the desired outcomes. It would bring to the assessment of alternative policies a knowledge of relative costs and benefits, so that decision-makers could select the options with the highest payoff. And once policies were in operation, it would provide objective evaluation of their effectiveness so that necessary modifications could be made to improve performance.

One manifestation of the scope, pervasiveness, and penetration of these hopes is the number of evaluation studies actually conducted. While it is impossible to identify all such studies, the 1976 Congressional Sourcebook on Federal Program Evaluations contains 1700 citations of program evaluation reports issued by 18 executive branch agencies and the general accounting office during fiscal years 1973 through 1975 (Office of Program Analysis, GAO, 1976: 1).

Just as by the late 1960s we had discovered that poverty would not go away as easily as we had hoped, so the visions of government based on rational decisionmaking undergirded by scientific truth were beginning to fade. No sooner had the crises of Great Society social programs given rise to calls for greater accountability than scientists responded that their research was not being used. The utopian hopes for a scientific and rational society, so imminent in the early 1960s, had somehow been postponed. The landing of the first man on the moon had come and gone, but there was still poverty and research was still not being used as the basis for government decisionmaking.

While the utilization crisis concerned all types of applied social science (cf. Weiss, 1977), nonutilization seemed to be particularly characteristic of evaluation studies. Ernest House (1972: 412) put it this way: "Producing data is one thing! Getting it used is quite another." Williams and Evans (1969: 453) wrote that "in the final analysis, the test of the effectiveness of outcome data is its impact on implemented policy. By this standard, there is a dearth of successful evaluation studies." Wholey et al. (1970: 46) concluded that "the recent literature is unanimous in announcing the general failure of evaluation to affect decision-making in a significant way." They go on to note (1970: 48) that their own study "found the same absence of successful evaluations noted by other authors." Cohen and Garet (1975: 19) found that "there is little evidence to indicate that government planning offices have succeeded in linking social research and decision-making." Seymour Deitchman, in his "Tale of Social Research and Bureaucracy," concluded that "the impact of the research on the most important affairs of state was, with few exceptions, nil" (1976: 390). Weidman et al. (1973: 15) concluded that "on those rare occasions when evaluations studies have been used . . . the little use that has occurred [has been] fortuitous rather than planned." In 1972, Carol Weiss (1972c: 10-11) viewed underutilization as one of the foremost problems in evaluation research:

> Evaluation research is meant for immediate and direct use in improving the quality of social programming. Yet a review of evaluation experience suggests that evaluation results have not exerted significant influence on program decisions.

This conclusion is echoed by four prominent commissions and study committees: the U.S. House Committee on Government Operations, Research and Technical Programs Subcommittee (1967); the Young Committee report published by the National Academy of Sciences (1968); the Report of the Special Commission on the Social Sciences for the National Science Foundation (1968); and the Social Science Research Council's prospective on the Behavioral and Social Sciences (1969).

British economist L. J. Sharpe reported that the situation is the same in Europe. He reviewed the European literature and commission reports on utilization of social scientific knowledge and concluded that "we are brought face to face with the fact that it has proved very difficult to uncover many instances where social science research has had a clear and direct effect on policy even when it has been specifically commissioned by government" (1977: 45).

We are called back, then, to the early morning scene which opened this chapter. Decisionmakers lament the disappointing results of evaluation research, complaining that the findings do not tell them what they need to know. And evaluators complain about many things, "but their most common complaint is that their findings are ignored" (Weiss, 1972d: 319). The question remains: what do we have to do to produce good evaluation studies that are actually used?

Utilization-Focused Evaluation Research: A Comprehensive Approach

The question of how to enhance the usefulness and actual utilization of evaluation research is sufficiently complex that a piecemeal approach based on isolated prescriptions for practice is likely to have only piecemeal impact. The overall problem of underutilization of evaluation research will not be solved by compiling and following some long list of evaluation proverbs and axioms. Real world circumstances are too complex and unique to be routinely approached through the application of isolated pearls of evaluation wisdom. It is like trying to live your life according to Ben Franklin's *Almanac* or any of the full range of proverbial gems that constitute our cultural heritage. At the moment of decision, you reach into your socialization and remember: "he who hesitates is lost." But then again: "fools rush in where angels fear to tread." Advice to young evaluators is no less confusing: "work closely with decisionmakers to establish trust and rapport," but "maintain distance from program decisionmakers to guarantee objectivity and neutrality."

What is needed is a comprehensive approach to program assessment that provides an overall framework within which the individuals involved can proceed to develop an evaluation design with a built-in utilization component appropriate to the unique circumstances they encounter. In evaluation research, as in life, it is one's overall philosophy integrated into pragmatic principles that provides a guide to action. It is to that end that this book is directed, i.e., to development of a comprehensive utilization-focused approach to evaluation.

The next chapter considers the question of how to define utilization. This problem is approached empirically by asking a sample of federal decisionmakers and evaluators about the actual impact of studies in which they have been involved. The results of our interviews suggest that what is typically characterized as underutilization or nonutilization of evaluation research can be attributed in substantial degree to a definition of utilization that is too narrow and fails to take into consideration the nature of actual decisionmaking processes in most programs.

Based on the redefinition of utilization in Chapter 2, the third chapter explores the power of evaluation. By considering the political practice of conducting and using evaluation research, a theoretical perspective for understanding utilization is developed. Chapter 4 expands this theoretical perspective by linking the processes of utilization to specific decisionmakers and information users. Based on data from the federal utilization study, a variable called "the personal factor" is identified as the key element in explaining the impact of evaluation research. That factor serves as the basis for identifying and describing the first step in utilization-focused evaluation.

Chapter 5 considers the problem of bringing focus to an evaluation study. This chapter develops a question-oriented component as a major part of utilization-focused evaluation. Within that component are a series of options available to evaluators as they interact with decisionmakers and information users to focus the evaluation question. Those options include utilization-focused goals clarification (Chapters 6 and 7), implementation evaluation (Chapter 8), and framing the evaluation question in the context of the program's theory of action (Chapter 9).

Chapter 10 explores a utilization-focused approach to evaluation methods. Alternative paradigms of evaluation measurement and design are described and discussed. Chapter 11 considers the analysis, interpretation, and dissemination of evaluation data. In particular, this chapter is a final illustration of the theme that runs throughout the book, namely, that utilization is affected by every aspect of an evaluation, from initial conceptualization to data analysis and interpretation. The final chapter integrates this theme and the separate ideas contained within it to present an overview of the utilization-focused approach to evaluation.

A modern version of an ancient Asian story (adapted from Shah, 1964: 64) is helpful in explaining the nature of the search for utilization contained in this book.

> It is said that a man once found his neighbor down on his knees under a street lamp looking for something.
>
> "What have you lost, friend?"
>
> "My key," said the man on his knees.
>
> "After a few minutes of searching, the neighbor asked, "Where did you drop it?"
>
> "In that dark pasture," replied his friend.
>
> "Then why, for heaven's sake, are you looking here?"
>
> "Because there is more light here."

The easy and, perhaps, obvious place to look for utilization is in the concrete decisions made by evaluators and decisionmakers after a study is completed. What we shall find, however, is that the search for utilization takes us into the "dark pasture" of decisions made before any evaluation data are ever collected. The reader will find very little in this book about what to do when a study is over. At that point the potential for utilization has been largely determined. Utilization-focused evaluation emphasizes what happens in a study to determine its eventual impact before a final report is produced. The key to utilization will be found on the path the evaluation takes before the findings are exposed to the general light of public scrutiny.

Review

This chapter opened at an early morning meeting of an evaluation advisory board that ended with the question, "what do we have to do to produce good evaluation research that actually gets used?" This was not a unique scene. The utilization of evaluation research as a public issue is larger than the local, parochial troubles of individual evaluation advisory boards. It has to do with the uses of social research in many milieux that overlap and interpenetrate to form a larger social and historical pattern. The public issue of utilization reflects an institutional crisis that involves our fundamental assumptions about societal progress, human rationality, and scientific truth. Gene Glass (1976: 9) succinctly captured the multiple origins of the present crisis when he described the historical emergence of evaluation:

> From the ambitions of the academic disciplines, from the convulsive reforms of the educational system, from the battleground of the War on Poverty, from the ashes of the Great Society, from the reprisals of an indignant taxpaying public, there has emerged evaluation.

But the emergence of evaluation research has not meant a corresponding utilization of evaluation findings for rational decisionmaking. The consensus in the evaluation literature is that research findings are ignored in program decisionmaking. The evaluation research approach to assessment of program effectiveness offers an alternative to the charity model and the purely political assessments of programs done in classical pork barrel style, but the acceptance of this research approach will depend at least partly upon its usefulness to those makers of decisions whose own charity, politics, and research understanding are uncertain from the perspective of social scientists.

Nor does the solution lie in the application of piecemeal wisdom, as expressed in evaluation proverbs and provisos. Producing good evaluation studies that actually get used will require a comprehensive approach to the conduct of evaluation research. It is to that end that this book is directed—to development of a utilization-focused approach to evaluation that is comprehensive enough to be generally applicable, and practical enough to make a difference in particular situations. The theme that runs throughout this book is that a comprehensive approach means considering how utilization is affected by every aspect of an evaluation, from initial conceptualization to data analysis and interpretation. In the next two chapters, we lay the foundation for such an approach by examining the nature and consequences of research utilization.

Chapter 2

UTILIZATION IN PRACTICE:

AN EMPIRICAL PERSPECTIVE

A Setting

Picture a middle-aged and aging man sitting in his overpadded and aging chair. He is slouched in front of the television set watching a football game. It appears he has been sitting there watching football games for several days—college games, all star games, playoff games, Monday night football—it is probably the December-January holiday, football marathon season. He has several days growth of beard on his face; a beer can is held loosely in one hand, with several empties on the floor around his chair. The only movement is from the images on the screen. Even upon close inspection it is hard to tell whether he is awake or asleep.

Stage left, enter his wife and her female neighbor. As they pass through the room, the wife pauses by his chair and reflects aloud to her neighbor, "the question I ponder is not whether there is life after death, but rather, whether there is life after birth."

The Ontogeny of Evaluation: A Question of Definition

The question here is not whether some evaluation heaven exists where the souls of virtuous studies ascend after their physical remains have been laid to rest in an agency library or other cemetery for public documents. The question is whether there is life after birth. From the moment of birth, nay, from the moment of conception, how does the evaluation grow and develop, and as it grows and develops, how does it make its presence felt in the world around it? Does the existence of that evaluation make a difference? Does it impact on its environment? Or do evaluators, as a species, have an overly glorified, anthropocentric image of the importance of their work?

One might well construct a metaphysics of evaluation from such questions. But my purpose is more immediate and practical: to define utilization. Tracing the utilization ontogeny of any particular evaluation necessitates a definition of utilization so as to be able to recognize its presence or absence in any given case. The evaluation literature reviewed in the last chapter is overwhelming in its agreement that evaluation studies are not used in decisionmaking. But how would we recognize utilization if it occurred? What would life after birth be like for an evaluation study? What is the opposite of nonutilization?

Most of the literature on evaluation research never explicitly defines utilization. But there is an implicit definition: utilization occurs when there is an immediate, concrete, and observable effect on specific decisions and program activities resulting directly from evaluation research findings. This definition stems from the stated purpose of evaluation research, which is to gather data that can be used to make judgments about program effectiveness. If such data is gathered, then a judgment ought to follow. That judgment leads somewhat directly to concrete action and specific decisions. Carol Weiss (1972c: 10) made this view explicit: "Evaluation research is meant for immediate and direct use in improving the quality of social programming." It is this immediate and direct use that Weiss was speaking of when she concluded that "a review of evaluation experience suggests that evaluation results have generally not exerted significant influence on program decisions" (1972c: 11).

A Study of Utilization

If utilization is to be increased, it might be helpful to try to find a few positive examples that deviate from this norm of nonutilization. We could then study those examples of excellence to learn how to increase utilization. In the fall of 1975, participants in an evaluation methodology training program at the University of Minnesota decided to do just that. The program was in its fourth year. For three years these students, with support from the National Institute of Mental Health, had been studying evaluation methodology, reading the evaluation literature, critiquing evaluation studies, and conducting their own fieldwork projects in evaluation. It was a multidisciplinary group with students and faculty representing background in sociology, psychology, political science, geography, educational psychology, statistics, economics, social work, philosophy, and public affairs. The issue of research utilization was a personal one for these students. Under the auspices of the federal government, they were preparing for careers in applying social science research to the study of program effectiveness in order to improve the delivery of human services. They did not want merely to study the problem of human services delivery; they wanted to impact on those problems. I was among them.[1] We shared

the basic premise of the research-for-policy literature that using social science research for public policy making is a good thing. Use is good, more use is better, and increasing the use of social research means improving the quality of government decisions (Weiss, 1977: 4).

Because of this basic premise, we wanted to talk directly to *users* of evaluation research and find out how they defined utilization. In effect, we used an inductive approach to this problem of determining what is the opposite of nonutilization. We began without our own definition of research utilization and let a conceputalization of what utilization looks like emerge from the responses of federal decisionmakers. That study and the interview responses of those decisionmakers marked the beginning of the formulation of a utilization-focused approach to evaluation.

We conducted followup studies of 20 federal health evaluations. We attempted to assess the degree to which these evaluations had been used and to identify the factors that affected varying degrees of utilization. Given the pessimistic nature of most writings on utilization, we began our study fully expecting our major problem would be to find even one evaluation that had had a significant impact on program decisions. What we found was considerably more complex and less dismal than our original impressions led us to expect. Evaluation research is used, but not in ways we anticipated. The definition of utilization which emerged from this study is central to the utilization-focused approach to evaluation presented in this book.

A Definition of Evaluation Research and a Sample of Evaluations

The 20 case studies that constitute the sample in this study are national health program evaluations. They were selected from among 170 evaluations on file in the Office of Health Evaluation, HEW.[2] The process of selecting evaluation studies for inclusion in the sample necessitated developing a definition of evaluation research:

> *Evaluation research is the systematic collection of information about the activities and outcomes of actual programs in order for interested persons to make judgments about specific aspects of what the program is doing and affecting.*

Operationally fewer than half of the 170 HEW health studies classified as evaluations met our criteria for evaluation research.[3] This was because a large number of those studies were nonempirical think pieces or policy research studies aimed at social indicators in general rather than evaluation of specific programs.

For reasons of confidentiality, neither the actual programs evaluated nor the titles of the evaluation studies can be reported. However, we can present a general description of the final random sample. The 20 cases in this study consisted of four evaluations of various community mental health centers' program activities, four health training programs, two national assessments of laboratory proficiency, two evaluations of neighborhood health center programs, studies of two health services delivery systems programs, a training program on alcoholism, a health regulatory program, a federal loan forgiveness program, a training workshop evaluation, and two evaluations of specialized health facilities.

The types of evaluation studies in the final group of 20 cases ranged from a three week program review carried out by a single internal evaluator to a four year evaluation that cost a million and a half dollars. Six of the cases were internal evaluations and 14 were external.

Data on Utilization: The Interviewees

Because of very limited resources, it was possible to select only three key informants to be contacted and intensively interviewed about the utilization of each of the 20 cases in the final sample. These key informants were (1) the project officer for the study,[4] (2) the person *identified by the project officer* as being either the decisionmaker for the program evaluated or the person most knowledgeable about the study's impact, and (3) the evaluator who had major responsibility for the study. Most of the federal decisionmakers interviewed had been or now are Office Directors (and Deputy Directors), Division Heads, or Bureau Chiefs. Overall, these decisionmakers each represented an average of over 14 years' experience in the federal government.[5]

The evaluators in our sample were a rather heterogeneous group. Six of the 20 cases were internal evaluations, so the evaluators were federal administrators or researchers. In one case the evaluation was contracted from one unit of the federal government to another, so the evaluators were also federal researchers. The remaining 13 evaluations were conducted by private organizations or nongovernment employees, though several persons in this group had either formerly worked for the federal government or have since come to do so. Evaluators in our sample each represented an average of nearly 14 years' experience in conducting evaluative research.[6]

Interviews ranged in length from one to six hours, with an average length of about two hours. Interviews were taped and transcribed for analysis. At this point we are concerned only with the section of the interview that asked directly about utilization. Our question was as follows:

> Now we'd like to focus on the actual impact of this evaluation study. We'd like to get at any ways in which the study may have had an impact—an impact on program operations, on planning, on funding, on policy, on decisions, on thinking about the program, and so forth.
>
> From your point of view, what was the impact of this evaluation study on the program we've been discussing?

Following a set of probes and additional questions, depending upon the respondents' initial answers, we asked a question about the nonprogram impacts of the evaluations:

> We've been focusing mainly on the study's impact on the program itself. Sometimes studies have a broader impact on things beyond an immediate program, things like general thinking on issues that arise from a study, or position papers, or legislation.
>
> Did this evaluation have an impact on any of these kinds of things?

The analysis of the interviews began with general discussions in which the 17 interviewers shared their perceptions about their own interviews. Three staff members then independently read all interviews looking for patterns and themes. These processes led to the formation of tentative hypotheses about dominant themes. The interview transcripts were then examined again, searching for evidence supporting these tentative hypotheses as well as looking for contradictory evidence and counterexamples. Quotes extracted from the interviews as examples of particular points were then independently examined by other staff members to check for context and accuracy. Only those findings about which there was a high degree of consensus are reported in the pages which follow.

The Findings on Utilization

In response to the first question on impact, 78 percent of responding decisionmakers and 90 percent of responding evaluators felt that *the evaluation had had an impact on the program*. Moreover, 80 percent of responding decisionmakers and 70 percent of responding evaluators felt these specific evaluation studies had had identifiable nonprogram impacts.

The number of positive responses to the questions on impact is quite striking considering the predominance of the theme of nonutilization in the evaluation literature. The main difference here, however, may be that the actual participants in each specific evaluation process were asked to define impact in terms that were meaningful to them and their situations. Thus, none of the impacts described was of the type where new findings from an evaluation led directly and immediately to the making of major, concrete program decisions. The more typical impact was one where the evaluation findings provided additional pieces of information in the difficult puzzle of program action, permitting some reduction in the uncertainty within which any federal decisionmaker inevitably operates.

The most dramatic example of utilization reported in our sample was the case of an evaluation of a pilot program. The program administrator had been favorable to the program in principle, was uncertain what the results would be, but was "hoping the results would be positive." The evaluation proved to be negative. The administrator was "surprised, but not alarmingly so. . . . We had expected a more positive finding or we would not have engaged in the pilot studies" (DM367: 13).[7] The program was subsequently ended with the evaluation carrying "about a third of the weight of the total decision" (DM367: 8).

This relatively dramatic impact stood out as a clear exception to the more typical pattern where evaluation findings constitute additional input into an evolutionary process of program action. One decisionmaker with 29 years' experience in the federal government, much of that time directing research, gave the following report on the impact of the evaluation study about which he was interviewed:

> It served two purposes. One is that it resolved a lot of doubts and confusions and misunderstandings that the advisory committee had. . . . And the second one was that it gave me additional knowledge to support facts that I already knew, and, as I say, broadened the scope more than I realized. In other words, the perceptions of where the organization was going and what it was accomplishing were a lot worse than I had anticipated . . . but I was somewhat startled to find out that they were worse, yet is wasn't very hard because it was partly confirming things that I was observing (DM232: 17).

He goes on to say that, following the evaluation,

> we changed our whole functional approach to looking at the identification of what we should be working on. But again I have a hard time because these things, *none of these things occurred overnight, and in an evolutionary process it's hard to say, you know, at what point it made a significant difference or what point did it merely verify and strengthen the resolve that you already had* (DM232: 17).

This decisionmaker had become highly involved in applied government research, including his initiation of the study in our sample, because he believed research can help reduce uncertainty in decisionmaking:

> As time went on I more clearly recognized that I was not satisfied with having to make program decisions that I was making or that others were making based on "professional judgment." Not that it's bad or anything, it's just that it's pretty shaky at times, and you know, you always sit back and say, "now if I hadn't done that and done something else, what would have been the result?" So it's nice to find that there are better ways of doing it (DM232: 25).

Still, his assessment of the actual impact of the evaluation was quite constrained: "it filled in the gaps and pieces that various ones really had in their orientation to the program" (DM232: 12) and "it verified my suspicions" (DM232: 24).

Respondents frequently had difficulty assessing the degree to which an evaluation study actually affected decisions made after completion of the evaluation. This was true, for example, in the case of a large-scale evaluation effort that had been extremely expensive and had taken place over several years' time. The evaluation found some deficiencies in the program, but the overall findings were quite positive. Changes corresponding to those recommended in the study occurred when the report was published, but those changes could not be directly and simply attributed to the evaluation:

> The staff was aware that the activities in the centers were deficient from other studies that we had done, and they were beefing up these budgets and providing technical assistance to some of the projects and improving mental health activities. Now I can't link this finding and that activity. Again that confirms that finding and you say, eureka, I have found [the program] deficient, therefore I will [change] the program. That didn't happen. [The] deficiency was previously noted. A lot of studies like this confirmed what close-by people knew and they were already taking actions before the findings. *So you can't link the finding to the action, that's just confirmation. . . . The direct link between the finding and the program decision is very diffuse.* [Its major impact was] confirming our setting, a credibility, a tone of additional credibility to the program (DM361: 12, 13).

Moreover, this decisionmaker felt that additional credibility for the program became one part of an overall process of information flow that helped to some degree reduce the uncertainty faced by decisionmakers responsible for the program: "People in the budget channels at OMB were, I guess, eager for and interested in any data that would help them make decisions, and this was certainly one useful bit of data" (DM361: 13).

The kind of impact we found, then, was that evaluation research provided some additional information that was judged and used in the context of other available information to help reduce the unknowns in the making of difficult decisions. The impact ranged from "it sort of confirmed our impressions . . . confirming some other anecdotal information or impression that we had" (DM209: 7,1) to providing a new awareness carrying over into other programs:

> Some of our subsequent decisions on some of our other programs were probably based on information that came out of this study. . . . The most significant information from this study that we really had not realized . . . made an impact on future decisions with regard to other programs that we carry on (DM209: 7).

And why did it have this impact?

> Well I guess I'll go back to the points I've already made, that it confirmed some impressionistic feelings and anecdotal information that we had about certain kinds of things. At least it gave us some hard data on which to base

some future programming decisions. It may not have been the only data, but it was confirming data, and I think that's important. . . . And you know at the time this study was conceived, and even by the time it was reported to us, we really had very little data, and you know, probably *when you don't have any data, every little bit helps* (DM209: 15).

This reduction of uncertainty emerged as highly important to decision-makers. In some cases it simply made them more confident and determined. On the other hand, where the need for change is indicated an evaluation study can help speed up the process of change or provide an impetus for finally getting things rolling.

Well I think that all we did was probably speed up the process. I think that they were getting there anyhow. They knew that their performance was being criticized by various parts of the government and the private sector. As I said earlier, we didn't enter this study thinking that we were going to break any new ground, and when we got finished, we knew that we hadn't. All we did was document what the people have been saying for a long time— that _____ are doing a lousy job, so what else is new? But we were able to show just how poor a job they were doing (EV268: 12).

Reducing uncertainty, speeding things up, and getting things finally started are real impacts—not revolutionary, organization-shaking impacts—but real, important impacts in the opinion of the people we interviewed. One administrator summarized this view both on the specific evaluation in question and about evaluation in general as follows:

Well I've worn several hats. I've been on evaluation teams. I've participated in extensive evaluation in-house of other organizational components. Myself, I have a favorable view toward evaluating. If nothing else it precipitates activity many times that could not be precipitated without someone taking a hard look at an organization. It did precipitate activity in [this program]. Some of it was not positive. Some of it was negative. *At least something occurred that wouldn't have occurred if the evaluation hadn't taken place* (DM312: 21).

Another evaluator made it quite clear that simply reducing the enormous uncertainty facing program administrators is a major purpose of evaluative research:

One of the things I think often is that the government itself gets scared . . . of whatever kinds of new ventures that they want to go into, and they're quite uncertain as to what steps they want to take next. So then they say, okay, let's have some outside person do this for us, or maybe an inside person do this, so at least we have some "data" to base some of our policies on (EV283: 34).

The view of evaluation research that emerged in our interviews stands in stark contrast to the image of utilization that is presented as the ideal in the bulk of the evaluation literature. The ideal held forth in the literature is one of major impact on concrete decisions. The image that emerged in our interviews is that there are few major, direction-changing decisions in most programming, and that evaluation research is used as one piece of information that feeds into a slow, evolutionary process of program development. Program development is a process of "muddling through" (Lindblom, 1959; Allison, 1971; Steinbruner, 1974), and evaluation research is part of that muddling.

Neither did we find much expectation that government decisionmaking could be or should be otherwise. One person with 35 years' experience in the federal government (20 of those years in evaluation) put it like this: "I don't think an evaluation's ever totally used. That was true whether I was using them as an administrator or doing them myself" (EV346: 11). Later in the interview he said:

I don't think the government should go out and use every evaluation it gets. I think sometimes just the insights of the evaluation feed over to the next administrative reiteration, maybe just the right way to do it. That is, [decisions aren't] clearly the result of evaluation. There's a feedback in some way . . . upgrading or a shifting of direction because of it. [Change] is, you know, small and slow (EV 346: 16).

Another evaluator expressed a similar view.

I think it's just like everything else in life, if you're at the right place at the right time, it can be useful, but it's obviously only probably one ingredient in the information process. It's rather naive and presumptuous on the part of the evaluation community and also it presumes a rationality that in no way fits (EV264: 18).

Our findings, then, suggest that the predominant image of nonutilization that characterizes much of the commentary on evaluation research can be attributed in substantial degree to a definition of utilization that is too narrow in its emphasis on seeing immediate, direct, and concrete impact on program decisions. Such a narrow definition fails to take into account the nature of most actual program development processes. In effect, social scientists have failed to find evidence of research utilization because their narrow definition of utilization excluded the kinds of more limited impacts described by the decisionmakers we interviewed. In the past, the search for utilization has often been conducted like the search for contraband in the famous Sufi story about Nasrudin the smuggler.

> Nasrudin used to take his donkey across a frontier every day, with the panniers loaded with straw. Since he admitted to being a smuggler when he trudged home every night, the frontier guards searched him again and again. They searched his person, sifted the straw, steeped it in water, even burned it from time to time. Meanwhile he was becoming visibly more and more prosperous.
> Then he retired and went to live in another country. Here one of the customs officers met him, years later.
> "You can tell me now, Nasrudin," he said. "Whatever *was* it that you were smuggling, when we could never catch you at?"
> "Donkeys," said Nasrudin (Shah, 1964: 59).

Utilization of evaluation is there to see, but not if one is looking only for impacts of great moment. As Weiss (1977: 7) points out, many social scientists have come into applied government research with high hopes of rationalizing the system. They entered the arena of applied research expecting to make great policy waves and are disillusioned to find that they have only provided a few cogs in the great gears of program change and development, helped with a decision here or there, made actions more certain for a few decisionmakers.

Yet the situation seems little different in basic research. Researchers in any field of specialization can count the studies of major impact on one hand. Most science falls into that great amorphous activity called "normal science." Changes come slowly. Individual researchers contribute a bit here and bit there, reducing uncertainty gradually over time. Scientific revolutions are infrequent and slow in coming (Kuhn, 1970).

The situation is the same in applied research. Evaluation research is one part of the normal "science" of government decisionmaking. Research impacts in ripples, not in waves. Occasionally a major study emerges with great impact. But most applied research can be expected to make no more than a small and momentary splash in the great pond of government. The utilization of most studies is likely to sound something like this:

> [We expected that it would be used] but in a way of providing background information around the consequences of certain kinds of federal decision-making options. But not necessarily in and of itself determining those

decisions. In other words you might have some idea of what the consequences of the decision are, but there might be a lot of other factors you'd take into account in how you would decide.

It's part of a total atmosphere, and in the balance of things it's contributing another bit of information about the importance of this particular process, but by no means is it the only thing entering into what's going on in a policy review (DM264: 8, 11).

The Life and Death of Evaluation Studies: A Review

This chapter began by asking whether or not there is life after birth for evaluations. It ends with what might be an epitaph for the typical evaluation.

EVALUATION EPITAPH

Didn't change the course of history,
But certainly I did live.
I was put in for input
And input I did give.

This epitaph essentially summarizes the findings from our study of the utilization of federal health evaluations. We found in interviews with federal decisionmakers that evaluation research is used by decisionmakers, but not in the clearcut, organization-shaking ways in which social scientists sometimes believe research should be used. Our data suggest that what is typically characterized as underutilization or nonutilization of evaluation research can be attributed in substantial degree to a narrow definition of utilization that fails to take into consideration the nature of actual decisionmaking processes in most programs. Utilization of research findings is not something that suddenly and concretely occurs at some one distinct moment in time. Rather, utilization is a diffuse and gradual process of reducing decisionmaker uncertainty within an existing social context (cf. Levine and Levine, 1977).

Finally, it is important to understand how the view of utilization that emerges in this chapter establishes a context for utilization-focused evaluation. The utilization-focused approach is aimed at increasing the likelihood that evaluation input will be substantial, meaningful, and relevant. In that respect, the degree of utilization of the evaluations reviewed in this chapter can help us be realistic without accepting such levels of utilization as normative. It is the premise of this book that utilization of evaluation research can be increased and more carefully targeted, but evaluation findings will seldom have the enormous kind of influence envisioned by social scientists who wanted to rationalize decisionmaking processes. The potential for enhancing utilization lies less in its capability for rationalizing decisionmaking than in its capacity to empower the users of evaluation information.

NOTES

1. At the time of the study, I was Director of the NIMH Evaluation Methodology Program, University of Minnesota. The study was conducted through the Minnesota Center for Social Research, University of Minnesota. The following trainees participated in the project: Dale Blyth, Nancy Brennan, James Cleary, Joan Dreyer, James Fitzsimmons, Barbara French, Steve Froman, Kathy Gilder, Patricia Grimes, Kathy Guthrie, David Jones, Leah Harvey, Gary Miller, Gail Nordheim, Julia Nutter, Darla Sandhoffer, Jerome Segal, and John Townsend. A shorter version of this study was published under the title "In Search of Impact: An Analysis of the Utilization of Federal Health Evaluation Research" (Patton et al., 1977).

2. The Office of Health Evaluation coordinates most evaluation research in the health division of HEW. In 1971, this office designed a new recordkeeping system that collected abstracts from all evaluations coming through that office; 170 evaluations were collected during the period 1971-1973. This became the universe of evaluations from which we chose our final sample. We wish to express our thanks to HEW officials for their assistance throughout this research project, particularly Harry Cain, Director, Office of Policy Development and Planning, Office of the Assistant Secretary for Health, and Isadore Seeman, Director, Office of Health Evaluation, Office of the Assistant Secretary for Planning and Evaluation, DHEW.

3. Operationally there were only two criteria actually applied in coding HEW studies: (1) existence of an actual program that was the subject of the study and (2) some type of systematic data collection in the study.

4. The term "project officer" refers to the person in the federal government who was identified as having primary responsibility for administering the evaluation. For studies which were done by organizations which are not a part of the federal government, the project officer was the person who administered the federal government's contract with that organization.

5. In two of our 20 cases we had no information on decisionmaker experience; this average is based on 18 respondents.

6. In four of our 20 cases we had no information on evaluator's experience; this average is based on 16 respondents.

7. Citations for quotes taken from the interview transcripts will use the following format: (DM367: 13) refers to the transcript of an interview with a decisionmaker about evaluation study number 367. The quote is taken from page 13 of the transcript. The study numbers and page numbers have been systematically altered to protect the confidentiality of the interviewees. The study numbers do not correspond to any codes used within DHEW. Thus (EV201: 10) and (PO201: 6) refer to interviews about the same study, the former was an interview with the evaluator, the latter was an interview with the project officer.

Chapter 3

THE POWER OF EVALUATION

A Setting

During the 1975-1976 school year, the Kalamazoo Education Association (KEA), Kalamazoo, Michigan, was locked in battle with the local school administration over the Kalamazoo Schools Accountability System. The accountability system consisted of 13 components, including teacher and principal performance objectives, fall and spring standardized testing, teacher-constructed criterion-referenced tests in high school, parent, student, and principal evaluations of teachers, and teacher peer evaluations. The system had received considerable national attention. For example, *The American School Board Journal* editorialized in April (1974: 40) that by the summer of 1974 "Kalamazoo schools probably will have one of the most comprehensive computerized systems of personnel evaluation and accountability yet devised."

Yet conflict over the school system's accountability program had been high for several years; charges and countercharges had been exchanged regularly between the Kalamazoo Education Association and the Office of the Superintendent of Schools. The KEA, for example, charged that teachers were being demoralized; the Superintendent argued that teachers didn't want to be accountable. Political statements flowed with increasing frequency, making constructive dialogue difficult.

A central issue concerned the degree to which teachers throughout the system were supportive of or hostile to the accountability system. The KEA claimed widespread teacher dissatisfaction. The superintendent countered that the hostility to the system came largely from a vocal minority of malcontent unionists. The newspapers hinted that the administration might be so alienating teachers that the system could not operate effectively. School board members were nervous; an election was approaching and uncertainty about the administration's ability to manage the schools in the face of what appeared to be growing teacher hostility was potentially a major political issue.

Ordinarily, a situation of this kind would continue to be one of charge and countercharge based entirely on selective perception, with no underlying data to clarify and test the reality of the opposing positions. But early in 1976, the KEA sought outside assistance from Vito Perrone, Dean of the Center for Teaching and Learning, University of North Dakota. The KEA proposed that Dean Perrone conduct public hearings where interested parties could testify on and be questioned about the operations and consequences of the Kalamazoo Accountability System. Perrone suggested that such a public forum might become a political circus; moreover, he was concerned that a fair and representative picture of the system could not be developed in such an openly polemical and adversarial forum. He suggested instead that a survey of teachers be conducted to describe their experiences with the accountability system and to collect a representative overview of teacher opinions about their experiences.

Perrone attempted to negotiate the nature of the accountability review with the Superintendent of Schools. However, the superintendent indicated that he and the administration of the schools "could not cooperate" during the spring of 1976. The administration wanted to postpone the survey until after the election, when everyone could reflect more calmly on the situation and when administrators would have more time to cooperate in a review.

After several unsuccessful attempts to involve the school administration in the review, Perrone, with the concurrence of KEA-MEA-NEA, made a decision to go forward. The review would include, as the major data source, teacher responses to a mail survey conducted independently by the Minnesota Center for Social Research. The evaluation, then, was limited to providing as concisely as possible a review of the accountability program *from the perspective of teachers.* The evaluation of the accountability system was based on teacher responses to a mail questionnaire sent to all members of the Kalamazoo Education Association the first week of June, 1976. The evaluation and research staff of the school system, which is responsible for the accountability system, previewed the survey instrument and made wording suggestions that were incorporated into the final revision of the questionnaire. Sixty-one percent of the teachers anonymously responded to the survey conducted during the last week of the school year.

The results removed the uncertainty about teacher experiences with and opinions about the accountability system. It was clear from the questionnaire results that teachers felt the Kalamazoo Accountability System was largely ineffective and inadequate. Ninety percent of the teachers disagreed with the school administration's published statement that "the Kalamazoo Accountability System is designed to personalize and individualize education." Eighty-eight percent reported that the system does not assist teachers to become more effective. Ninety percent responded that "the accountability system has not improved educational planning in Kalamazoo." Ninety-three percent believed that "accountability as practiced in Kalamazoo creates an undesirable atmosphere of anxiety among teachers." Ninety percent asserted that "the accountability system is mostly a public relations effort."

Teachers felt that the school administration had failed to develop a useful, positive approach to educational accountability. Ninety percent reported that "administrators do *not* use accountability data in a positive, constructive manner." Likewise, 95 percent disagreed with the statement: "The accountability system is a positive force in Kalamazoo schools." Eighty-three percent rated the "overall accountability system in Kalamazoo" either "poor" or "totally inadequate."

The full analysis of the data, including teachers' openended comments, suggested that the underlying problem was a hostile teacher-administration relationship created by the way in which the accountability system was developed (without teacher input) and implemented (forced on teachers from above). The data also documented serious misuse of standardized tests in Kalamazoo.

The school board election eroded the school administration's support, and during the summer of 1976, the superintendent resigned. The new superintendent and school board in 1976-1977 used the Perrone/MCSR report as a basis for starting fresh with teachers. The KEA officials reported a new environment of teacher-administration cooperation in developing a mutually acceptable accountability system.

The evaluation report did not directly cause the changes. Many other factors came to play in Kalamazoo at that time. But the evaluation report was information that reduced the uncertainty about the scope and nature of teachers' feelings. A full meeting of the school board was devoted to discussion of the report. Candidates for the job of Kalamazoo superintendent called Dean Perrone to discuss the report and increase their understanding of the system. The evaluation report became part of the political context within which administration-teacher relations developed throughout the 1976-1977 school year. It became information that had to be taken into consideration, and information that had an observable impact on the Kalamazoo school ssytem. The evaluation data were used by teacher union officials to enhance their political position and to increase their input into the accountability system.

The Political Context of Evaluation

The previous chapter stated that social scientists fail to find evidence of research utilization because their definition of utilization is overly grandiose and rational. In particular, the rational social scientific model assumes an objective truth that is above and beyond political perception or persuasion. Scientists become uneasy when one group adopts a set of findings to further their own political purposes, as happened in Kalamazoo. They much prefer that the data serve all parties equally in a civilized search for the best answer. The evidence is, however, that the Kalamazoo example of utilization conditioned by a political context is the norm rather than the exception.

This chapter begins by presenting evidence about the linkages between political processes and evaluation research. Data from the study on utilization of federal health evaluations are used to describe and document the political nature of evaluative research. Six reasons why the evaluation process is inherently political are presented. This serves as the basis for development of a theoretical perspective on the power of evaluation derived from its impact both on particular decisionmakers and on program and organizational dynamics. Finally, we consider three limits on the proposition that knowledge is power. Overall, this chapter is aimed at elaborating the utilization-focused evaluation assumption that evaluation research is a highly political process from initial conceptualization to ultimate utilization, and that the evaluator shares responsibility for the content and direction of the political processes inherent in the power-laden nature of program evaluation.

An Empirical Look at the Political Nature of Evaluation Research

In studying the utilization of federal health evaluation research (Chapter 2), we asked evaluators and decisionmakers about the political factors that affected the impact of the specific studies we were investigating. Early in the interview, after questions on the role of the respondent in the study, the purpose of the study, and its origins, we asked the following question:

> Thinking about the study as a whole, it would be helpful for us to have some understanding of the political context within which this particular study took place. Were there any political considerations that you feel directly affected this study?

Near the end of the interview, a question about political considerations was asked again. This time the question came as one of a number asked about factors that influenced the degree of utilization of the findings:

> Many writers discuss the importance that political factors can have on the utilization of evaluation research. Evaluations sometimes get caught up in the external politics of programs—or the internal politics of the program. Evaluations can be either used for political purposes—or ignored for political reasons. Were there any political considerations that seem to have affected how this study was used, that affected its impact?

Nine decisionmakers and ten evaluators said that political considerations had affected how the study was used. In combination, at least one person interviewed in 15 of the 20 cases felt that politics had entered into the utilization process. Nine decisionmakers and seven evaluators felt that political considerations had been "very important" as a factor explaining utilization.

The types of politics involved included intra and interagency rivalries; budgetary fights with the Office of Management and Budget, the Administration, and Congress; power struggles between Washington administrators and local program personnel; and internal debates about the purpose or acomplishments of pet programs. Budgetary battles seemed to be the most political. One evaluator was particularly adamant about the political nature of his evaluation from the initiation of the study to the final report: "This was a really hot political issue, and I think that was the really important factor [explaining utilization]" (EV264: 17). The decisionmaker concurred.

While many evaluators responded affirmatively to the questions on political influences in the evaluation process, their full answers reveal a hesitancy and uneasiness that reflect the tensions between political and scholarly functions. The data from the interviews suggest that many evaluators resolve this tension by disassociating themselves from the political side of evaluation, despite evidence throughout their interviews that they are necessarily a part of the politics of evaluation. Because the utilization-focused approach to evaluation is based on the assumption that evaluation is a highly political process, and that the evaluator shares responsibility for the nature of that process, it is important to understand the implications of evaluators' attempts to disassociate themselves from the political process. The federal health evaluation utilization interviews provide rich source material for this purpose.

Political Innocence and Ignorance

In one of our interviews with an evaluator of mental health programs, the research scientist was particularly forthright about his lack of political sophistication. When asked about the political context of the stu;dy, he at first attempted to help the interviewer by suggesting that maybe there were pressures from Congress for evaluation, but then he stopped and said: "We had no knowledge or feeling about political relationships. We are quite innocent on such matters. We may not have recognized it" (EV5: 7). This was from a research scientist with 12 years' experience, "primarily evaluations and then I have done community studies and surveys as incidental to a program operating job" (EV5: 20).

Of the ten evaluators who felt that political considerations had affected utilization, only a few could clearly specify the nature of the political factors involved. For others, there was a vague expectation that politics was involved, but they were not sure just how: "Internally I expect there was. . . . I merely speculate. I expect the director could use it in any number of ways; he may not have done it at all" (EV119: 18). On another study, the decisionmaker stated that the study had not been used because program funding had already been terminated before the evaluation was completed. When asked about this in a later interview the evaluator replied:

No, I wasn't aware of all that. Nor was I aware that it was under any serious threat. . . . I'd say the communication on political matters related to the evaluation was not something that came up with us. It was not dis-

cussed to my recollection before or after, no, not before, during, or after
the conduct of the study (EV97: 12-13).

Part of evaluators' innocence or ignorance about the political processes
of utilization stems from a definition of politics that includes only happen-
ings of momentous consequences. Evaluators frequently answered our
questions about political considerations only in terms of the overall climate
brought on by President Nixon's attacks on HEW programs. They did not
define the day-to-day activities out of which programs and studies evolve
as "politics." One evaluator explained that no political considerations
affected the study because "this was not a global kind of issue. There were
vested interests all right, but it was not what would be considered a hot
issue. Nobody was going to resign over whether there was this program
or not" (EV145: 12).

Nine decisionmakers and five evaluators reported that political considerations played *no* part in the utilization process. It is instructive to
look at these cases of "apolitical" evaluations, because on close inspection many were quite political. Consider, for example, the case of an
academic researcher who became involved in the study of citizen boards
for community mental health programs. At points in the interview, the
researcher respondent objected to the term "evaluation" and explained
that his was a basic research study, not an evaluation—thus its apolitical
nature. When asked early in the interview whether political considerations
or political factors of any kind affected the study in any way, he replied:
"No. No. I would say no" (EV4: 6). The researcher went on to explain
that he required absolute autonomy in the study and no external political
pressures were brought to bear. Near the end of the interview, when
asked if political considerations in any way affected the utilization of
findings, the researcher again responded with a firm "no." In this
researcher's mind, the study was clearly an example of academic
research—nonpolitical in conception, implementation, and utilization.
Consider, then, his responses to other questions in the interview.

Data on the Political Nature of Evaluation

Item: When asked how the study began, the evaluator described a set
of personal contacts that he and colleagues made to find NIMH funding
for the project:

We got in touch with some people . . . and they were rather intrigued by
this. . . . It came at year's end as usual, and they had some funds left over

from year end type of things, and they were wondering, you know, who
would be willing to take a small amount, and our project was really small
in terms of dollars, $26,000-$27,000, somewhere around in there. . . . I'm
pretty certain we were not competing with other groups; they felt a sole bid
kind of thing wasn't going to get other people angry and all this (EV4: 1, 5-6).

Item: When asked about the purpose of the study, the evaluator replied:

Well, a couple of things. We were wondering about conflict patterns in
different programs' citizen boards. NIMH at that time was somewhat
concerned because many of their centers were in high density ghetto areas,
not only cutting across the black population, but Mexican Americans or a
mix of the two, or a mix of the three, that is, Puerto Ricans thrown in
there. . . .
   The other thing that we were interested in, and to some extent NIMH
was also interested in, is that up until the time of the study many of the
agencies had boards which were pretty middle class type boards and what
they were wondering, what we were wondering, is that now you put in
"poor people," people of other kinds of mixes and all of this, how is that
going to work? Is that going to enhance the thing, or is that really going
to disturb the system as far as the middle class people were concerned
(EV4: 4)?

Item: The interviewer followed the above response by probing, "were
there any other issues articulated by people at NIMH?" The evaluator
responded:

Oh, yeah. They had a young guy who was very much concerned. He, you
could say in some ways, was an advocate for, not so much for citizen
participation, but just for loosening up the system so to speak . . . and he was
very much into this thing, as many of them were, in fact, so he tried to push
some of the people to look at things this way. Some of them I felt were
pretty conservative and they were afraid that we were rocking the boat by
looking at some of this (EV4: 4).

He then described some of the personalities and interactions involved.
   Item: The research study included a set of recommendations about
how citizen boards should be organized and better integrated into
program activities.
   Item: The researcher described considerable long-range impact of
this study on local centers, on NIMH policy, on later studies, and even
on legislation.

The influence is certainly not a direct outcome as far as the study was concerned, but it's a very important byproduct of the study in which at that time we kept people talking about citizen evaluation; what does citizen participation truly mean, and so forth. You see, that generated a lot of thinking (EV4: 14).

Item: On release of results, the evaluator said:

We only released the results in a report and we wrote one paper out of it. Now, the fascinating thing, like reverberation, like throwing a pebble in a pond, and then what happens [was that] *Psychology Today* picked up this report and wrote a glowing little review. . . . They looked at seven or eight different NIMH reports and ours seemed to come through for the cheapest amount of money; then they made some nasty comments about the cost of government research (EV4: 10-11).

Item: The researcher recounted a lengthy story about how a member of Ralph Nader's consumer protection staff got hold of the study and then figured out the sample and wrote their own report. He and his colleagues talked with their lawyers but were unable to stop Nader's staff from using and abusing their data and sources, some of whom were identified incorrectly. They were unable to fight Nader's group.

We just don't have that kind of money, so we were furious. Various of us have friends who are lawyers that, you know, we thought that we would go to our lawyer friends and see if they couldn't do something. And they all came back with pretty much the same kind of response. Again, what finally happened was that when their big report came out, using our stuff, parts of our stuff, they gave it to the New York *Times* and various newspapers (EV4: 11-12).

Item: Since the study, the researchers have been involved in a number of regional and national meetings where they have reported their findings.

We go to enormous numbers of meetings. We see all kinds of people in all kinds of different settings, and it's not that we want to trumpet this particular study, but you know how it is at meetings, "what are you doing now?" kind of thing, "what have you been doing?" And so we talk about some of these sorts of things . . . and through this study we've sort of become known in a limited circle as "the experts in this sort of thing" (EV4: 20).

He described one such meeting where he became involved in an argument with local medical staff.

The doctors and the more middle class type of people in mental health work said we were just making too much of a fuss, that things were really, by and large, pretty nice, pretty quiet, going along pretty well. And I remember distinctly in that room, which must have had 200 people that day, the blacks and some of the, well, you might call them militant liberals, whatever labels one would put on them, were whispering to each other . . . and I began to get the tension, feel the tension and the kind of bickerings that were going on (EV4: 19).

Politics By Any Other Name

It is difficult to understand on what basis this researcher can report that the study was above political considerations. By his own testimony, the study must be considered highly politicized from conception to utilization. Personal influence was used to get funding. The research question was conceived in highly value-laden terms, i.e., "middle class boards" versus "poor people boards." Internally there were concerns about "rocking the boat by looking at some of this." The study made controversial recommendations, was cited in national publications, and was used indirectly in legislative processes. The researchers became expert advocates for a certain view of citizen participation, a view about which there was less than complete consensus. *Personal contacts, value-laden definitions, controversial recommendations, subtle pressures to please, advocacy—of such things are politics made.*

The traditional academic values of many social scientists lead them to want to be nonpolitical in their research. Yet they always want to affect government decisions. The evidence is that they cannot have it both ways. To be innocent of the political nature of evaluation research is to become a pawn in someone else's game, wittingly or unwittingly—or perhaps more commonly, to miss the game all together. Yet, there has been a "rejection of systematic valuative discourse by the contemporary social sciences" (MacRae, 1976: 55).

Gideon Sjoberg (1975: 30), in his comprehensive review of the relationships between politics, ethics, and evaluation research, suggests that most social scientists fail to understand the political nature of evaluations because they continue to have

an unrealistic view of the research process. . . . The conceptualization of the scientific process as expresesd in most treatises on social research makes it impossible to grapple with the political and ethical issues that arise (Sjoberg and Nett, 1968), especially in the area of evaluation research.

Social scientists find it difficult to see beyond their own notions of logical and rational judgments about truth, despite the fact that there is now a large body of evaluation case studies and experience documenting the political nature of evaluation research (e.g., Cohen, 1970; House, 1973, 1974; Weiss, 1970, 1972, 1975, 1977; Levine and Levine, 1977). The problem is integrating that experience into evaluation practice and "understanding social research as a social enterprise" (Sjoberg, 1975: 30).

The Sources of Evaluation's Political Inherency

The political nature of the evaluation process stems from several factors:

1. The fact that people are involved in evaluation research makes it a political process. Social research as a social enterprise means that the values, perceptions, and politics of everyone involved (scientists, decision-makers, funders, program staff) impinge on the evaluation process from start to finish.

2. The fact that classification systems and categories are involved in evaluation makes it a political process. People perceive things through filters called classification systems and categories. The concepts, methods, theories, and propositions of scientific research are normative and value-laden. The way in which an evaluation problem is stated necessarily includes value orientations, specialized cognitive interests, and subjective perceptions about both the nature of social "reality" and what is important to know about that social reality (cf. Mayntz, 1977; Gouldner, 1970). The categories and classification systems used directly affect the nature of the data collected. One of the evaluators interviewed in our utilization study was particularly conscious of the political nature of research categories. When asked how political considerations affected the study, he responded:

> Well, certainly our decision to look at urban and rural reflected the political
> considerations at the time . . . it reflected the consideration that there are
> problems in the city that are different from problems in rural areas, and
> that this was a national program, so we didn't want to concentrate solely on
> problems in the city and not pay any attention to problems in rural areas . . .
> And then our decision to use the percent nonwhite, to look at the black
> and white issue as one of the dimensions on which we stratified, that
> certainly reflects, you know, the attention to poor, minority areas and to
> the whole, well the political and socioeconomic distribution of the popula-
> tion and the projected interpretation of the proportion of mental illness
> that exists. . . . So to the extent that we used factors that were important at
> the moment of the study in the politics and the socioeconomic condition of
> the nation, to that extent we were very much influenced by political con-

siderations. . . . What we tried to do in our sample was to reflect the political and social and economic problems we thought were important at the time (EV12: 7-8).

3. The fact that empirical data are involved in evaluation research makes it a political process. Data always require interpretation. Social science is a probabilistic enterprise. Social scientific data presents probabilities and patterns, not final conclusions and facts. Interpretation is only partially a logical, deductive process; it is also a value-laden, political process. Actions taken and decisions based on such data are necessarily best guesses.

4. The fact that actions and decisions are the desired result of evaluation research makes it a political process. As described in the last chapter, any given programmatic action or decision is a result of multiple factors and influences, a process of "satisficing" rather than maximizing (Simon, 1957; March and Simon, 1958; Cyert and March, 1963). Evaluation research is just one input into the complex system of programmatic and organizational functioning. Weighting those inputs is a political activity.

5. The fact that programs and organizations are involved makes evaluation research a political process. Organizations are decisionmaking systems and as such, there are tensions between rational and political forces.

> [Organizations] may have substantial elements of rationality in the sense of possessing an ordered set of preferences, the procedures for revealing available alternative courses of action and the ability to choose between them in terms of the preference. Rationality is limited, however, by the existence of many preference orders within an organization" (Silverman, 1970: 204-205).

There is conflict both within organizations and between organizations, conflicts over the distribution of resources, status, and power. One of the weapons employed in these organizational conflicts is information.

6. The fact that information is involved in evaluation research makes it a political process. Information leads to knowledge; knowledge reduces uncertainty; reduction of uncertainty facilitates action; and action is necessary to the accumulation of power. While the actual role of information in decisionmaking is not always obvious or direct, there is evidence (as demonstrated in Chapter 2) that information can make a difference. Cohen (1970: 214) states the linkage between information and decision-making quite succinctly:

Decision-making, of course, is a euphemism for the allocation of resources—money, position, authority, etc. Thus, to the extent that information is an instrument, basis, or excuse for changing power relationships within or among institutions, evaluation is a political activity.

The "Is" and the "Ought" of Evaluation Politics

In effect, what we have been saying is that evaluation research is partly a political process. We have not been discussing whether or not it should be political. The evidence indicates that regardless of what ought to be—and social scientists have largely argued that utilization of scientific findings ought to be apolitical—the utilization of evaluation research is and will be partially political in nature. The degree of politicalization varies, but it is never entirely absent.

In our study of the utilization of federal health evaluations, we found that political factors consistently emerged to affect the utilization process, whether or not the decisionmakers and evaluators were fully aware of the political implications of the study from the outset. Moreover, many decisionmakers seemed to feel that political awareness is part of the responsibility of being an evaluator. Social scientists, they explained, will not change the political nature of the world, and while several respondents were quite cynical on this point, the more predominant view seemed to be that government would not be government without politics. One highly experienced and particularly articulate decisionmaker expressed this view quite explicitly:

> A substantial number of people have an improper concept of how politics works and what its mission is. And its mission is not to make logical decisions, unfortunately for those of us who think program considerations are important. Its mission is to detect the will of the governed group and express that will in some type of legislation or government action. And that will is very rarely, when it's pooled nationally, a rational will. It will have moral and ethical overtones, or have all kinds of emotional loads (DM328: 18).

This decisionmaker clearly believes that politics is in the nature of things. But he also believes that, in terms of a democratic system of government, government decisionmaking ought to be political.

> [Government decisionmaking] is not rational in the sense that a good scientific study would allow you to sit down and plan everybody's life.

And I'm glad it's not, by the way. Because I would be very tired, very early, of something that ran only by the numbers. Somebody'd forget part of the numbers. So I'm not fighting the system, but I am saying that you have to be careful of what you expect from a rational study when you insert it into the system. It has a tremendous impact. . . . It is a political, not a rational process. . . . Life is not a very simple thing (DM328: 18-19).

The key work here is process—political process. Evaluation information feeds into and is also part of the process. During our interviews, evaluators in particular tended to separate politics from evaluation, so that evaluation information is perceived as rational and objective while other inputs into the decisionmaking process are subjective and political. One evaluator expressed this view as follows:

Well, as I said earlier, it didn't have very much impact, in our opinion. The why is very simply that the politics of situations usually outweigh the results of evaluations. . . . It takes a lot of time to satisfy oneself that the grounds for the evaluation were legitimate . . . and that it wasn't colored. And I think if you work in this business long enough, you recognize that evaluations are an input to decisionmakers . . . politics have an input to a decisionmaker, and politics probably carry more weight than evaluation (EV131: 8).

Such a dichotomy between evaluation and politics contributes to social scientists' ineffectiveness in attempts to enhance utilization of their findings because they fail to recognize the fundamentally political and power-laden nature of the information they have collected. In the next section, a theoretical basis for this perspective is explored.

Reducing Uncertainty and Enhancing Power Through Evaluation Information

The utilization-focused approach to evaluation research assumes that evaluation research is and necessarily will be political in conceptualization, design, implementation, and utilization. Indeed, this approach assumes that utilization of evaluation findings will occur in direct proportion to the evaluation's power-enhancing capability. Power-enhancing capability is determined as follows: *The power of evaluation varies directly with the degree to which the findings reduce the uncertainty of action for specific decisionmakers.*

This view of the relationship between evaluation information and power is adapted from the organizational theories of Michael Crozier (1964) and James Thompson (1967). Crozier developed his theory from the study of organizational structure and dynamics in a French clerical agency and a tobacco factory. He found that power relationships develop around those aspects of organizational functioning and personal interaction that are closely related to uncertainty about things upon which the organization depends, i.e., their central goals. Groups within an organization try to limit their dependence on others and, correspondingly, enlarge their own areas of discretion. They do this by making their own behavior unpredictable in relation to other groups.

Crozier begins the interpretation of what he found by using Robert Dahl's (1957) definition of power: "the power of a person A over a person B is the ability of A to obtain that B do something he would not otherwise have done." Systems attempt to limit power conflicts through rationally designed, highly routinized structures, norms, and tasks. Crozier found, however, that even in a highly centralized, routinized bureaucratic and monopolistic organization, it was impossible to eliminate uncertainties.

> In such a context, the power of A over B depends on A's ability to predict B's behavior and on the uncertainty of B about A's behavior. As long as the requirements of action create situations of uncertainty, the individuals who have to face them have power over those who are affected by the results of their choice (Crozier, 1964: 158).

The use of information as a means for manipulating and reducing uncertainty emerges clearly in Crozier's analysis. Supervisors in the clerical agency had no interest in passing information on to their superiors, the section chiefs. There were several section chiefs in the organization who competed with each other for attention from their superior, the division head. Section chiefs distorted the information they gave to the division head to enhance their own position. Section chiefs could make such distortions partially because the lower level supervisors were interested in keeping what they know to themselves. The division head used the information he got to schedule production and to assign work. The division head only had available to him information that others were willing to give. His decisions were thus highly tenuous and aimed only at safe, minimal levels of achievement because he knew he lacked sufficient information to take narrow risks:

The power of prediction stems to a major extent from the way information is distributed. The whole system of roles is so arranged that people are given information, the possibility of prediction, and therefore control, precisely because of their position within the hierarchical pattern (Crozier, 1964: 158).

The power that comes with information is most clearly illustrated in the government's complex system of documents classification. "Limited distribution," "Confidential," " Secret," and "Top Secret," are only a few of the designations used to limit the distribution of information. This system is a clear recognition of the power of information and knowledge.

While Crozier's analysis centers on power relationships and uncertainties within organizations, James Thompson argues that a similar set of concepts can be applied at the level of the whole organization in relationship to other organizations and its larger environment. He argues that organizations are open systems that need resources and materials from outside, and that "with this conception the central problem for complex organizations is one of coping with uncertainty" (Thompson, 1967: 13). He is primarily concerned with industrial, production-oriented, profit organizations. Thompson suggests that assessment and evaluation are used by organizations as mechanisms for reducing uncertainty and enhancing their control over the multitude of contingencies with which they are faced. They evaluate themselves to assess their fitness for the future, and they evaluate the effectiveness of other organizations to increase their control over the maintenance of crucial exchange relationships.

Dornbusch and Scott (1975) have presented an empirically grounded theory that authority relations are based on the process of personnel evaluation. Evaluation is a control mechanism. To be effective, however, the evaluation mechanism must be agreed to by both subordinates and superordinates. Workers can sabotage evaluation systems. Thus, evaluations as part of authority systems work most effectively when the evaluation content and procedures are considered fair, important, and stable by workers. If the personnel evaluation information is to be used in making actual personnel decisions, this use of power must be authorized from below and above. The theory was tested in five settings—a basic research organization, a large hospital, a student newspaper, a university football team, and a factory. In all five organizations they found that evaluation (in this case personnel evaluation) was the central process around which authority relations developed and through which organizational control mechanisms functioned. In this context, organizations use personnel evaluations to reduce uncertainty and increase predictability about worker/employee/member performance. *Information for prediction is information for control: thus the power of evaluation.*

While this analysis of the power of evaluation has thus far been derived from perspectives recently developed by sociologists of organizations, social judgment theory can also be used to establish the same framework. As early as 1935, Tolman and Brunswick discussed the effects of "causal ambiguity" on human judgment and decisionmaking. Social judgment theory assumes an environment of causal ambiguity. Indeed, as Kenneth Hammond et al. explain (1975: 272), the existence of such an environment is the raison d'etre for the exercise of human judgment:

> Knowledge of the environment is difficult to acquire because of causal ambiguity—because of the probabalistic, entangled relations among environmental variables. . . . The organism in its normal intercourse with its environment must cope with *numerous, interdependent, multiformal relations* among variables which are *partly relevant* and *partly irrelevant* to its purpose, which carry only a *limited amount of dependability*, and which are organized in a variety of ways. The problem for the organism, therefore, is to know its environment under these circumstances. In the effort to do so, the organism brings a variety of processes (generally labeled *cognitive*), such as perception, learning, and thinking, to bear on the problem of reducing causal ambiguity. As a part of this effort, human beings often attempt to manipulate variables (by experiments, for example) and sometimes succeed—in such a manner as to eliminate ambiguity (italics in original).

Evaluation research is one of the processes certain organisms (decision-makers) use to manipulate variables and reduce uncertainty. Thus Hammond's advice to "the student of human judgment" is equally relevant to the student of evaluation utilization: "his first step must be to learn about and to understand the texture (and by that we mean the causal ambiguity) of the relationships among variables in the tasks which require human judgement (Hammond et al., 1975: 273). It is in the arena of causal ambiguity that the cognitive processes of evaluation operate to generate information for prediction, information for control—and power.

The Political Practice of Evaluation

The Kalamazoo Accountability System evaluation with which this chapter opened is a good illustration of the political practice of evaluation. The accountability system was initiated to reduce uncertainty about teacher and student performance. The hostility of teachers to the account-ability system led to uncertainty concerning management's ability to manage. The superintendent actively worked to stop the study that would establish the degree to which teacher opposition was widespread and crystallized. Once the study clearly established the failure of the account-ability system in the opinion of teachers, union officials used that informa-tion to help force the superintendent's resignation, to mobilize public opinion, and to gain influence in the new administration. In particular, teachers won the right to participate in developing the system that would be used to evaluate them. The Kalamazoo evaluation was precisely the kind of political enterprise that Cohen has argued characterizes evaluation research: "to evaluate a social action program is *to establish an information system* in which the main questions involve the allocation of power, status, and other public goods" (Cohen, 1970: 232; italics added).

Limits on Knowledge as Power

There is, however, a countering perspective to this notion of knowledge as power. A British colleague, L. J. Sharpe, cogently represents this opposing point of view. In trying to explain why social scientists of the 1960s so grossly overestimated their potential influence on government decisionmaking, he argued that one "important cause of this overopti-mism is the widespread assumption that governments are always in need of, or actively seek, information. But it seems doubtful whether this is the case. It is more likely that government has too much information, not too little—too much, that is, by its own estimation" (Sharpe, 1977: 44). Sharpe argues that information delays and complicates government decisionmaking. He then quotes Keynes to the effect that information avoidance is a central feature of government: "there is nothing a govern-ment hates more than to be well-informed; for it makes the process of arriving at decisions more complicated and difficult."

The perspectives of Keynes and Sharpe demonstrate the necessity of limiting the generalization that "knowledge is power." There are three qualifiers on this maxim that will take us closer to understanding how to approach evaluation with a utilization-focus.

1. *Not all information is useful.* To be power-laden, information must be relevant and in a form that is understandable to users. Crozier (1964: 158) introduces this qualifier in his discussion of power derived from differential control over uncertainties: "one should be precise and specify *relevant* uncertainty. . . . People and organizations will care only about

what they can recognize as affecting them and, in turn, what is possibly within their control." A similar point is made by Dornbusch and Scott (1975) when they conclude that authority relations develop around personnel evaluation only to the extent that workers believe the evaluations are important, soundly based, fairly applied, and central to their work.

Evaluation research is not useful just because it is information. Government may well have too much irrelevant, trivial, and useless information. One evaluator in our interviews made this point in contrasting short-term, highly focused evaluations with the long-term work of the National Center for Health Services Research.

> I mean they don't respond quick enough, they can't bring their resources to bear on the issues of the day quickly enough, and when they do provide an answer—well, that's yesterday's question. . . . Gee, they're nice people out there looking at pretty global questions but what have they done for me lately? And there's not a whole lot you can point to (EV81: 17).

Our study of the utilization of federal health evaluations indicates that in political practice, decisionmakers are anxious to have relevant information that will reduce the uncertainties they face.

2. *Not all people are information users.* Social science is essentially a story of the social tendency toward patterning and routinizing behavior. Habits, norms, rules, custom, tradition—this is the stuff of basic social science. The socialization process into society at large as well as into work organizations is aimed at limiting those things about which individuals make decisions. Different components or parts of an organization limit individual discretion to varying degrees, depending on the routineness of task and technology (c.f. Perrow, 1970: 50-91). At the same time, individuals vary in their aptitude for handling uncertainty and their ability to exercise discretion; socialization, education, and experience emphasize and magnify such differences.

In the political practice of evaluation, this means simply that information is power only in the hands (minds) of people who know how to use it and are open to using it. If the organization's need for the exercise of discretion is differentially distributed, and the ability of individuals to exercise discretion using information to reduce uncertainty is also differentially distributed, then the problem for utilization is at least partly one of matching: getting the right information to the right people.

Widespread notions about "the bureaucratic personality" and "organization man" are now part of our organizational folklore, affirming this assertion that not all people are information users. Many, perhaps most people rely on the predispositions of their socialization and the pressure of peers to chart their daily course of action. But there are those people who can and do make information part of their decisionmaking frame of reference. One evaluator in our utilization of federal health evaluation interviews made this point quite succinctly. This person had had 35 years' experience in government, 20 of those years directly involved in research and evaluation. He had also worked for several years as a private evaluation research contractor, during which time he had been involved in evaluating some 80 projects for HEW. Throughout his response to our questions on the importance of various specific factors in affecting utilization he returned to the theme of individual variability in the ability to use information. He tied this to his idea of the good manager.

The good manager is aggressive, open, confident, anxious to interchange ideas. He's not defensive. Rather, "he's interested in finding out what your views are, not defending his. . . . You know my sample is relatively small, but I'd say probably there are a quarter (25%) of what I'd call good managers" (EV346: 15). *These, he believes, are the people who use evaluation research.*

3. *Until actually used, information is only potential power, not actual power.* One of the critical uncertainties of decisionmaking and "muddling through" is that it is difficult to know in advance of immediate contingencies what information will be needed. In the battle for control over uncertainty one thing is certain—no one wants to be caught with less information than competitors for power. A lot of information is collected "just in case." One evaluator we interviewed explained the entire function of his office in these terms.

I wouldn't want to be quoted, but there was a real question as to whether we were asked for these reports because they wanted them for decisionmaking. We felt that the five foot shelf that we were turning out may actually have had no particular relevance to the real world. Again, that's something you don't know, you're never in a position to find out.

A list of OMB questions were dealt with in here and we didn't know why we were being asked those questions. They were not questions that we would have asked about the program, for example. We all worked for Richard Nixon. We'd produce answers to questions. It's a political aspect, but it's probably the form political effects take inside a bureaucracy.

This operation made it impossible for NIMH, some Congressman, or someone, it made it impossible for him to say that the issue had never been studied. Therefore, it would be a fairly standard administration ploy to study the issue so that it is not possible for somebody to insist you never even looked at this issue. And one did wonder to what extent we were turning out paper for that purpose (EV152: 18).

It is possible to become quite cynical about the "just in case" approach to data gathering. The utilization-focused approach is not aimed merely at potential utilization but rather at actual utilization. It is simply impossible to collect data on every possible future contingency, so evaluators might as well attempt to study questions where the odds favor utilization. Utilization-focused evaluation is aimed at more than producing pages of reports "just in case." One HEW official described the "just in case" approach as follows:

> Yeah, it can be put in crude terms, that evaluation studies are just to cover your ass. But that's kind of misunderstanding when it's put that crudely because they do more than that. They also give you information by which you could make changes if you want to make changes or by which you can test if you're doing things that are really wrong and so they would exercise some controlling function even though, in fact, you never use them. They could also serve as a way of checking out options so that if contingencies come up where certain kinds of information would be useful, then that information would be there. Just because that condition doesn't come up doesn't mean that they haven't served a purpose (DM4: 13).

Utilization-focused evaluation aims at closing the gap between potential utilization and actual utilization. Lazarsfeld and Reitz (1975) call this the gap between knowledge and action. Bridging that gap, they believe, is the most important translation step in the utilization process. Bridging that gap is a creative process that generates power. In the next chapter, we shall explore the locus of this process of generating actual power through the creative use of evaluative information.

Politics As Usual, Evaluation Research As Different

We know from the literature on utilization that the usual practice of traditional scientific research has left social scientists frustrated that their findings are not used. We also know from the experiences of the last 20 years that social scientists are not about to rationalize government. Government decisionmaking will continue to be political. Because politics will continue as usual, it is the evaluation research process that must change if relevant information is going to get into the hands of decisionmakers able to use evaluation research.

Political naivete can no longer be an excuse for social scientists who find their research ignored or abused. The political nature of applied social science research has been well-documented. The challenge is to apply this understanding to the research utilization process. As Sjoberg (1975: 29) put the problem,

Although a number of social scientists have in recent years become sensitive to various ethical and political aspects of the research process, they have not incorporated the issues involved into their methodology, or, more narrowly, into their methodology for evaluation research.

It is the task of the remainder of this book to do precisely that, to describe a utilization-focused approach to evaluation that incorporates the realities of the political nature of decisionmaking and the potential power of evaluation as information that facilitates the reduction of decisionmaker uncertainty.

Chapter 4

THE PERSONAL FACTOR:

IDENTIFICATION AND ORGANIZATION OF RELEVANT

DECISIONMAKERS AND INFORMATION USERS

A Setting

It is shortly after 8 A.M. on a damp summer morning at Snow Mountain Ranch near Rocky Mountain National Park. Some 40 human service and education people from all over the country have gathered in a small, dome-shaped chapel to participate in an evaluation workshop. The session begins like this:

Okay, lets get started. Instead of beginning by my haranguing you about what you should do in program evaluation, we're going to begin with a short evaluation exercise to immerse us immediately in the process. That is, we're going to take an experiential or simulation approach to learning about the stages of program evaluation.

So what I'm going to do is ask you to engage in an exercise as both participants and evaluators (since that's the situation most of you find yourself in anyway in your own agencies and programs—where you have both program and evaluation responsibilities). We're going to share an experience through this exercise to loosen things up a bit . . . perhaps warm you up, wake you up, and allow you to get more comfortable. The exercise will also allow us to test your participant observer skills and provide us with a common experience as evaluators. We'll generate some personal data about the process of evaluation that we can use for discussion later.

So what I want you to do for about the next five minutes is to move around this space, to get up and move around in any way you want to, to explore this environment. You can explore the environment in any ways you want to—touch things, move things, experience different parts of this setting. And while you're observing the physical environments, watch what others do. Then after about five minutes I'll ask you to find a place where you feel comfortable to write down your observations about the exercise, what you observed, and also to evaluate the exercise. Experience, explore, observe, and evaluate. That's the exercise.

Oh yes, there are two rules. First, I'd prefer that you not talk to anyone, and secondly, I'd prefer that no one leave the room. The exercise works best if people hang around for it! But otherwise, you're free to explore, and remember, while you are participating in this experience, this exercise, you're also evaluating it.

At the end of the exercise the participants were asked to write an evaluation report based on their own observations of what had occurred. Several people were then asked, on a voluntary basis, to share with the group what they had written.

First Observer: "People slowly got up. Everybody looked kind of nervous 'cause they weren't sure what to do. People moved out toward the walls, which are made of rough wood. The lighting is kind of dim. People sort of moved counter-clockwise. Every so often there would be a nervous smile exchanged between people. The chairs are fastened down in rows so it's hard for people to move in the center of the room. A few people went to the stage area, but most stayed toward the back and outer part. The chairs aren't too comfortable but it's a quiet, mellow room. The exercise showed that people are nervous when they don't know what to do."

Second Observer: "The room is hexagonally shaped with a dome shaped ceiling. Fastened-down chairs are arranged in a semicircle with a stage in front that is about a foot high. A podium is at the left of the small stage. Green drapes hang at the side. Windows are small and triangular. The floor is wood. There's a coffee table in back. Most people went to get coffee. A couple people broke the talking rule for a minute. Everyone returned to about the same place they had before after walking around. It's not a great room for a workshop, but it's okay."

Third Observer: "People were really nervous about what to do because the goals of the exercise weren't clear. You can't evaluate without clear goals so people just wandered around. The exercise shows you can't evaluate without clear goals."

Fourth Observer: "I said to myself at the start, this is a human relations thing to get us started. I was kind of mad about doing this because we've been here a half hour already and we haven't done anything that has to do with evaluation. I came to learn about evaluation not to do T-group stuff, or nonverbal communications stuff. So I just went to get coffee and I talked to someone because I didn't like the rule about not talking, but the other person was really nervous about breaking the rule. I didn't like wasting so much time on this."

Fifth Observer: "I felt uneasy too, but I think it's natural to feel uneasy when you can't talk and aren't sure what to do. But I liked walking around looking at the chapel and feeling the space. I think some people got into it, but we were stiff and uneasy. People avoided looking at each other. Sometimes there was a nervous smile when people passed each other, but by kind of moving in a circle most people went the same direction and avoided looking at each other. I think I learned something about myself and how I react to a strange, nervous situation."

The five observers had five different perspectives on the same experience. The exercise and reports were followed by a discussion of what it would take to produce a more focused set of observations and evaluations. Suggestions included establishing clear goals; making up criteria for what is being evaluated; figuring out what is supposed to be observed in advance so everyone can observe it; giving clearer directions of what to do; stating the purpose of evaluation; and training the evaluators so that they all know how to observe the same thing.

The problem is that before any of these things can be done a prior step is necessary. This prior step constitutes the first stage in utilization-focused evaluation. It is this first step that is the concern of this chapter.

The First Step in the Evaluation Process

It is clear from the literature on evaluation research that most evaluations are aimed at assessing the relative degree of program goal attainment, i.e., how effective is a program in attaining measureable goals? It is also clear that the purpose of the evaluation should be explicitly stated; that concrete evaluative criteria for program success should be established; and that the measurement procedures and instruments should be appropriate to the goals. All of these are important issues in any evaluation. The question is: who will make decisions about these issues?

The first step in the utilization-focused approach to evaluation is IDENTIFICATION AND ORGANIZATION OF RELEVANT DE-CISIONMAKERS FOR AND INFORMATION USERS OF THE EVALUATION.

Consider the workshop exercise that opened this chapter. The participants observed different things and were unable to evaluate what happened partly because they did not know for whom they were writing. There are several potential information users and decision-makers in relation to an evaluation of the exercise:

(1) As workshop leader, I might want to evaluate whether or not the exercise accomplished my objectives.

(2) Each individual participant might conduct a personal evaluation in terms of his or her own criteria.

(3) The group could establish consensus goals for the exercise which would serve as focus for the evaluation.

(4) The bosses, agency directors, and funding boards who paid for participants to attend might want an assessment of the exercise in terms of a return on the resources they have invested for staff training.

(5) The Snow Mountain Ranch director might want an evaluation of the exercise in terms of the appropriateness of the chapel for such workshop activities.

(6) The building architects might want an evaluation of how participants responded to the space they designed.

(7) A group of professional workshop facilitators might want to evaluate the exercise as to its effectiveness for opening a workshop.

(8) Ecological psychologists or human relations trainers might want to assess the effects of the exercise on participants.

(9) Experiential learning educators might want an assessment of the use of such an exercise as an experiential learning tool.

(10) The janitors of the chapel might want an evaluation of the work engendered for them by an exercise that permits moving things around (which sometimes occurs to destructive proportions when the exercise has been used with loose furniture).

This list of potential decisionmakers and information users could be expanded. The evaluation research question in each case would likely be different. I would have different evaluation information needs as workshop leader than would the camp director; the architects' information needs would differ from the janitors' evaluation question; the evaluation criteria of individuals would differ from those reached by the total group through some consensus-formation process.

This long discourse on the nature of differential perception is not aimed at simply making the point that different people see things differently and have varying needs. I take that to be on the order of a truism. *The point is that this truism is regularly and consistently ignored in the design of evaluation studies.* To target an evaluation at the information needs of a specific person or at a group of identifiable and interacting persons is quite different from what is usually referred to as "identifying the audience" for an evaluation. Audiences are amorphous, anonymous entities. Nor is it sufficient to identify an agency or organization as recipient of the evaluation report. Organizations are an impersonal collection of hierarchical positions. People, not organizations, use evaluation information. I shall elaborate on these points later in this chapter, when discussing how most evaluations manage to avoid identification and organization of relevant decisionmakers and information users. First, I want to present data from our utilization of federal health evaluations study that illustrate and elaborate this first step in the utilization-focused approach to evaluation. In the course of presenting these data, I hope it will become clear who are "relevant" decisionmakers and information users and why they are the key to the utilization process.

Factors Affecting the Utilization of Evaluation Research and the Emergence of the Personal Factor

In designing the interview instruments used with federal decisionmakers and evaluators in our study of the utilization of health evaluations (see Chapter 2), we reviewed the evaluation literature in a search for possible variables related to utilization. This research literature offers a number of factors to explain variations in utilization of findings, among them poor methodological quality (Bernstein and Freeman, 1975); the differing values, languages, reward systems, and reference groups of researchers and bureaucrats (Caplan et al. 1975); differential relevance of findings for various levels of a program (Alkin et al. 1974); degree of dissemination of findings (Halpert, 1969); communication patterns in organizations (Jain, 1970); the positive or negative nature of findings (Weiss, 1972c); and the reputation and legitimacy of the evaluator (Archibald, 1970).

In our interviews with federal decisionmakers and evaluators, we asked questions about the relevance of these factors extracted from the literature as well as more openended questions about utilization. The questioning sequence worked as follows. Once the respondents had discussed their perceptions about the nature and degree of utilization of the specific evaluation study under investigation, we asked the following open-ended questions:

> Okay, you've described the impact of the study. Now we'd like you to think about *why* this study was used in the ways you've just described. Some of this you've already done, but now we'd like to explore this in more detail. What do you feel were the important reasons why this study had the level of impact it did? [Probe, if necessary]

The literature on evaluation studies suggests a lot of reasons why some evaluations are used while others are ignored. Most of the literature, however, is based on speculation. A major objective of the interviews we're doing is to find out directly from people who are in a position to know, what factors they consider important in explaining how specific studies are used.

Following additional probes, we asked respondents to comment on how, if at all, each of 11 factors extracted from the literature on utilization had affected utilization of their study. These factors were methodological quality, methodological appropriateness, timeliness, lateness of report, positive or negative findings, surprise of findings, central or peripheral program objectives evaluated, presence or absence of related studies, political factors, decisionmaker-evaluator interactions, and resources available for the study. Finally, we asked respondents to "pick out the single factor you feel had the greatest effect on how this study was used."

From this long list of questions only two factors emerged as consistently important in explaining utilization: (1) the political considerations factor discussed in Chapter 3 and (2) a factor we have called "the personal factor." This latter factor was unexpected and its clear importance to our respondents has, we believe, substantial implications for the utilization of evaluation research. *None of the other specific literature factors about which we asked questions emerged as important with any consistency.* Moreover, when these specific factors were important in explaining the utilization or nonutilization of a particular study, it was virtually always in the context of a larger set of circumstances and conditions related to either political considerations or the personal factor.

The personal factor refers to the presence of an identifiable individual or group of people who personally cared about the evaluation and the information it generated. Where such a person or group was present, evaluations were used; where the personal factor was absent, there was a correspondingly marked absence of evaluation impact. The personal factor represents the leadership, interest, enthusiasm, determination, commitment, aggressiveness, and caring of specific, individual people. In terms of power of evaluation discussed in the preceding chapter, these are the people who are actively seeking information to reduce decision uncertainties so as to increase their ability to predict the outcomes of programmatic activity and enhance their own discretion as decisionmakers. These are the users of evaluation research.

Data on the Importance of the Personal Factor

The personal factor emerged most dramatically in our interviews when, having asked respondents to comment on the importance of each of our 11 utilization factors, we asked them to identify the single factor that was most important in explaining the impact or lack of impact of that particular study. Time after time, the factor they identified was not on our list. Rather, they responded in terms of the importance of individual people:

> *Item:* "I would rank as the most important factor this division director's interest, [his] interest in evaluation. Not all managers are that motivated toward evaluation" (DM353: 17).
>
> *Item:* [The single most important factor that had the greatest effect on how the study got used was] the principal investigator. . . . If I have to pick a single factor, I'll pick people any time (DM328: 20).
>
> *Item:* That it came from the Office of the Director—that's the most important factor. . . . The proposal came from the Office of the Director. It had had his attention and he was interested in it, and he implemented many of the things (DM312: 21).
>
> *Item:* [The single most important factor was that] the people at the same level of decisionmaking in [the new office] were not interested in making decisions of the kind that the people [in the old office] were, I think that probably had the greatest impact. The fact that there was no one at [the new office] after the transfer who was making programmatic decisions (EV361: 27).
>
> *Item:* Well, I think the answer there is in the qualities of the people for whom it was made. That's sort of a trite answer, but it's true. That's the single most important factor in any study now that's utilized (EV232: 22).
>
> *Item:* Probably the single factor that had the greatest effect on how it was used was the insistence of the person responsible for initiating the study that the Director of _____ become familiar with its findings and arrive at judgment on it (DM369: 25).
>
> *Item:* [The most important factor was] the real involvement of the top decisionmakers in the conceptualization and design of the study, and their commitment to the study (DM268: 9).

While these comments concern the importance of interested and committed individuals in studies that were actually used, studies that were not used stand out in that there was often a clear absence of the personal factor. One evaluator, who was not sure how his study was used but suspected it had not been, remarked:

> I think that since the client wasn't terribly interested . . . and the whole issue had shifted to other topics, and since we weren't interested in doing it from a research point of view . . . nobody was interested (EV264: 14).

Another highly experienced evaluator was particularly adamant and articulate on the theory that the major factor affecting utilization is the personal energy, interests, abilities, and contacts of specific individuals. When asked to identify the one factor that is most important in whether a study gets used, he summarized his viewpoint as follows:

> The most important factor is desire on the part of the managers, both the central federal managers and the site managers. I don't think there's [any doubt], you know, that evaluation should be responsive to their needs, and if they have a real desire to get on with whatever it is they're supposed to do, they'll apply it. And if the evaluations don't meet their needs they won't. About as simple as you can get. *I think the whole process is far more dependent on the skills of the people who use it than it is on the sort of peripheral issues of politics, resources.* . . . Institutions are tough as hell to change. You can't change an insitution by coming and doing an evaluation with a halo. Institutions are changed by people, in time, with a constant plugging away at the purpose you want to accomplish. And if you don't watch out, it slides back (EV346: 15-16).

His view had emerged early in the interview when he described how evaluations were used in OEO.

> In OEO it depended on *who* the program officer was, on the program review officials, on program monitors for each of these grant programs. . . . Where there were aggressive program people, they used these evaluations whether they understood them or not. They used them to affect improvements, different allocations of funds within the program, explanations of why the record were kept this way, why the reports weren't complete or whatever. Where they, where the program officials in OEO were unaggressive, passive —*nothing!*
>   Same thing's true at the project level. Where you had a program director who was aggressive and understood what the hell the structure was internally, and he used it as leverage to change what went on within his program. Those who weren't—nothing (EV346: 5).

At another point he said, "The basic thing is how the administrators of the program view themselves, their responsibilities. That's the controlling factor" (EV346: 8), and later he commented:

> It always falls back to the view of the administrator and his view of where his perogatives are, his responsibilities. A good manager can manage with or without evaluations and a poor one can't, with or without evaluations. It just gives him some insights into what he should or shouldn't be doing, if he's a good manager. If they're poor managers, well . . . (EV346:11).

The same theme emerged in his comments about each possible factor. Methodological quality, positive or negative findings, the degree to which the findings were expected—he always returned eventually to the themes of mangerial interest, competence, and confidence. *The person makes the difference.*

Our sample included another rather adamant articulation of this premise. An evaluation of a pilot program involving four major projects was undertaken at the instigation of the program administrator. He made a special effort to make sure that his question (i.e., were the pilot projects capable of being extended and generalized?) was answered. He guaranteed this by personally taking an active interest in all parts of the study. The administrator had been favorable to the program in principle, was uncertain what the results would be, but was hoping the program would prove effective. The evaluation findings were, in fact, negative. The program was subsequently ended with the evaluation carrying considerable weight in that decision (DM367: 8).

The evaluator interview on this case completely substantiated the administrator's description. The findings were specific and clear. The program was not refunded. Thus the evaluation had a substantial, direct impact on that decision. The question then becomes why this study had such significant utilization. The answer from the decisionmaker was brief and to the point:

> Well, [the evaluation had an impact] because we designed the project with an evaluation component in it, so we were expected to use it and we did. . . . Not just the fact that [evaluation] was built in, but the fact that we built it in on purpose. This is, *the agency head and myself had broad responsibilities for this, wanted the evaluation study results and we expected to use them. Therefore they were used. That's my point.* If someone else had built it in because they thought it was needed, and we didn't care, I'm sure the use of the study results would have been different (DM367: 12).

The evaluator (an external agent selected through an open request-for-proposal process) completely agreed:

> *The principle reason [for utilization] was because the decisionmaker was the guy who requested the evaluation and used its results. That is, the organizational distance between the policymaker and the evaluator was almost zero in this instance.* That's the most important reason it had an impact.
>
> Well, I guess the point is that the project was really monitored by the decisionmaker rather than the project offficer. . . . *It was the fact that the guy who was asking the question was the guy who was going to make use of the answer* (EV367: 12).

What emerges here is a picture of a decisionmaker who knew what information he wanted, an evaluator committed to answering the decisionmaker's question, and a decisionmaker committed to using that information. The result was a high level of utilization in making a decision contrary to the decisionmaker's initial personal hopes. In the words of the evaluator, the major factor explaining utilization was

> that the guy who's going to be making the decision is aware of and interested in the findings of the study and has some hand in designing the questions to be answered, that's a very important point (EV367: 20).

The decisionmaker's conclusion is so similar that it sounds like collusion:

> Evaluation research. Well I guess I would affirm that in many cases it has no impact for many of the reasons that the literature has suggested. But if I were to pick out factors that made a positive contribution to its use, one would be that the decisionmakers themselves wanted the evaluation study results. I've said that several times. If that is not present, it is not surprising that the results aren't used (DM367: 17).

This point was made often in the interviews. One highly placed and highly experienced administrator offered the following advice at the end of a four hour interview:

> Win over the program people. Make sure you're hooked into the person who's going to make the decision in six months from the time you're doing the study, and make sure that *he* feels it's his study, that these are *his* ideas, and that it's focused on *his* values. . . . I'm sure it enters into personality things (DM283: 40).

The personal factor applies not just to utilization but to the whole evaluation process. Several of the studies in our sample were initiated completely by a single person because of personal interests and information needs. One study in particular stands out because it was initiated by a new office director with no support internally and considerable opposition from other affected agencies. The director found an interested and committed evaluator. The two worked closely together. The findings were initially ignored because there was no political heat at the time, but over the ensuing four years the director and evaluator personally worked to get the attention of key Congressmen. They were finally successful in using personal contacts. The evaluation contributed to the eventual passing of significant legislation in a new area of federal control. From beginning to end, the story was one of personal human effort to get evaluation results used.

The specifics vary from case to case but the pattern is markedly clear: where the personal factor emerges, where some individual takes direct, personal responsibility for getting the information to the right people, evaluations have an impact. Where the personal factor is absent, there is a marked absence of impact. Utilization is not simply determined by some configuration of abstract factors; it is determined in large part by real, live, caring human beings.

This conclusion is supported by other studies on the utilization of applied research. Glazer and Taylor (1969: iii) studied utilization by comparing five applied research projects rated as successful by NIMH staff and five rated as unsuccessful. They concluded that successful applied research is

characterized by *high communication;* awareness and *involvement* with persons and groups within and outside the immediate environment from its *earliest moments.* . . . The research was *designed by* the *principal investigator,* who devoted *full time* to the project. The host agency indicated its *commitment* by *contributions* of services and supplementary funds. The focus of the research was aimed at a *felt need* which enjoyed a shared interest from other people. Ipso facto, therefore, the product was readily marketable. Potential consumers were involved and informed. They encouraged *early efforts* at *dissemination* of findings, and were ready to consider implications for utilization (italics in original).

Charles Windle of NIMH investigated factors that affected the success of 15 evaluation studies of NIMH's Community Health Centers Program. These were evaluations contracted from the one percent monies of the Community Mental Health Centers Act, funds authorized specifically for program evaluation by the 90th Congress. He reviewed all such evaluations that had products available by the summer of 1972. His investigation revealed that

the factor most closely related to ratings of success was closeness of relationships between the contractor and N.I.M.H. staff. This closeness seemed both to orient the research toward potential utility and to enhance the likelihood that N.I.M.H. staff would utilize the products (Windle, n.d.: 11).

Such findings are sometimes interpreted as meaning simply that the *amount* of contact between decisionmakers and evaluators should be increased. But our data on the personal factor suggest that increased contact with the wrong persons (i.e., people who are not oriented towards the use of evaluative information) is likely to accomplish little. It is the nature and quality of interactions between evaluators and decisionmakers that is at issue. My own experience suggests that where the right people are involved, (i.e., people who care about the evaluation and its utilization) the amount of direct contact can sometimes be reduced because the interactions that do occur are of such high quality.

In a quite different and more systematic way, Ronald Havelock (1968) has demonstrated the highly personal nature of knowledge utilization. Drawing heavily on the vast diffusion of innovations literature (cf. Rogers, 1962; Rogers and Shoemaker, 1971), he identifies particular roles that are fulfilled in a utilization or dissemination process. There are "leaders," "defenders," "innovators," "conveyors," "linking agents" and others who provide the personal mechanisms for information transmittal and use. What emerges quite clearly in Havelock's analysis is that the qualities and characteristics of individual people make a difference in the utilization process.

The linkage between evaluation information and decisionmaking can best be made at the level of individual people because it is individuals who experience uncertainty and seek ways to increase their discretion. As demonstrated in the preceding chapter, the utilization process is highly political. The personal factor intersects with the political factor most clearly at the point where it is necessary to bridge the gap between knowledge and action. As Lazarsfeld and Reitz (1975: 98) argue, "this gap can only be filled by creative thinking which responds with guesses of varying degrees of risk." This creativity resides in individuals. Attention to the personal factor is the mechanism for identifying both creative decisionmakers and creative evaluators.

The Focus on People Who Can Use Information

The focus in the utilization-focused approach to evaluation research is on identification and organization of relevant decisionmakers and information users. First, this means finding and bringing together people who want to know something. It means locating people who are able and willing to use information. Researchers and decisionmakers who care about seeing evaluation results utilized must take seriously the importance of identifying who needs what information under what conditions for what purposes. Relevant decisionmakers and information users are the specific individuals who want evaluative information. Relevancy in the context of the personal factor means finding people who have a genuine interest in research data—persons who are willing to take the time and effort to interact with evaluators about their information needs and interests. Thus, the first step in utilization-focused evaluation is to answer seriously and searchingly the question posed by Marvin Alkin (1975a): "Evaluation Who Needs It? Who Cares?"

Second, formal position and authority are only partial guides in identifying relevant decisionmakers and information users. Evaluators must find the strategically located person or persons who are enthusiastic, committed, competent, interested, and aggressive. Our data suggest that more may be accomplished by working with a lower level person displaying these characteristics than in working with a passive, disinterested person in a higher position.

Third, regardless of what a request-for-proposal (RFP) calls for, the most valuable information with the highest potential for utilization is that information that directly answers the questions of the individual(s) identified as the relevant decisionmaker(s). RFPs may be written by individuals other than the decisionmakers who really need and want the evaluation information. It behooves evaluators to clarify the degree to which an RFP fully reflects the information needs of interested government officials.

Fourth, attention to the personal factor can not only assist evaluators' efforts to increase the utilization of their research, but can also aid decisionmakers' efforts to find evaluators who will provide them with relevant and useful information. Evaluators who are both interested in and knowledgeable about what they are doing *and* who are committed to seeing their findings utilized in answering decisionmaker's questions will provide the most useful information to those decisionmakers.

Fifth, there are political implications for both evaluators and decisionmakers in explicitly recognizing and acting on the importance of the personal factor. To do so is also to accept the assumption that decisionmaking in government is likely to continue to be a largely personal and political process rather than a rationalized and scientific process. Under personal or political conditions, the actions and interests of individual people make a difference. People are more than the positions they occupy.

In the remaining chapters of this book we shall explore the implications of the personal factor and the utilization-focused approach to evaluation for other steps in the applied research process. Prior to that, however, it may be helpful to contrast our first step in conceptualizing evaluation with other beginning strategies. There are several ways of doing evaluation without identifying who will make decisions with the information obtained, but most of these reduce the study's utilization potential.

Avoiding Identifying Real Information Users

First, and most common, evaluators avoid identification and organization of real information users and decisionmakers by themselves becoming the major decisionmakers for the evaluation. This can happen by default (no one else is willing to do it), by intimidation (clearly the evaluator is the expert), or simply by failing to think about or seek alternatives. This means that the evaluators answer their own questions according to their own interests, needs, criteria, and creativity. Others may have occasional input here or there, but it is essentially an evaluation by the evaluator, for the evaluator, and of the evaluator. These conditions are a great boom for conducting basic scientific research under the funding guise of evaluation research, but such studies are seldom of use to program people, whose reaction is likely to be: "it's a great study, really well done. We can see you did a lot of work. But it doesn't tell us anything we want to know."

The second usual approach for avoiding identification and organization of relevant decisionmakers and information users is to use the standard "identification of audience" approach. Audience, however, is not an identifiable group of people organized to have regular and systematic input into the evaluation. Audience refers to groups of largely anonymous faces: the "feds," state officials, the legislature, funders, clients, the program, the public, and so forth. The audience approach recognizes that "it is important to distinguish among the possible audiences for the evaluation study. It is important because we gather different information for different audiences. Different people have different appetites for different information" (Stake, 1973: 304). But specific individuals are not identified from these audiences and organized in a manner that permits continuous input into the evaluation process.

In the absence of specific, identifiable individuals and information users, the evaluator must speculate on the audience's information needs and, in effect, remains the decisionmaker for the evaluation. This de facto control of the evaluation by the researcher remains paramount. Carol Weiss' popular *Evaluation Research* is a good example. After an excellent discussion on how different groups, audiences, and decisionmakers need different information and of the impossibility of any one evaluation answering everyone's questions, she counsels: "with all the possible uses for evaluation to serve, the evaluator has to make choices" (Weiss, 1972b: 15).

What fundamentally distinguishes the utilization-focused approach to evaluation from other approaches is that the evaluator does not alone carry this burden for making choices about the nature, purpose, content, and methods of evaluation. These decisions are shared by an identifiable and organized group of decisionmakers and information users.

A third way of conducting evaluations without identification and organization of decisionmakers and information users is to focus on decisions and information instead of on decisionmakers and information users. This approach is epitomized by Mark Thompson (1975: 26, 38), who defines evaluation as "marshalling of information for the purposes of improving decisions" and makes the first step in an evaluation "identification of the decision or decisions for which information is required." Thompson simply assumes throughout his model that decisionmakers and information users are already identified and organized. Thus the issue is the decision itself.

This approach has the advantage of appearing to be utilization-oriented and politically neutral without the evaluator becoming personally involved. Carol Weiss (1972b: 16) describes this approach as follows:

> Some researchers say that to try to satisfy a multiplicity of demands and uses under usual field conditions invites frustration. The evaluator who identifies the key decision pending and gears his study to supplying information relevant to that issue is on firmer ground. Others believe that there are ways . . . to study a range of issues concurrently. Nevertheless, it remains important for the evaluator to know the priority among purposes. If the crunch comes, he can jettison the extra baggage and fight for essentials.

Again, it is left up to the evaluator to decide what data are actually needed. This decision-oreinted approach stems from the rational social scientific model of how decisionmaking occurs, i.e., there is a clearcut decision to be made; information is needed to make the decisions; the social scientist supplies the information; and the decision is then made in accordance with that information. But this model fits neither the real world utilization process (described in Chapter 2) not the political nature of evaluation (Chapter 3).

It can indeed be important, even crucial, to orient evaluations toward future decisions. But identification of such decisions and the implications of those decisions for the evaluation are best made in conjunction with specific information users who come together to decide how the evaluation can gather what data for what purposes. Discussion of future uses of the evaluation is an important component of building up a commitment on the part of decisionmakers to actually use the information gathered during the evaluation. But determining what information is needed for what purposes is not left solely to the discretion of the evaluation researcher. Such an approach, I believe, differs substantially from Stake's (1973: 305) advice to evaluators:

> The evaluator, I think, has a responsibility to snoop around and to guess at what decisions may be forthcoming. He should use these guesses to orient his evaluation plan. He should try to develop some of the objectives of the evalu-

ation study so as to aid those future decisions. We evaluators should try to understand the local situation well enough so that we can suggest some of the decisions that may come up and so that we can gather data that are relevant to those decisions.

Under this advice the evaluator not only recommends which course to choose on a particular issue, but even decides what things to make decisions about in the first place. It is my position that utilization of evaluation research is enhanced not by increasing the social scientist's control and expertise mystique, but by fundamentally altering the evaluation decision process so that the evaluator shares power and expertise with an identifiable and organized group of decisionmakers and information users at every step along the way. The responsibility for making program decisions is theirs. The responsibility for determining what information they need in order to make future decisions is also theirs. If they are unwilling to meet those responsibilities prior to data collection, there is no reason to believe that they will take them on after the data are available.

A fourth way that utilization potential is diminished at the outset of an evaluation is simply to decide automatically that the funders of the evaluation, of the program, or both, are the relevant information users. In some cases this is accurate: funders may be among those interested in using evaluative information. But there are many other reasons why evaluations are funded—to give the appearance of being interested in evaluation, because legislation or licensing requires evaluation, or because someone thought it had to be written into the budget proposal. Just because someone controls evaluation purse strings does not mean that they have an evaluation question. Often they simply believe that evaluation is a good thing, ought to be done, helps programs, and keeps people on their toes. They do not care about the content of a specific evaluation, they only care that an evaluation—any evaluation—takes place. They mandate the process, but not the substance. Under such conditions (which are the rule rather than the exception) there is considerable opportunity for real information user-type decisionmakers to formulate the evaluation question and design.

Finally, a fifth way utilization potential is diminished during the conceptualization of the process is to target evaluations at organizations rather than at individuals. When the organization is the identified consumer of evaluation, specific decisionmakers and information users do not have to be identified and organized, and usually are not. For sociologists, the major characteristic which distinguishes modern from traditional societies is that " 'modern' societies carry on much more of their life in special-purpose organizations than do 'traditional' societies" (Stinchcombe, 1965: 145). Indeed, the process of modernization is characterized by "the growth of large-scale and multi-purpose—i.e., nonecological and nonkinship—groups and associations" (Eisenstadt, 1966: 53). Organizations are ubiquitous, and as Hage and Aiken (1970: 5) point out:

> The ubiquitousness of organizations is easily explained; they are the *major* mechanisms for achieving man's goals. . . . Whenever there is some specific objective to be accomplished, the realization of that goal requires the development of an organization.

Sociologists have a very precise view of how best to understand and study organizations. It is a view that has had substantial impact on evaluation researchers, management analysts, and administrative sciences. It is also a view largely devoid of individual people: indeed, the personal factor is anathema to sociology. Organizations are made up of positions. Skills, powers, rules, roles, and rewards attach to these positions. Since Max Weber's seminal essay on bureaucracy, sociologists have viewed the interchangeability of people in organizations as the hallmark of organizational rationality in modern society. Under their ideal norms of bureaucratic rationality, it does not matter who is in a position but only that the position be filled using universalistic criteria. The position, the set of positions, and the organizational social structure mold the individual to function rationally in that position. Weber argued that bureaucracy makes for maximum efficiency precisely because the organization of role-specific positions in an unambiguous hierarchy of authority and status renders action calculable and rational without regard for personal considerations or particularistic criteria.

It is this view of the world that has permeated the minds of evaluators when they say that their evaluation is "for the federal government" or any other organizational entity. Organizations do not consume information; people do—individual, idiosyncratic, caring, uncertain, searching people. Who is in a position makes all the difference in the world from the perspective of utilization of information. To ignore the personal factor is to diminish utilization potential from the outset. To target evaluations at organizations is to target them at nobody in particular—and, in effect, not to really target the evaluation at all.

Beyond Just Beginning

In this chapter the personal factor is identified as a critical determinant of utilization. The personal factor is a basis for establishing the first step in a utilization-focused approach to evaluation: identification and organization of relevant decisionmakers and information users. Once identified and organized, evaluators can interact with these decision-makers and information users throughout the evaluation, not just at the beginning. For there is a sixth approach to evaluation that also diminishes utilization potential, namely, to identify and organize relevant decision-makers and information users at the outset of the study, and then ignore them until the final report is ready.

Identification and organization of relevant decisionmakers and information users is not just an academic exercise performed for its own sake. The purpose of identifying and organizing real people who can use information is to enable them to establish direction for and have input into every step along the way. The personal factor is important from initiation of the study through the design and data collection stages as well as in the final report and dissemination parts of the process. If decisionmakers have shown little interest in the study in its earlier stages, our data suggest that they are not likely to suddenly show an interest in using the findings at the end of the study. Thus, utilization considerations are important through-out a study, not just at the stage where study findings are disseminated. The remaining chapters explore the implications of this perspective.

Chapter 5

FOCUSING THE EVALUATION QUESTION

A Setting

In 1976, the Northwest Regional Educational Laboratory contracted with the Hawaii State Department of Education to evaluate Hawaii's innovative 3-on-2 Program. The 3-on-2 Program is a team teaching approach in which three teachers work with two regular classrooms of primary-age children. Some classes combined children in multiage groupings. Walls between classrooms were removed so that three teachers and 40 to 60 children shared one large space. The program was aimed at greater individualization, greater cooperation and planning among teachers, and increased diversity of resources available to students in a single classroom.

The Northwest Lab research team proposed an advocacy-adversary evaluation model. Two teams were created; by coin toss one was designated the advocacy, the other the adversary team. The task of the advocacy team was to make the program look as good as possible. The advocates were charged with supporting the proposition that Hawaii's 3-on-2 Program is effective and ought to be continued. The adversaries were to attack the program; they were charged with marshalling all possible evidence demonstrating that the program ought to be terminated. The evaluation project director served as arbiter between the two teams (NWREL, 1977).

The advocacy-adversary model was a combination debate-courtroom approach to evaluation. As concern about the politics and pressures of evaluation grew in the early 1970s, and as critics of evaluation argued with increased vociferation that single evaluators could not maintain neutrality and objectivity throughout the evaluation process, support for the notion of the advocacy-adversary grew (cf. Wolf, 1975; Kourilsky, 1974; Owens, 1973). It was an intriguing idea and an alluring prospect.

I became involved as a resource consultant on classroom structure in November of 1976. The two teams were about to begin site visits to observe classrooms, and I was asked by the project director to assist them in developing a framework for systematically observing 3-on-2 classrooms.

When I arrived on the scene, I perceived and personally felt the exhilaration of the competition. I said to myself:

> These are no staid academic scholars. They are athletes training for the contest that will reveal who is best. These are lawyers prepared to use whatever means necessary to fully represent their clients. These are two teams that have become openly secretive about their respective strategies. Each team wants to present the best case it can. These are highly experienced and professional evaluators engaged in a battle not only of data but also of wits. The prospects are interesting indeed.

Just before I left Hawaii, the two teams began to prepare their final reports. As they discussed the content of the report among themselves and various information users, a concern emerged among some of the evaluators about the narrow focus of the evaluation question. As the evaluators addressed the primary issue of whether the Hawaii 3-on-2 program should be continued or terminated, the question was raised as to whether other information about how to change the program, how to make it better without terminating it, might not be more useful given the political realities of the situation. Was it possible that a great amount of time, effort, and money was directed at answering the wrong question?

Two members of the evaluation teams summarized the problem in their published *post mortem* of Hawaii's 3-on-2 advocacy-adversary evaluation.

> As we became more and more conversant with the intricacies, both educational and political, of the Hawaii 3-on-2 Program, we realized that Hawaii's decision-makers should not be forced to deal with a simple save-it-or-scrap-it choice. Middle ground positions were more sensible. Half-way measures, in this instance, probably made more sense. But there we were, obliged to

do battle with our adversary colleagues on the unembellished question of whether to maintain or terminate the 3-on-2 Program (Popham and Carlson, 1977: 5).

As planned and hoped for the results of the Hawaii 3-on-2 evaluation did focus on the right question and the results were used by the originally identified upper level decisionmakers. The results of a survey of Hawaii education officials reported by William Wright and Thomas Sachse at the 1977 Meeting of the American Educational Research Association showed that decisionmakers got the information they wanted. But the most important evidence that the evaluation focused on the right question comes from actions taken by decisionmakers following the evaluation. In the summer of 1979 Dean Nafziger, NWREL's Director of Evaluation, Research and Assessment wrote me to provide an update on the Hawaii 3-on-2 evaluation. After noting that the decisionmakers were clearly identified as state legislators, members of the State Board of Education, and the superintendent, he wrote:

> Their clear charge was that we should help them make a decision about maintaining the program or dropping it entirely. On the basis of the evaluation, the decision makers decided to eliminate the 3 on 2 program. The final phasing out of the program is scheduled for the upcoming year. As you can see then, we maintained attention to the information needs of the *true* decision makers, and adhered to those needs in the face of occasional counter positions by other evaluation audiences. . . .
>
> If a lesson is to be learned it is this: an evaluator must determine who is making the decisions and keep the information needed by the decision makers as the highest priority. In the case of the Hawaii 3 on 2 evaluation, the presentation of program improvement information would have served to muddle the decision making process.

The Hawaii 3-on-2 evaluation is exemplary in showing how the right information to the right people can make a difference. But it's seldom easy to know just what the right information is.

An Evaluation Fantasy

As I listened to the conversations in Hawaii I began to fantasize about how a conversation might go between program officials and evaluators if it had turned out, as Popham and Carlson worried it might, that an advocacy-adversary evaluation would not provide needed information for making program changes. My fantasy, which really deserves the touch of an Art Buchwald, went something like this:

Program officials: "We are very much looking forward to the results of your study. As you know, we have been experiencing a high rate of inflation and a declining school-age population. Under these conditions, with reduced federal aid, our program is simply too expensive to maintain as is."

Evaluators: "Do you mean you've already made the decision to terminate the program before the evaluation is completed?"

Program officials: "Oh, no! Nothing like that. All we've decided is that the program has to be changed. In some schools the program has been very successful and effective. Teachers like it; parents like it; principals like it. How can we terminate such a program? Other schools have only gone along because they were forced to, or because of getting extra money, or to save a teacher position when enrollments declined. In some places the two-class-room space has been subdivided into what is essentially three self-contained classrooms. We know that.

"What's more, it's the kind of program that has some strong political opposition and some strong political support. So, there's no question of terminating the program, and there's no question of keeping the program the same."

Evaluators: "I see. But you realize that the evaluation has two teams. One team will present data to show why the program should be continued. The other will present data to show why the program should be ended."

Program officials: "Ah, yes, we know. And that will be very interesting. We are looking forward to the presentation. But afterwards we trust you will give us answers to our practical questions. We hope you will tell us how to reduce the size of the program, how to make it more cost-effective where possible, and how to increase the overall quality of the program by setting up ways for eliminating ineffective sites and increasing support to successful sites. We don't want to interfere with your evaluation presentation. After all, you are the evaluators. But after the evaluation, maybe you can tell us the answer to these questions, too."

Evaluators: "Of course we want to be helpful in any way we can, but you realize those aren't the questions we've been studying. We've been studying the question of whether to keep the program or end the program. That's what the final reports will deal with."

Program officials: "Yes, yes, the final reports should be very interesting. But afterwards you can answer our real questions. There's no question of ending the program or keeping it the same. So afterwards we hope you will tell us how to improve the program, make it better. You can do that, can't you?"

Evaluators: "We can try, but at the moment we have nothing to say on those issues. We haven't thought about how to improve the program. We haven't gathered data on those questions. That hasn't been our job . . . !"

Identifying and Focusing the Evaluation Question

The practice of evaluators answering the wrong question, or no question at all, is widespread. The most common complaint I hear about evaluation research is that "it didn't tell me what I needed to know. It didn't answer my question." Such a response is not, however, inevitable.

Once relevant decisionmakers and information users have been identified and organized, *the second step in utilization-focused evaluation is to IDENTIFY AND FOCUS THE RELEVANT EVALUATION QUESTION.* This is an interactive process between evaluators and relevant decisionmakers or information users. It can be a difficult, even painful process, because deciding what you will study also means deciding what you will not study. Programs are so complex and have so many levels, goals, and functions that there are always more potential study foci than there are resources to examine them. Moreover, as human beings we have a limited capacity to take in data and juggle complexities. We can deal effectively with only so much at one time. The alternatives have to be narrowed and a choice made about which way to go.

This problem of focus is by no means unique to evaluation research. Management consultants find that a major problem for executives is focusing their energies on priorities. The trick in meditation is learning to focus on a single mantra, koan, or image. Professors have trouble getting graduate students to analyze less than the whole of human experience in their dissertations. And evaluators have trouble getting program staffs to delineate clear, specific goals.

But the delineation of clear, specific, and measureable goals is only one option in approaching the task of question focusing. In the next two chapters I shall discuss goal specification in utilization-focused evaluation. At this point I am talking about what happens at the very first meeting of selected decisionmakers and information users. I want to suggest some very practical ways of focusing the evaluation question so as to enhance utilization potential.

Identifying and focusing the evaluation question means dealing with several basic concerns. What is the purpose of the evaluation? How will the information be used? What will we know after the evaluation that we do not know now? What can we do after the evaluation that we cannot do now for lack of information? These are not simply rote questions. The answers to these and related questions will determine everything else that happens in a utilization-focused approach to evaluation. As evaluators and decisionmakers or information users interact around these questions, the evaluation begins to take shape.

Formative and Summative Evaluation Questions

First, it is important to clarify at the outset whether the primary purpose of the evaluation is to make an overall judgment about the effectiveness of a program or to collect information that can be used primarily for program development and improvement. The labels for this distinction were introduced by Michael Scriven (1967: 40-43) in discussing evaluation of educational curriculum. He called the former "summative evaluation" and the latter "formative evaluation." The distinction has since become a fundamental evaluation typology and the terms are now applied more broadly than they were by Scriven.

Summative evaluations are aimed at determining the essential effectiveness of programs and are particularly important in making decisions about continuing or terminating an experimental program or demonstration project. As such, summative evaluations are often useful to funders. Formative evaluations, in contrast, focus on ways of improving and enhancing programs not only in their initial development, but at any point in the life of a program. Formative information is particularly useful to program administrators and staff.

In his seminal article on formative versus summative evaluation, Scriven introduced these terms in the hope of reducing the positive connotations associated with "evaluation for improvement" versus the negative connotations associated with "evaluation to determine effectiveness." He was arguing against Cronbach's (1964) assertion that evaluation for improvement is more important and useful than evaluations to test a finished product. Considering the extent to which Scriven's formative-summative terminology is now a deeply entrenched and important distinction in evaluation research, it is ironic that the thrust of the article defining that terminology actually blurs the importance and implications of the distinction. While his overall position was essentially an argument in favor of outcomes evaluation for summative purposes, Scriven conceded that evaluation can and usually should play several roles—as long as its goal or purpose is clearly understood to be that of making judgments about performance. The implications of the formative-summative distinction were lost when he went on to seek a middle ground in the polemic over evaluation's most important role: "educational projects, particularly curricular ones, clearly must attempt to make best use of evaluations in both these roles" (Scriven, 1967: 41).

For any given evaluation, however, this distinction can be critical. Formative and summative evaluations involve significantly different research foci. The same data seldom serve both purposes well. When a program evaluation question is framed in summative terms and summative data are collected, program decisionmakers may not receive much-needed formative information for program change and improvement. They fail to receive the needed information because the evaluation question is not framed in formative terms.

While Scriven is right that any given data may be used for several purposes and that a final report may play various roles, it is also true that not all those purposes and roles can be served equally well. It is thus important to identify the primary purpose of the evaluation at the outset. In this way you are sure of fulfilling at least one evaluative function relatively well. Other decisions about what to do in the evaluation can then be made in accordance with how well the primary purpose will be served.

This point is similar to the rationale for identifying relevant decision-makers and information users as the first step in the evaluation process. Once assembled, this group does not represent all possible consumers of evaluation findings. A wide variety of people may have some interest in some aspect of a study. But these identified information users represent the primary users of the evaluation; they have responsibility for establishing direction and for determining the evaluation's purpose. Failing to identify people to fulfill these responsibilities means running the risk of serving a variety of evaluation functions poorly, or of serving some roles better than others without consciously planning which roles will be given priority. A more effective approach is to enhance utilization by focusing on ful-filling one purpose extremely well, so that at least the decisionmakers' central questions are answered.

Criteria for Utilization-Focused Evaluation Questions

From a utilization point of view, the right evaluation question has several characteristics:

(1) It is possible to bring data to bear on the question.

(2) There is more than one possible answer to the question, i.e., the answer is not predetermined by the phrasing of the question.

(3) The identified decisionmakers *want* information to help answer the question.

(4) The identified decisionmakers feel they *need* information to help them answer the question.

(5) The identified and organized decisionmakers and information users want to answer the question for themselves, not just for someone else.

(6) They care about the answer to the question.

(7) The decisionmakers can indicate how they would use the answer to the question, i.e., they can specify the relevance of an answer to the question for future action.

A brief elaboration of these major criteria follows.

THE EMPIRICAL CRITERION

Utilization-focused evaluation questions are empirical questions, i.e., it is possible to bring data to bear on them and the answer is not predetermined by the phrasing of the question. Evaluation research involves systematically collecting and analyzing empirical information for the purpose of making judgments and decisions about programs. The making of those judgments and decisions necessarily involves values. But value questions in and of themselves are not answerable empirically. It is critical, therefore, to separate the empirical question from the values question in the phrasing of the evaluation issue.

Let me illustrate this point with an example from teacher centers. Teacher centers have emerged as an alternative to isolated in-service programs on a school-by-school basis. A teacher center is a program aimed at providing resources, ideas, assistance, direction, and encouragement to teachers. Through the Office of Education, the federal government is now putting a great deal of money into teacher centers. The federal program requires evaluation. For many, the evaluation issue centers on the question of *improvement.* Are schools improving? Are teachers being helped? Are children doing better? In a review of the program's development, one teacher center planner and advocate has argued that assessment of program effectiveness "will have to be in terms of verifying individual teacher's improvement in classroom performance over time" (Devaney, 1977: 7; italics added).

Assessing improvement involves making a judgment about whether or not an observed impact is desirable or undesirable. It is important to separate the issue of improvement from the related but quite different issue of impact or change. Improvement involves a judgment about whether or not something is better, whereas impact involves the more limited question of whether or not something is different. An observed difference may or may not constitute improvement, depending on who is making the value judgment about whether or not the change is for better or worse. It is crucial throughout the evaluation process that empirical observations about program impact be kept separate from judgments about whether or not such impact constitutes improvement.

Suppose a teacher center conducts a series of workshops on the use of resources outside the classroom. As a result, a group of teachers increase field trips by an average of three hours a week. The time spent outside the classroom leads to an average reduction of two hours per week in time spent on reading and arithmetic in class. Clearly the teacher center has had an impact. Change has occurred. But has teaching improved? The answer depends on how much one values supervised reading and arithmetic compared to other stimulating activities.

Questions of right and wrong, better or worse, are not simple empirical questions. To formulate evaluation questions solely in value terms can sabotage an evaluation from the beginning. The empirical question is not improvement but change. Has the program been effective in changing teachers? Do they think differently? Can they do things now that they could not do before? Do they feel differently? Are different things occurring in classrooms? These are empirical evaluation questions. Data from such questions can then be used to determine whether or not such changes and differences constitute progress or improvement.

This is not an esoteric, semantic distinction, but a practical suggestion for distinguishing between that which can be observed (by whatever methods) and that which cannot be observed. Failure to make this distinction can lead to serious misunderstandings throughout the evaluation process. Questions which cannot be answered empirically do not provide a clear focus for utilization-focused evaluation.

QUESTIONS DECISIONMAKERS WANT ANSWERED

Utilization-focused evaluation questions focus on issues of *interest* to identified decisionmakers and information users. The question is something they want information about. This means avoiding questions that decisionmakers or information users do not want answered. In almost any program, there are questions of enormous political and personal sensitivity. You can tell when you have stumbled onto such a question because of the uneasy silence it produces, followed by the staff's groping for a way to tactfully change the subject. The most common questions in this category concern opinions about the performance of specific personnel. Personnel evaluation is quite different from program evaluation. Personnel evaluations involve gathering information about the performance of individuals. Program evaluations focus on structural and treatment characteristics of programs. At times there is a narrow line between the two because personnel performance can, of course, affect program effectiveness. Nevertheless, they represent quite distinct evaluation foci.

I recall one human service program in particular where we were asked to evaluate the staff development component of the program. In accordance with Peter's Principle, the person in charge of staff development had risen to her own level of incompetence: she was tenured; she had territoriality on that component of the program; she could not be fired and there was no place to which to promote her; she seemed likely to be impervious to change. No one wanted to know what staff, clients, or administrators thought about her—that was data they did not want and could not use. We focused instead on concrete, changeable program activities (e.g., frequency and length of training sessions, content of sessions, participant input, style of training, use of outside resources, and so on).

Research focus is always a difficult issue. Some evaluators seem to have a talent for honing in on personally sensitive questions; their instinct is to go for the kill. Whatever program staff do not want answered, the evaluators do want answered. They are investigators uncovering incompetence and rooting out ineffectiveness. While I personally take a different approach, I do not deny the right of evaluators to do what they feel they must do—or else resign their commission. But the utilization potential of such evaluators is low. If decisionmakers and information users do not want a question answered, they will find ways to ignore or discredit the answers proffered. The evaluator can feel righteous about having produced the information, but is not likely to have the satisfaction of seeing it used. There is probably a proverb to express this viewpoint, something to the effect that "you can lead decisionmakers to information but you can't make them swallow it." They have to be interested.

QUESTIONS THAT NEED ANSWERING

Utilization-focused questions are those that decisionmakers feel they need information to answer. This means the answer is not already known.

In some cases the reason why program staff do not want a question asked is because they already know with considerable certainty what the answer is. From a utilization point of view, there is no reason to spend a lot of time and money gathering information to tell people things they already know. This is particularly true when a program is relatively chaotic—staff are going in different directions, management ineffective, clients unhappy. Everyone involved knows things are a mess. The last thing such a program needs is more information to deal with: managerial help, yes; planning assistance, indeed; staff training, without a doubt; but program evaluation, no. Such a program does not suffer from lack of evaluative information, it suffers from a lack of action.

This is a point that must be stressed with decisionmakers, information users, and program staff. Unless a lack of knowledge and information is part of the problem, evaluation research will not help an organization. All evaluation research can do is tell you something you do not already know, or increase your certainty about something of which you were unsure. Evaluations are no panacea for program problems.

An example of this is a daycare program in Minneapolis that was losing clients and money. The board knew that the program was poorly located and poorly organized. But instead of relocating and reorganizing, they got a grant to conduct an evaluation. During the evaluation the program folded.

Part of the evaluation interaction process, then, should be aimed at determining what things are already known, what actions can already be taken without further study—and on what aspects of program functioning evaluative information is really needed.

THE PERSONAL INTEREST CRITERION

Utilization-focused questions are of direct personal interest to identified and organized decisionmakers and information users. They want to answer the question for themselves, not just for someone else: they personally care about the answer to the question. The reason for identifying and organizing relevant decisionmakers and information users is to be sure that the people who are going to be the primary users of evaluation findings are the same people who decide what the focus of the evaluation will be. This means that the evaluation should focus on their information needs—not on their speculations about what someone else wants to know. If the evaluation is for someone else, it behooves the evaluator to make that person part of the identified and organized evaluation task force. A brief example may help illustrate this point.

I sometimes have the opportunity to work at the classroom level with individual teachers. My mandate is to help them improve their teaching, in which case the individual teacher is my decisionmaker and information user. The teacher, however, does not necessarily see it that way:

> *Evaluator:* "What would you like to have me help you gather information about?"
> *Teacher:* "Well, I guess we should evaluate student achievement in basic skills."
> *Evaluator:* "Do you know how well your students are doing in basic skills?"
> *Teacher:* "Sure, I know how well they're doing. But the principal and parents don't know."
> *Evaluator:* "Well now, as I understand this evaluation it's purpose is to help you improve your teaching. If there's nothing you need to know and if the evaluation is for the principal, then I should talk to the principal and find out what she wants evaluated. She may already know how well the students are achieving basic skills. Likewise with the parents. If the evaluation is for them, I ought to get them together and find out what they want to know."

At this point we can decide if there is anything the teacher wants to study, or if someone else should become the decisionmaker or information user for the evaluation. My experience is that once people really catch onto the idea that it is all right for them to ask their own questions, *questions about which they care,* and that they can conduct evaluations for themselves, not just for someone else, then they become quite excited about and committed to the evaluation process.

QUESTIONS AIMED AT FUTURE ACTION

The utilization potential of an evaluation is enhanced if decisionmakers and information users can indicate during conceptualization how they plan to use information obtained during an evaluation. If they cannot indicate future usefulness at the outset, there is no reason to believe they will be able to do so after the evaluation.

Identification of future decisions to be made based on evaluation data sometimes constitutes the first step in an evaluation model, e.g., Mark Thompson's (1975) "evaluation for decision" approach. There are two problems with this approach to conceptualizing evaluation questions. First, unless relevant decisionmakers and information users have been identified and organized, the evaluator ends up deciding what future decisions ought to be affected. Second, our findings on the actual ways in which evaluation information is used (Chapters 3 and 4) show that in real programs there are very few decisions of the concrete, single point in time, this-is-the-day-to-make-a-decision variety. Rather, evaluation information feeds into a process of programmatic change, development, and "muddling through" (cf. Suchman, 1972: 57-58).

Thus, to say that evaluation questions ought to be framed in a future action context does not mean that they need be aimed at some single future decision, though on occasion that may be possible and appropriate. Rather, more generally, decisionmakers and information users ought to be able to indicate where their knowledge uncertainties lie, what activities, actions, and options are clouded by those uncertainties, and how evaluative information would increase their potential for doing a better job and making the program more effective. In short, the evaluator attempts to "frame the decision context for the evaluation" (Alkin, 1976b).

One way to help guarantee that evaluation studies are geared to collecting information with future action potential is to focus on what Amitai Etzioni calls "moveable" or "malleable" variables. These are factors that are subject to human intervention. Etzioni conceptualizes a continuum from highly immutable conditions (laws of nature) to highly manipulable elements (symbols):

> The first and single most important methodological consideration for a policy researcher is an interest in moveable variables. . . . Within the social realm you can rank order all the variables which characterize the social world as to what is more moveable and what is less moveable. . . . The reason I emphasize this so much is that most of our non-evaluation, non-policy research tends to zero in on the non-moveable variable (Etzioni and Patton, 1976).

In the same vein, Etzioni argues that jobs are usually more malleable than people. He suggests, for example, that rather than trying to make lower socioeconomic persons into punctual, routine-oriented workers, jobs ought to be changed so that employees can carry out their work on a flexible schedule: "generally I would think that you can demonstrate empirically that jobs can be restructured more readily than people's personalities" (Etzioni and Patton, 1976).

This distinction recalls the point made earlier in this chapter about the difference between personnel evaluation and program evaluation. Program elements are more malleable than personnel. In focusing the evaluation question on future action potential, it is helpful to be sure that the question is aimed at malleable aspects of programmatic activity. From a utilization point of view there is little value in studying a question that would generate information about conditions which are impervious to change.

Duncan MacRae (1976: 283) suggests that the focus on manipulable variables may be too narrow. Nonmanipulable variables are also important because "the consequences of policy choice or of action depend in an *interactive* fashion on manipulated and nonmanipulated variables." The real point is to focus the evaluation on future action potential. Edward Suchman (1972: 55) has emphasized the importance of this orientation:

> Much too often evaluation studies are undertaken when there is very little likelihood that anything will change regardless of how the evaluation comes out. The attitude seems to be "let's do the evaluation and then decide what to do with the results." In such a case, the evaluation is probably unnecessary and certainly inadequately conceived.

Generating Questions

Given these criteria for how to focus on evaluation questions with high utilization potential, there remains the problem of how to get started. How can an evaluator facilitate the framing of evaluation questions without imposing his or her own questions? I shall suggest one process that I have found particularly helpful. I first used it in an evaluation of the Frontier School Division, Manitoba, Canada.

The Frontier School Division is a geographically immense school district that encompasses much of northern Manitoba. The Deputy Minister of Education in Manitoba thought evaluation might be a way to shake things up, so he asked me to come and meet with them. His own goal was simply to get something started. The actual form and content of the evaluation was to be determined internally, within the Frontier School Division. So I went up to Winnipeg and met with the division administrators, a representative from the parents' group, a representative from the principals' group, and a representative from the teachers' union. I had asked that all constituencies be represented in order to establish a base with all the people who might be involved in using the evaluation. This was to be the initial group of decisionmakers and information users.

Inasmuch as I had been brought in from outside by a superordinate official, it was not surprising that I encountered an atmosphere ranging from defensiveness to outright hostility. They had not asked for the evaluation, and the whole idea sounded unsavory and threatening. In short, the utilization potential for my services seemed minimal.

I began by asking the group to tell me what kinds of things they were interested in evaluating. One administrator responded: "okay, to begin with we'd like to see the evaluation instruments you've used in assessing other school districts."

I replied that I would be happy to share those instruments with them if they should prove relevant, but it would be helpful to know first what they wanted to evaluate, what kind of information they wanted. They were very appreciative of my concern for their input, so one participant suggested, "we didn't mean that you needed to show us all the instruments. Just show use one so we have an idea of what's going to happen."

I again replied that it was too early to really start talking about instruments. First, we had to identify the evaluation question. Then we would talk about instruments. By then I could tell that I was intensifying their initial suspicions and fears. I was confirming the worst and heightening their resistance by my secretiveness about the content of *my* evaluation scheme. One superintendent decided to try a different tack: "okay, well, we don't need to see everything at once. How about just showing us one part, say the part that asks about superintendents in the teacher interviews you use."

At that point I was about to throw in the towel, give them some old instruments, and let them use what they wanted out of other evaluations. But I decided to try one other approach first: "look, maybe your questions will be the same as questions I've used on surveys elsewhere. But I'm not even sure at this point that any kind of survey is appropriate. Maybe you don't need an evaluation. I certainly don't have any questions I need answered about your operations and effectiveness. Maybe you don't either. In which case I'll tell the Deputy Minister that evaluation isn't the way to go. But before we decide to quit, let me ask you to participate with me in a simple little exercise. It's an old complete-the-blank exercise from grade school." I then turned to the blackboard and wrote a sentence in capital letters.

I WOULD LIKE TO KNOW _____ ABOUT FRONTIER SCHOOL DIVISION.

"What I want each of you to do individually is to complete the blank ten times. What are ten things about Frontier School Division that you'd like to know, things you aren't certain about, things that might make a difference in what you do if you had more information? Take a shot at it, without regard to methods, measurement, design, resources, precision— just ten basic questions, real questions about this division."

They did that. Then I divided them into three groups of four people each and asked them to combine their lists together into a single list of ten things that each group wanted to know. They found that there were a lot of items that were very similar, that were easily combined. Then we got back together and generated a single list of ten basic things that they would like to know—things that they did not have information on but that they wanted to have information on, information that might make a difference in what they were doing.

The questions generated were somewhat similar to other district-wide educational evaluations because there are only so many things one can ask about a school division. But the questions were phrased in their terms, incorporating important local nuances of meaning and circumstance.

It was important to have a list of questions. The questions needed some additional work to fit all the criteria for high utilization potential, but at least we had some questions they cared about—not my questions but their questions, because during the course of the exercise it had become *their* evaluation. The whole atmosphere had changed. This became most evident as I read aloud the final list of ten items they had generated that morning. One of the items read: "we would like to know what teachers think about the job superintendents are doing and how often superintendents ought to be out in the teachers' classrooms." One of the superintendents who had been most hostile when I first came in said, "that would be dynamite information. We have no idea at all what teachers think about us and what we do. I have no idea if they want me in their classrooms or if they don't want me in the classroom, or how often they think I ought to visit. That could just turn my job around. That would be great to know." We went on down the list and came to a question about the relationship between the classroom and the community. Both the teacher and parent representatives said that nobody had ever thought about that in any real way: "we don't have any policy about that. We don't know what goes on in the different schools. That would be important for us to know."

We spent the rest of the day refining questions, prioritizing, formalizing evaluation procedures, and establishing an agenda for the evaluation process. The hostility had vanished. By the end of the day they were anxious to have me make a commitment to return. They had become excited about doing their evaluation. The evaluation had credibility because the questions were their questions. A month later they found out that budget shifts in the Ministry meant that the central government would not pay for the evaluation. The Deputy Minister told them that they could scrap the evaluation if they wanted to, but they decided to pay for it out of local division funds.

The evaluation was completed in close cooperation with the task force at every step along the way. The results were disseminated to all principals and teachers. The conclusions and recommendations formed the basis for staff development conferences and division policy sessions. The evaluation process itself impacted on the Division. Over the last three years Frontier School Division has gone through many changes. It is a very different place in terms of direction, morale, and activity than it was on my first visit. Not all those changes were touched on in the evaluation, nor are they simply a consequence of the evaluation. But generating a list of real and meaningful evaluation questions played a critical part in getting things started.

Alternatives to Utilization-Focused Evaluation Questions

There are other ways to solve the problem of focus in the evaluation process. One typical solution to the problem of what to study is for the evaluator to frame questions based largely upon his or her own interests, disciplinary tradition, and theoretical perspective. The evaluator's research agenda is most likely to be paramount where relevant decisionmakers and information users have *not* been identified and organized. Under such circumstances who else is there but the evaluator to determine the real focus of the evaluation? The answer to the evaluator's questions may be of some use to the evaluator, but rarely will such an evaluation answer the questions of those who face the day-to-day uncertainties of determining program effectiveness and guiding program improvement.

Decisionmakers bear considerable responsibility for making sure that their questions are the focus of the evaluation. In our study of the utilization of federal health evaluations, one decisionmaker described quite cogently the effort involved in making sure that the right question was evaluated.

> The initial design stages went round and round because they [the evaluators] kept trying to answer a different question than the one we wanted answered. . . . If we had dropped it with them right then and said go ahead and do your own thing with it, it would not have been useful. . . . I have a feeling I'm becoming redundant. The greatest single factor [explaining utilization] was that the question *we* wanted answered was the question they did at least try to answer in the study (DM367: 16).

When funds for basic research are scarce, resourceful academicians have found that evaluation funds serve just as well for research support. At a 1975 Theory Symposium sponsored by the University of Minnesota Department of Sociology, Peter Rossi called this the "Robin Hood" approach to evaluation: stealing from the rich (those with evaluation funds) to give to the poor (those in need of basic research funds). A tipoff that scholarly Robin Hoods are on the loose is their long and frequent soliloquies about the importance of using applied research to contribute to basic scientific knowledge. Since the researcher is in a better position than program staff to know what will contribute to basic scientific knowledge, and since one can no more be against contributing to basic scientific knowledge than one can be against progress (sometimes operationalized as increased motherhood, more apple pie, and larger doses of baseball), the evaluation researcher is in the optimal position to determine the research question.

Another closely related way of determining what to study in an evaluation is to let the available methods shape the question. Whatever question can be answered with available evaluator skills, that is the question that will be answered. The usefulness of studying a particular question is thus not at issue. Economists pose questions in cost-benefit terms; sociologists frame questions that are amenable to study using survey methods; anthropologists think in terms of their own field methods to shape the question; and psychologists look for evaluation questions that will necessitate the use of some test to measure effects on the program's target population.

Another approach to the problem of focus is to try to look at everything at once. This approach can emerge from enthusiastic proponents of evaluation who believe that evaluation is so important it should be applied to everything. At other times the decision to look at multiple issues emerges as a political compromise when consensus about a more limited focus cannot be found. As often as not, evaluations aimed at everything are simply a result of poor conceptualization and failure to think about the issues involved.

There are two dangers in taking on too much. First, as suggested earlier in this chapter, once the evaluation is actually under way some things end up getting more attention than others. Regardless of intentions, not everythink will be studied equally. The second danger is that those participating in the evaluation can become overwhelmed by the complexity and endlessness of it all, particularly if they are new to research. One of the advantages of at least beginning with relatively small-scale, highly focused, and manageable evaluations is that they can provide some immediate reinforcement (through visible results) for demonstrating the utility of evaluation, thereby building staff support for larger scale, longer term, and more complex evaluation efforts.

The opposite case is illustrated by a Manitoba Ministry of Education evaluation system where every seven years each school division undertakes a comprehensive study of student achievement, school climate, teacher development, curriculum, administrative effectiveness, community values about education, the school lunch program, the division bus transportation system, extracurricular activities, and basic skills. In short, each division conducts a comprehensive, systematic review of its entire educational mission, using both internal resources and external consultants—thus its name, "the Internal-External Model of Evaluation." At a two day conference held to introduce the plan to three pilot school divisions, local school officials soon felt overwhelmed by the enormity of the task. They quickly dubbed the system "the internal-external-eternal" model of evaluation. The experiences of that interminable first year bore out the wisdom of the revised label. Without focus, one can generate a great deal of activity with very little useful product.

Evaluation Questions in Review

The second step in a utilization-focused approach to evaluation is *identifying and focusing the relevant evaluation questions.* One way of beginning this process is to clearly establish the formative and summative purpose of the evaluation. The case of the Hawaii 3-on-2 Program's adversary-advocacy evaluation illustrates how utilization is affected when relative summative-formative emphases are not clarified.

Not all questions establish a framework for program evaluation equally well. From a utilization point of view, the right question has several characteristics:

(1) It is possible to bring data to bear on the question.

(2) There is more than one possible answer to the question, i.e., the answer is not determined by the phrasing of the question.

(3) The identified decisionmakers want information to help answer the question.

(4) The identified decisionmakers feel they need information to help them answer the question.

(5) The identified and organized decisionmakers and information users want to answer the question for themselves, not just for someone else.

(6) They care about the answer to the question.

(7) The decisionmaker can indicate how they would use the answer to the question, i.e., they can specify the relevance of an answer to the question for future action.

The Frontier School Division evaluation experience illustrates a technique for generating evaluation questions through structured interaction with relevant decisionmakers and information users. There are, however, alternatives to focusing the question according to utilization criteria: let the researcher determine the question; let the methods available determine the question; or, try to look at everything at once with no focused evaluation question.

The point of paying such close attention to identifying and focusing the evaluation question is that utilization potential is thereby enhanced. But a note of temperance may be in order. Increasing utilization potential does not guarantee utilization of findings. There are no guarantees. All one can really do is increase the likelihood of utilization. Utilization-focused evaluation is time consuming, exhausting, and frequently frustrating. It is a process filled with options, ambiguities, and uncertainties. When things go wrong, as they often do, you may find yourself asking a personal evaluation question: how did I ever get myself into this craziness?

But when things go right, when decisionmakers care, when the evaluation question is important, focused, and on target, when you begin to see programs changing even in the posing of the questions—then evaluation research can be exhilarating, energizing, and fulfilling. It is a creative, challenging process. It involves people in that most splendid of human enterprises—the application of intellect and emotion to the search for answers that will improve human effort and activity. It seems a shame to waste all that intellect and emotion studying the wrong question. Thus it is worth taking the time to identify and focus on relevant evaluation questions.

Chapter 6

THE GOALS CLARIFICATION GAME

A Setting

This chapter is a critical review of strategies for identifying and clarifying program goals. Evaluation questions are typically framed in relation to the goals and objectives of a program. Peter Rossi (1972: 18) has stated that "a social welfare program (or for that matter any program) which does not have clearly specified goals cannot be evaluated without specifying some measurable goals. This statement is obvious enough to be a truism." In a major review of the evaluation literature in education, Worthen and Sanders (1973: 231) concluded that

> if evaluators agree in anything, it is that program objectives written in unambiguous terms are useful information for any evaluation study. Thus, program objectives and specifications become an extremely important consideration when an evaluation study is constructed.

And Carol Weiss (1972b: 24-26) has noted that "the traditional formulation of the evaluation question is: to what extent is the program succeeding in reaching its goals?" This question assumes that goals can be identified, but goal identification and clarification can be a difficult process. Weiss has explained that "the goal must be clear so that the evaluator knows what to look for." But clarity is itself an elusive goal: "the evaluation question sounds simple enough in the abstract. . . . But what looks elementary in theory turns out in practice to be a demanding enterprise. . . . Thus begins the long, often painful process of getting people to state goals in terms that are *clear*, *specific*, and *measurable*" (italics in original).

Discussions of program and organizational goals are characterized by solemnity. One cannot read much evaluation literature without encountering serious treatises on the centrality and importance of identifying and clarifying program goals, and this solemnity seems to carry over into evaluators' discussions of goals with program staff.

There may be no more deadly way to begin a program staff meeting than by stating that the purpose of the meeting is to identify and clarify program goals and objectives. If evaluators are second only to tax collectors in the hearts of program staff, I suspect that it is not because staff fear evlauators' judgments about program success, but because they hate constant questioning about goals.

Goals clarification meetings are frequently conducted like the twenty questions game played at parties. Someone thinks of an object in the room and then the players are allowed 20 questions to guess what it is. In the goals clarification game, the evaluator has an object in mind (a clear, specific, and measurable goal). Program staff are the players. The game begins with the staff writing down some statement they think is a goal. Then the evaluator inspects the statement and tells the staff how close they have come to the goal he or she has in mind. This process is repeated in successive trys until the game ends. The game can end in one of three ways: the staff gives up (so the evaluator wins and writes the program goals for staff); the evaluator gives up (so the staff gets by with vague, fuzzy, and unmeasurable goals); or, in rare cases, the game ends when staff actually stumbles on a statement that reasonably approximates what the evaluator had in mind. There are at least five reasons why program staff have come to hate this game so much:

(1) They have played the game hu;ndreds of times, not just for evaluators, but for funders, advisory boards, in writing proposals, and even among themselves.

(2) They have learned that when playing the game with evaluators, the evaluators almost always win.

(3) They always come out of the game knowing that they appear fuzzyminded and inept to the evaluator.

(4) It is a boring game.

(5) It is an endless game because each new evaluator comes to the game with a different object in mind. (Clarity, specificity, and measurability are not clear, specific, and measurable criteria, so each evaluator can apply a different set of rules in the game!)

In recent years, however, program staff have become more astute at certain aspects of the goals clarification game. They have developed gambits, gambles, and gammons to counter the traditional goals clarification strategies of evaluators. Such strategies as the goals clarification shuffle, the goals conflict approach, and switching from goals clarification to goals war have made the problems of conceptualizing an evaluation research design increasingly more difficult. Evaluators have responded with their own new techniques to counter the strategic moves of program staff. Thus, the evaluator who wants to excel at the goals clarification game must include in his or her repertoire the Delphi technique, multiattribute-utility measurement, the decision-theoretic approach, fuzzy sets theory, social-judgment theory and goal-free evaluation.

Before discussing the goal of goals in the utilization-focused approach to evaluation, it will be helpful to review these precursory moves and countermoves from the evaluation literature. While my treatment of these ploys and counterploys will be somewhat on the light side, the attempt to show that discussions of goals can be fun will do the reader a severe disservice if its sarcasm completely disguises the serious nature of the underlying issues involved. It is well to remember that the stakes in this game of values clarification can include the allocation of millions of dollars for health, education, welfare, and other programs, i.e., decisions that can affect the basic provision of needed services to hundreds of thousands of people. Under such conditions evaluation and decision-making efforts can often be viewed as either tragic or ridiculous. For my own sanity I choose to see the humor.

The Goals Clarification Shuffle

The ploy of the goals clarification shuffle is employed most often by program staff who lose the first round of play but later find that they do not like the goal priorities established by the evaluator. This strategy can also be used by funders, administrators, advisory boards, or any other group of people who want to create evaluation havoc. Like many other dance steps (e.g., the Harlem shuffle, the hustle) this technique has the most grace and style when executed simultaneously by a full group of people. The goals clarification shuffle involves a sudden change in goals and priorities after the evaluator is firmly committed to a certain set of measuring instruments and to a research design. The choreography for this technique is quite simple. The top priority program goal is moved two spaces to either the right or left and four spaces backward. Concurrently, all other goals are shuffled randomly but with style and subtlety. Many variations are possible here. The only stipulation is that the first goal must end up somewhere in the middle, with other goals reordered by new criteria.

The goals clarification shuffle first came into national prominence in 1969, when it was employed as a daring counterthrust to the Westinghouse-Ohio State University Head Start Evaluation. That study evaluated cognitive and affective outcomes of the Head Start Program and concluded that Head Start was largely ineffective (Westinghouse Learning Corporation, 1969; Cicarelli, 1971). However, as soon as the final report was published the goals clarification shuffle was executed before enthusiastic congressional audiences, thus establishing the belief that Head Start's health, nutrition, resource redistribution, cultural, and community goals ought to have been in the spotlight (cf. Williams and Evans, 1969; Evans, 1971: 402). The result was that despite the negative evaluation findings, Congress expanded the Head Start program and the evaluators were thrown on the defensive. (It was about this same time that serious concerns over nonutilization of evaluation findings started to be heard on a national scale.)

In the case of Head Start, the goals clarification shuffle was only partially effective because the technique was not employed until after the evaluation had been completed. This permitted data to be collected on the goals preferred by the evaluators. The technique has the greatest impact if used just as the evaluation is getting underway. At this point evaluators will have committed themselves to a definitive ordering of program outcomes. By executing the goals clarification shuffle, the program staff essentially reopens play precisely when evaluators think the goals clarification game has already been won. This technique confuses evaluators, sometimes makes them angry, and always makes them defensive: "but I thought we had reached agreement on program goals!" If carried out with the proper precision and timing, the goals clarification shuffle can completely discredit an evaluation from the start and, on occasion, sabotage the entire effort. Evaluators have recently begun protecting themselves from the goals clarification shuffle at the outset by having program staff produce official, written goal statements to which allegiance is made in some public fashion. (A newspaper article stating the goals as having been leaked by a well-placed, usually reliable source is a particularly effective strategy.) The effectiveness of the shuffle is seriously diminished if staff has produced such an official list of goal priorities in the first round of play. Lists of goals are easier to shuffle if they were prioritized and written by evaluators, not staff.

Conflict Over Goals and the Delphi Counter

Conflict arises from many sources and can sometimes be functional (cf. Coser, 1964), but conflict over program goals is frequently a major source of irritation for evaluators trying to identify and clarify those goals. In criminal justice programs, there can be conflict over whether the purpose of the program is punitive (punish criminal offenders for wrongdoing), custodial (keep criminal offenders off the streets), or to provide treatment (rehabilitate and return to society). In education and training programs, there is often conflict over whether the goal of the program is attitude change or behavior change. In welfare agencies, there may be disagreement concerning whether the purpose of the program is to provide long-term services to the needy or short-term crisis intervention services. In health settings, staff dissension may emerge over the relative emphasis to be placed on preventive versus curative medical practice. Virtually anytime a group of people assemble to determine program goals there is potential for undermining the goals clarification process if a "conflict configuration" emerges. The emergence of a conflict configuration can be either pre-meditated or spontaneous; either way it usually results in lengthy, frustrating, and inconclusive meetings. In the goals clarification game a conflict configuration is usually an easy play to execute. Someone on the staff simply counters the evaluator's attempts to identify and clarify goals by playing on differences in members' personal values and otherwise engendering disagreements, arguments, and dissensus.

For inexperienced evaluators, a conflict configuration can be devastating. The novice evaluator can get caught up in the conflict and lose all credibility by joining one side or the other. More experienced evaluators have learned to remain calm and neutral in hopes that group members will eventually resolve the conflict themselves. But this is a dangerously passive technique. As with other sports, the best offense is a good defense. One option is for the evaluators to call a halt to the game by asserting that they, as neutral observers, are the only participants sufficiently objective and skilled to be able to write and prioritize goals for the group. This counter, however, leaves the evaluators vulnerable to the goals clarification shuffle at some later point in time.

A more elaborate defense against the goals conflict configuration is the Delphi Technique (Helmer, 1966; Dalkey, 1969). This technique is quite popular among evaluators who hate dealing with committees:

> The Delphi technique, a method of developing and improving group consensus, was originally used at the RAND Corporation to arrive at reliable predictions about the future of technology; hence its oracular name. . . . Delphi essentially refers to a series of intensive interrogations of samples of individuals (most frequently, experts) by means of mailed questionnaires concerning some important problem or question; the mailings are interspersed with controlled feedback to the participants. The responses in each round of questioning are gathered by an intermediary, who summarizes and returns the information to each participant, who may then revise his own opinions and ratings. . . . However antagonistic the initial positions and complex the questions under analysis—competing opinions apparently converge and synthesize when this technique is used (Rosenthal, 1976: 121).

The trick in this goals clarification technique is that participants never meet face-to-face. Thus, disagreements and arguments never get a chance to surface on a personal, interface level. Moreover, the participants in the process remain anonymous. At the end of the process, a master list of prioritized goals is produced to which everyone consents and for which no one has to take responsibility.

> The technique has proved so successful in producing consensus . . . it is now often adopted in many kinds of situations where convergence of opinion is advisable or desirable . . . avoiding as it does the sundry prima donna behaviors that may vitiate round table discussions (Rosenthal, 1976: 121-122).

The Technology of Conflict Resolution: Multiattribute-Utility Measurement and the Decision-Theoretic Approach

One requirement of the Delphi approach is that people be willing to make choices. As Adelson et al. (1967: 28) found in their national use of the Delphi technique for education planning, people are very uncomfortable about making choices . . . even people who should be adept and comfortable with the need to decide can find making the required choices—even hypothetically—extremely painful. Moreover, the choices are made very differently by different people . . . and there were some recorded dissensuses that did not seem to be resolved in the number of iterations used.

In some programs the evaluators encounter dissensus so intense that the situation constitutes an open war over goals and values. A "goals war" usually occurs when two or more strong coalitions are locked in battle to determine which group will control the future direction of some public policy or program. Such wars over goals are sparked by highly emotional issues that involve deepseated values. Evaluations of school busing programs to achieve racial balance are a good example. By what criteria ought busing programs be evaluated? Changed racial attitudes, changed interracial behaviors, changed student achievement, changed property values, and changed neighborhood demographics are all candidates for the honor of being primary program goals. Are school busing and other antiracist programs supposed to achieve desegregation (representative proportions of minority students in all schools) or integration (positive interracial attitudes, cooperation, and interaction)? Many communities, school boards, and school staffs are in open warfare over these issues. Included in such arguments are basic disagreements about the appropriate evaluation criteria to apply (cf. Cohen and Garet, 1975; Cohen and Weiss, 1977).

In the goals clarification game, an evaluator can anticipate a goals war when two or more coalitions emerge; these coalitions represent fundamentally contrasting values and refuse to agree on goal statements and priorities. The goals war is posed as a fight to the finish, elevating conflict to a level where the participating coalitions are so suspicious of each other that they would never allow a list of goals to emerge without face-to-face confrontation (which amounts to saying they would never allow a list of consensus goals to emerge). The goals war opponents insist on open meetings where interpersonal vendettas can be publicly aired. Efforts to establish consensus about the goals of public housing and land use regulation programs are usually of this order. Environmentalists clash with industrial developers over the purposes of these programs. Hearings on environmental impact statements are another excellent opportunity to observe the goals war strategy in full mobilization. In the health and welfare area, program staffs and funding bodies have recently found themselves on various sides of the war over whether or not abortions come under the mandate of medicaid.

Evaluators have recently developed a counterstrategy to neutralize goals war machinations. Drawing on the conceptual work of decision analysts and using techniques embodied in Bayesian statistics, a goals clarification "technology" called "multiattribute-utility measurement" is now being used to counter intense values conflicts (cf. Gardiner and Edwards, 1975). The most direct adaptation of multiattribute-utility measurement for evaluation research is the "decision-theoretic approach." This approach permits an option concerning whether or not to use face-to-face groups. Where conflict is not intense, face-to-face interaction is preferred because "individuals frequently agree more about values than they would predict" (Edwards et al., 1975: 172). Where conflict is intense, separate coalitions can work independently throughout the process.

Multiattribute-utilities measurement begins by identifying the persons or organizations whose utilities are to be maximized. Next is identification of the issues to which the needed utilities are relevant, followed by identification of the entities to be evaluated. After these more or less philosophical steps, the relevant dimensions of value are identified. Relevant dimensions of value are the goals of the program. These goals are ranked in order of importance and then rated to establish the relative distance between goals. At this point the so-called technology becomes more sophisticated. The ratings are mathematically transformed to a set of probabilities and "experts" are used to "measure the location of each entity being evaluated on each dimension"—i.e., goals are operationalized. Utilities are calculated for each entity, using the equation for a weighted average. Then, using the results, decisions can be made about which utilities to maximize. (These steps are outlined in virtually identical language by Edwards et al., 1975: 153-157; and Gardiner and Edwards, 1975: 14-19). In the "decision-theoretic" adaptation of this model to program evaluation, the first five steps are assumed to be already manifest in the program's statement of goals: "typically, program goals are consistent with the decision maker's values, and it is possible to make explicit the program's goals and their relative importance to the decision maker" (Edwards et al., 1975: 174).

The power of multiattribute-utility measurement or the decision-theoretic approach is that it allows the evaluator to deal with goals wars by providing separate information to each competing coalition in terms of the values of that coalition:

This is useful for three reasons. First, each group builds a consensus about its own values vis-à-vis the programs. . . . Second, the same evaluation data can be fed back to each group. . . . Thus, a number of groups can, using the same data, come to very different conclusions about whether a program or programs are meeting their goals. This then provides them with a substantive basis for discussions with one another. Third, consensus is not a sine qua non of the evaluation process. If a number of different groups generate different values, then data must be gathered which indicate how contemplated actions bear on every one of the values. This forces the evaluator into multiple measurement. In addition, it means that decision makers receive research data on issues that may be foreign to their own values, but quite germane to the values of other groups (Edwards, Guttentag, and Snapper, 1975: 172).

In effect, this approach postpones the war until data are gathered to be used as additional ammunition in each side's fight. The evaluators are technicians who provide modern technology for warfare to both sides of the conflict. The evaluators remain neutral. The issue for conflicting parties is whether or not it is to their advantage to have information to use in the battle. Many groups continue to prefer conventional street fights to the cleaner warfare of computer technology. Thus where several coalitions or agencies are involved, it may be difficult to get them all to make their values explicit using the same utilities analysis system. Edwards et al. (1975: 171) experienced this difficulty in a project that involved several HEW offices, only one of which used the utilities analysis system. If each had used the system,

it would have been possible for each of these agencies to know precisely where the differences and similarities in values between them lay. But the simultaneous conversion of several government agencies to a new methodology is too much to ask!

Multiattribute-utility measurement and the decision-theoretic approach are mechanisms aimed at rationalizing decisionmaking processes. They are sophisticated and complex methods that have high utilization potential when participants understand the process and commit themselves to it in advance. They are most useful where applied to specific, concrete decisions. As Gardiner and Edwards (1975: 33) have explained:

This approach offers a clear set of the rules of debate and an orderly way to proceed from information and data to values, to decisions which represent quite an improvement over the folkways. Even this will seldom reduce disagreements to zero, however. . . . If there is no individual or group decisionmaker to resolve disagreement, we can carry through the evaluation separately for each of the disagreeing individuals or groups, hoping that the disagreements are small enough to have no action implications. And if that hope is not fulfilled, we have no suggestions to offer beyond the familiar political processes. . . . We offer technology, not miracles!

Fuzzy Goals and Fuzzy Set Theory

The "fuzziness gambit" may be the most common opening gambit in the goals clarification game. A gambit is an opening chess move in which a pawn or other piece is sacrificed to get an advantage in position. The fuzziness gambit is executed by having program staff appear uncertain about their goals throughout the first round of play. Fuzziness is a lot like dizziness: one is not quite sure where he is or where he is going. After one or two meetings filled with fuzziness about program goals, the staff give in, admitting that they cannot come up with the goal the evaluator has in mind, and the evaluator wins the right to write the statement of program goals. Then, once the evaluator is fully committed to certain measuring instruments and a solid research design, the players announce that they are ready to reopen play because they have now figured out what their goals are. They express appreciation for the evaluator's efforts in writing their statement of goals, but state that he or she did not quite capture what the program is all about. If the evaluator continues with his or her original goals statement, the evaluation is discredited as irrelevant and biased. If the evaluator agrees to reopen play, the evaluation is delayed, a lot of time is lost, and the instruments developed may prove worthless. Moreover, there is no guarantee that the fuzziness gambit will not be used again in the second round, because now the tables are turned and the evaluator is in the unfortunate position of trying to guess what the staff has in mind as the goals of the program. By reopening play, the evaluator has conceded the right of staff participants to state their own goals for the program. Therein lies the gambit: the staff sacrifice a pawn in the opening round in order to gain an advantage in position later in the evaluation. Executed with finesse (and poker faces throughout) the fuzziness gambit is poetry in motion. Evaluators cannot be certain whether they are the victims of staff dedication or devilishness. As Carol Weiss (1972b: 27) has pointed out, there is always more than one possible explanation for fuzziness:

Fuzziness of program goals is a common enough expression to warrant attention. Part of the explanation probably lies in practitioners' concentration on concrete matters of program functioning and their pragmatic mode of operation. They often have an intuitive rather than an analytical approach to program development. But there is also a sense in which ambiguity serves a useful function: It may mask underlying divergences in intent . . . glittering generalities that pass for goal statements are meant to satisfy a variety of interests and perspectives.

The fuzziness gambit differs from the goals clarification shuffle in that the former calls a foul because the evaluator has stated program goals incorrectly or inaccurately, while in the latter instance a foul is claimed because the evaluator has wrongly prioritized the right goals. Both techniques, however, have the same effect. Evaluators are made to feel angry, defensive, and confused. The Delphi technique, multiattribute-utility measurement, and the decision-theoretic approach are inadequate defenses against the fuzziness gambit because all three approaches assume an accurate initial list of possible goals. These techniques are all aimed at clarifying the relationships among the goals on the list. If those goals turn out to be inaccurate, inappropriate, or lacking quite the right nuance after the initial orderings have been established, the evaluator can only proceed at risk of losing credibility—or yield to the gambit.

There was no sure counter to the fuzziness gambit until 1965, when Zedeh et al. (1975: ix) introduced fuzzy set theory:

Fuzzy sets appear to play an essential role in human cognition, especially in relation to concept formation, pattern classification, and logical reasoning. . . . The theory of fuzzy sets is finding applications in a wide variety of fields in which the phenomena under study are too complex or too ill defined to be analyzed by conventional techniques. Thus, by providing a basis for a systematic approach to approximate reasoning, the theory of fuzzy sets may well have a substantial impact on scientific methodology in the years ahead, particularly in the realms of psychology, economics, law, medicine, decision analysis, information retrieval, and artificial intelligence.

One indication of the importance of fuzzy set theory is provided by Manfred Kochen of the Mental Health Research Institute, University of Michigan. Based on conclusions drawn from careful laboratory experiments, Kochen (1975: 407) concludes that "on the whole, fuzzy set theory does seem appropriate for conceputalizing certain aspects of the behavior of perhaps half the population." No wonder evaluators have so much trouble getting clear, specific, and measurable goals! No wonder the fuzziness gambit is so common!

One thing ought to be made clear immediately: fuzzy set theory is not likely to be of much use to that half of the population that is fuzzyminded. Fuzzy set theory is highly mathematical, with its own calculus of fuzzy restrictions, compatability matrices of fuzzy relations, paradigmatic definitions, axioms, propositions, and rules, (such as the rules of implied conjunction and maximal restriction). In short, it is a highly quantitative, complex, and serious approach to the problems of approximate reasoning, and therein lies its advantages in the goals clarification game. Fuzzy set theory is aimed at allowing the not-so-fuzzyminded to understand and control the fuzzyminded, i.e., it permits evaluators to understand and control program staff.

Fuzzy set theory can be used not only to grasp fuzzy goals and decisions, but also to understand entire fuzzy programs as well. Chang (1976: 191) defines a fuzzy program

> through a flowchart where each arc is associated with a fuzzy relation (called a fuzzy branching condition) and a fuzzy assignment. Input, program and output variables occurring in a fuzzy program represent fuzzy subsets. A fuzzy program is interpreted as implicitly defining a tree, and the execution of the fuzzy program is equivalent to searching a solution path in the tree, i.e., tree searching.

The real advantage of fuzzy set theory is that analysts can accept fuzzy goals as a normal state in social program evaluations. Rather than trying to turn a fuzzy goal into a clear, specific, and measurable one, the fuzzy set theorist is willing to deal directly with fuzzy goals, fuzzy decisions, and fuzzy environments. However, this in no way diminishes the centrality of goals in the evaluation process.

> Although many decisions in real world problems arising from public, governmental, and industrial systems have been made, it does not seem that the goal associated with a decision has been clearly shown. . . . In our problems a decision X_c does not make sense without some estimated goal X_g and conversely an estimated goal X_g does not make sense without some decision X_c. There are many problems in a fuzzy environment where it is necessary to decide a present estimated goal such as the federal air quality act proposed by Edward Muskie in 1970. Hence it is necessary to formulate decision problems in such a sense that we can decide *an estimated goal* (Asai, 1976: 258-259; italics added).

Some evaluators, however consider this necessity to decide even "an estimated goal" as too much of an opening for the fuzziness gambit, and recommend employing a new technique that circumvents goals entirely.

Goal-Free Evaluation

In the goals clarification game one of the most daring moves is to "goal-free evaluation." This method immediately stops play in the goals clarification game. Philosopher-evaluator Michael Scriven first proposed the idea of goal-free evaluation. Goal-free evaluation essentially means gathering data on a broad array of *actual effects* and evaluating the importance of these effects in meeting demonstrated needs. The evaluator makes a deliberate attempt to avoid all rhetoric related to program goals: no discussion about goals are held with staff and no program brochures or proposals are read; only the program's outcomes and measurable effects are studied.

There are four reasons for doing goal-free evaluation:

(1) to avoid the risk of narrowly studying stated program objectives and thereby missing important unanticipated outcomes;

(2) to remove the negative connotations attached to the discovery of unanticipated effects, because "the whole language of 'side-effect' or 'secondary effect' or even 'unanticipated effect' tended to be a put-down of what might well be the crucial achievement, especially in terms of new priorities" (Scriven, 1972b: 1-2);

(3) to eliminate the perceptual biases introduced into an evaluation by knowledge of goals; and

(4) to maintain evaluator objectivity and independence through goal-free conditions.

In Scriven's own words (1972b: 2):

It seemed to me, in short, that consideration and evaluation of goals was an unnecessary but also a possibly contaminating step. I began work on an alternative approach—simply the evaluation of *actual* effects against a profile of *demonstrated* needs. I call this Goal-Free Evaluation. . . .

The less the external evaluator hears about the goals of the project, the less tunnel-vision will develop, the more attention will be paid to *looking* for *actual* effects (rather than checking on *alleged* effects).

Scriven (1972b: 3) distrusted the grandiose goals of most projects. Such great and grandiose proposals "assume that a gallant try at Everest will be perceived more favorably than successful mounting of molehills. That may or may not be so, but it's an unnecessary noise source for the evaluator." He saw no reason to get caught up in distinguishing alleged goals from real goals: "why should the evaluator get into the messy job of trying to disentangle that knot?" He would also avoid goals conflict and goals war: "why try to decide which goal should supervene?" He even countered the goals clarification shuffle. "Since almost all projects either fall short of their goals or over-achieve them, why waste time rating the goals, which usually aren't what is achieved? Goal-free evaluation is unaffected by—and hence does not legislate against—the shifting of goals midway in a project." Finally, he undermined the fuzziness gambit: "goals are often stated so vaguely as to cover both desirable and undesirable activities, by almost anyone's standards. Why try to find out what was really intended—if anything?"

Essentially, then, goal-free evaluation means gathering data directly on program effects and effectiveness without risking contamination by goals. Sometimes the result of goal-free evaluation is a statement of goals, i.e., rather than being the initial focus of the evaluation process, a statement of operating goals becomes its outcome. Scriven, however, considered this inappropriate:

> It often happens in goal-free evaluation that people use this as a way of working out what the goals are, but I discourage them from trying to do that. That's not the point of it. The outcome is an assessment of the merit of the program. A better way to put the trouble with the name goal-free is to say that you might put it better by saying it is needs-based instead of goal-based. It is based on something, namely the needs of the client or recipient, but it isn't based on the goals of the program people and you never need to know those and you shouldn't ever look at them. As far as the idea that you finally come up with them as a conclusion you'd be surprised the extent to which you don't (Scriven and Patton, 1976: 13-14).

By removing goals from the evaluation process, Scriven completely changed the nature of the interactions between evaluators and program staff. In the language of games, this constitutes a stunning gammon. The term gammon here designates a victory in which the winner overwhelms the opponent by getting rid of all pieces before the opponent gets rid of any. Goal-free evaluation rids an evaluation of goals before program staff have a chance to counter them through fuzziness, conflict, war, or shuffling priorities. Nor can staff disguise real goals by promoting public relations ideals to which they have no operating commitment. The evaluator wins the game by establishing rules that exclude even an entry by opponents. This may be the ultimate gammon in the goals clarification game.

There is another sense in which goal-free evaluation can be considered a gammon. Critics of Scriven, however, are more likely to be referring to the colloquial meaning of gammon: "nonsense intended to deceive," because goal-free evaluation only appears to get rid of goals. The only goals really eliminated are those of local project staff. Scriven replaced staff objectives with more global goals based on societal needs and basic standards of morality. The real cunning in this gammon is that only the evaluator knows for sure what those needs and standards are, though Scriven (1972b: 3-4) considered such standards to be as obvious as the difference between soap and cancer:

> Another error is to think that all standards of merit are arbitrary or subjective. There's nothing subjective about the claim that we need a cure for cancer more than a new brand of soap. The fact that some people have the opposite preference (if true) doesn't even weakly undermine the claim about which of these alternatives the *nation* needs most. So the Goal-Free Evaluation may use needs and not goals, or the goals of the consumer or the funding agency. Which of these is appropriate depends on the case. But in no case is it proper to use *anyone's* goals as the standard unless they can be *shown* to be the appropriate ones *and* morally defensible.

As a philosopher, Scriven may feel comfortable specifying what "the nation needs" and designating standards as "morally defensible." But from a utilization perspective, this simply begs the question of who is served by the information collected. The issue is not which goals are better or worse, moral or immoral, appropriate or inappropriate in any objective sense. The issue is whose goals will be evaluated. Scriven's goal-free model eliminates only one group from the game: local project staff. He directs data in only one clear direction—away from the stated concerns of the people who run the program. He addresses a national audience, legislative funders. But since these audiences are ill defined and lack organization, I am unconvinced that the standards he applies are other than his very own preferences about what program effects are appropriate and morally defensible. Scriven's denial notwithstanding (cf. Scriven, 1972b: 3), goal-free evaluation simply substitutes the evaluator's goals for those of the project. It is a skillful gammon. Marvin Alkin (1972: 11) is kinder, but makes essentially the same point:

> This term, Goal-Free Evaluation, is not to be taken literally. The Goal-Free Evaluation *does* recognize goals (and not just idiosyncratic ones), but they

are to be wider-context goals rather than the specific *objectives* of a program.
. . . By "goal-free" Scriven simply means that the evaluator is free to choose
a wide context of goals. By his description he implies that a goal-free
evaluation is always free of the goals of the specific program and *sometimes*
free of the goals of the program sponsor. In reality, then, goal-free evaluation
is not really goal-free at all but is simply directed at a different and usually
wide decision audience. The typical goal-free evaluator must surely think
(especially if he rejects the goals of the sponsoring agency) that his evaluation
will extend at least to the level of "national policy formulators." The question
is whether this decision audience is of the highest priority.

It should be noted that Scriven's goal-free proposal assumes both
internal and external evaluators. Thus, part of the reason the external
evaluators can ignore program staff and local project goals is because the
internal evaluator takes care of all that. Thus, again, goal-free evaluation
is only partially goal-free. Someone has to stay home and mind the
goals while the external evaluators muck around in search of any and all
effects. As Scriven (1972b: 4) has argued,

> Planning and production require goals, and formulating them in testable
> terms is absolutely necessary for the manager as well as the internal evaluator
> who keeps the manager informed. That has nothing to do with the question
> of whether the external evaluator needs or should be given any account of the
> project's goals.

It is ironic that in goal-free evaluation Scriven proposed for evaluators
precisely that approach which program staff have long advocated for
themselves. This is illustrated by a classic reaction from program staff
when evaluators announce that it is necessary to begin by clarifying goals:
"we're too busy running the program to spend time clarifying goals.
We're trying to accomplish a lot of things in this program. Why should
we be tied down to a narrow set of specific, clear, and measurable objectives? Goals will only serve to bias the program and hinder what we're
trying to do. This is an action program serving lots of individuals in lots
of ways. We don't have time to check some master list of goals all the time
to see if what this person needs is on the list. What good are goals, anyway?
Has a goal ever fed anyone? Can you get clothes with goals if you're naked?
Will goals heal you if you're sick, get you a job if you're unemployed, or
educate you if you're nonliterate?"
It would be little wonder if program staff responded negatively to
Scriven's double standard that program staff must clarify goals but
external evaluators do not have to. Scriven (1972b: 5) anticipated a
hostile reaction:

now it's important to see why goal-free evaluation is *more* of a threat [than goal-based evaluation]. Primarily this is because the goal-free evaluator is less under the control of management; not only are the main variables no longer specified by management, but they may not even *include* those that management has been advertising. . . . The idea of an evaluator who won't even *talk* to you for fear of contamination can hardly be expected to make the producer rest easy.

But Scriven goes on to admonish local staff that they have no right to fear that goal-free evaluators will misrepresent and harm programs by applying irrelevant and inappropriate criteria derived from some global morality. His final word is quite final; program staff are excluded and their criteria are irrelevant. He completes the gammon with a touch of finesse to which there would seem to be no reply: "if a producer really cares about quality control it won't do to insist that the project's definition of quality must be used" (Scriven, 1972b: 5).

There have been several serious critiques of goal-free evaluation (cf. Stufflebeam, 1972; Alkin, 1972; Popham, 1972; and Kneller, 1972), and as Popham (1972: 13) has predicted, goal-free evaluation may become very popular: "I can see future evaluators clamoring for specifically designed goal-free evaluation blinders to protect them from the taint of project goals." In the face of such clamoring, the best strategy for program staff may be emulation rather than hostility or criticism. As many parents of teenagers have discovered, double standards teach most effectively those behaviors which the parents practice but have forbidden to the child. If children learn by example, so may program staff. If evaluators need not know where a program was headed to evaluate where it ended up, why should program staff? They can work backwards as easily as evaluators can. Program staff need only wait until Scriven determines what the program has accomplished and then proclaim those accomplisments as their original goals. Ken McIntyre (1976: 39) has eloquently described just such an approach to evaluation. For the final coup de grace on the part of program staff, he suggests that

> One step remains: your program's goals you need a way of knowing;
> You're sure you've just about arrived, but where have you been going?
> So like the guy who fired his rifle at a ten-foot curtain
> And drew a ring around the hole to make a bull's-eye certain.

> It's best to wait until you're through and then see where you are:
> Deciding goals before you start is riskier by far.
> So if you follow my advice in your evaluation,
> You'll start with certainty, and end with self-congratulation.

Taking Goals Seriously

I noted at the beginning of this chapter that I choose to see the humor in the problem of goal specification. But seeing the humorous side of a situation is not the same thing as taking it lightly. The identification and clarification of program goals can be an important part of a comprehensive evaluation. The techniques described in the preceeding pages are serious proposals for dealing with the problems encountered by evaluators as they have attempted to identify and clarify program goals. Those problems are well documented from the experiences of evaluators: vague goals, multiple goals, conflicting goals, public relations goals versus real goals, general versus specific goals, central versus peripheral goals, funder goals versus program staff goals, overt versus covert goals, long-term and short-term goals, matching of evaluation goals to program stages, immeasurable goals, changing goals, subsidiary goals, appropriate and inappropriate goals, nominal and operational goals, morally putrescent or quintessential goals—the list is almost endless.

Evaluators have responded to these problems with a variety of proposals. The Delphi technique (Dalkey, 1969), multiattribute-utility measurement (Gardiner and Edwards, 1975) and the decision-theoretic approach (Edwards et al., 1975) are all strategies for dealing with the problems of multiple and conflicting goals. Behavioral objectives have been advocated as the answer to problems of vagueness and immeasurability (cf. Popham, 1969). "Differential evaluation" is a model for deriving objectives at three different stages of program development: the initiation stage, the contact stage, and program implementation (Tripodi et al., 1971). Suchman's proposal (1967: 51-56) for constructing "a chain of objectives" addresses the problem of goals that are too global or general as well as the long-range versus short-range issue. And, of course, goal-free evaluation (Scriven, 1972) attempts to deal with all of these issues by focusing on actual program effects instead of staff intentions.

All of this attention to goals is a clear indication of the importance evaluators attach to goals identification and clarification. The question that has yet to be answered (or even asked) is to what extent all this attention to goals clarification increases the likelihood that evaluation research will be useful. What is the goal of goals in utilization-focused evaluation? In order to answer, we must first briefly consider a fundamental and prior question: do program goals exist in any real sense or is the whole notion of program goals a figment of evaluators' imaginations? The answer is far from obvious. Consideration of this question takes us into that seldom penetrated inner chamber where our basic assumptions about the nature of social reality reside.

Reification of Goals

To reify is to treat an abstraction as if it were real. There is much debate in the social sciences about which concepts are reified. The idea of goals has been a special target of social scientists concerned with concept reification in organizational analysis. This special interest in reification of organizational goals arises from the centrality of goals in the very definition of organizations (cf. Parsons, 1960: 17; Blau and Scott, 1962: 1-8; Price, 1968: 3). Cyert and March (1963: 28) assert that *individual people have goals, collectivities of people do not.* They likewise assert that only individuals can act; organizations or collectivities, as such, cannot be said to take action. The future state desired by an organization (its goals) is nothing but a function of individual "aspirations." Silverman (1971: 9) agrees but adds a special condition:

> To say that an organization has a "goal" may be to involve oneself in some of the difficulties associated with reification. . . . It seems doubtful whether it is legitimate to conceive of an organization as having a goal except where there is an ongoing consensus between the members of the organization about the purposes of their interaction.

Etzioni (1968: 6), on the other hand, argues that collectivities do act and that organizations do have goals, defining an organizational goal as "a desired state of affairs which the organization attempts to realize." This is the dominant structural view in sociol gy, where the very conception of "structure implies that the component units stand in some relation to one another and that the whole is greater than simply the sum of its parts" (Blau and Scott, 1962: 2). Far from reification of the concept of organizational goals, structuralists argue that one cannot understand organizations simply as a collection of individuals with personal goals. Organizations develop a Gestalt; "the concept of *Gestalt* means that the organized arrangement of elements in a larger whole has a significance of its own, not attributable to the specific character of its elements" (Blau, 1967: 346).

To fully understand the issue of goals reification, it is necessary to frame it in the assumption of rationality that dominates social science perspectives on organizations and decisionmaking. The bureaucratic model of organizations in the tradition of Max Weber (1947) represents most completely the rational view of organizations aimed at maximizing efficiency and effectiveness in attaining goals. The "goal-model of organizations" (Etzioni, 1964: 16-18) is a direct manifestation of assumed bureaucratic rationality:

The basic elements of the goal model are that (1) the organization exists to achieve stated goals; (2) the organization develops a rational procedure for the achievement of the goals; and (3) the organization is assessed in terms of the effectiveness of goal attainment (Champion, 1975: 40-41).

As evaluators might anticipate, the rational-goals model of organizations has encountered serious operational problems. Sociologists have discovered that organizational goals are extremely difficult to determine. The fact that goals may be considered from so many different points of view for so many different analytical purposes has led to a proliferation of attempts at classifying goals (e.g., Etzioni, 1961; Perrow, 1968, 1970; Hage and Aiken, 1969; Gross, 1969). Studies of organizations usually find it convenient to *assume* organizational goals rather than to study them (cf. Price, 1968: 4). Azumi and Hage (1972: 414) note that

> Organizational sociologists have found it useful to assume that organizations are purposive. . . . However, it has been much more difficult to actually measure the goals of an organization. Researchers find the purposive image helpful but somehow elusive.

Champion (1975: 41-42) reviewed the sociological literature and concluded:

> The consensus seems to be that organizational goals are difficult to define and that the effectiveness of goal attainment is equally difficult to evaluate. A primary implication for the meaningful application of the goal model in organizational analysis is that it is too complex to use on a large scale.

In brief, social scientists who study goals are not quite sure what they are studying. Goals analysis as a field of study is complex, chaotic, controversial, and confusing. There can be no consensus about the goal of goals because there is not even consensus about the existence of goals. As Thompson (1967: 127) put the dilemma,

> There is obvious danger in reifying the abstraction 'organization' by asserting that it, the abstraction, has goals or desires. There is little to be gained, however, by swinging to the other extreme of insisting that the goals of an organization are somehow the accumulated goals of its individual members.

In the end, most researchers follow the pragmatic logic of Perrow (1970: 134):

For our purposes we shall use the concept of an organizational goal as if there were no question concerning its legitimacy, even though we recognize that there are legitimate objections to doing so. Our present state of conceptual development, linguistic practices, and ontology (knowing whether something exists or not) offers us no alternative.

Evaluators, like Perrow, are likely to come down on the side of practicality. The language of goals will continue to dominate evaluation. There is no final answer to the question of reification because the issue is one of perception, situational usage, and personal assumptions about the nature of reality. But different perspectives about the goal of goals in evaluation have real consequences for the entire evaluation process. Thus, my purpose in introducing the issue of goals reification was twofold. First, I hoped by this discussion to induce at least a modicum of caution and humility among evaluators before they impose goals clarification exercises on program staff. Social scientists who study organizations have demonstrated that classical notions of goal-based organizational rationality have severe limitations in practice. *Difficulties in defining program goals are more likely due to problems inherent in the notion of goals than in staff incompetence, intransigence or opposition to evaluation.* Failure to appreciate these difficulties, however, can quickly create staff resistance, which is likely to be detrimental to the entire evaluation process.

Secondly, this chapter on the problem of goals clarification in general and the discussion of goals reification in particular have, hopefully, established a context for understanding why utilization-focused evaluation does not depend on clear, specific, and measurable objectives as the sine qua non of evaluation research. Clarifying goals is neither necessary nor appropriate in every evaluation. In utilization-focused evaluation, framing the evaluation question in the context of program goals is only one option in efforts to identify and focus the relevant evaluation questions. The next three chapters consider a variety of alternatives for focusing evaluation questions, beginning with a discussion of goal-based options in utilization-focused evaluation.

Chapter 7

THE GOAL OF GOALS

A Setting

The last chapter challenged the universality of the standard evaluation dictum that program goals must be stated in clear, specific, and measurable terms before a program can be evaluated. A utilization-focused approach to evaluation consists of options and alternatives rather than universal prescriptions. Still, proverbs and dicta can be one important medium for passing accumulated research wisdom from evaluator to evaluator, generation to generation.

Another medium for passing on wisdom is the Sufi story. These are stories that have emerged over time through journeys into and out of a variety of rich cultural traditions. Sufi stories, particularly those about the adventures and follies of the incomparable Mulla (Master) Nasrudin, are a means of communicating ancient wisdom:

> Nasrudin is the classical figure devised by the dervishes partly for the purpose of halting for a moment situations in which certain states of mind are made clear. . . . Since Sufism is something which is lived as well as something which is perceived, a Nasrudin tale cannot in itself produce complete enlightenment. On the other hand, it bridges the gap between mundane life and a transmutation of consciousness in a manner which no other literary form yet produced has been able to attain (Shah, 1964: 56).

What, then, can we learn from Nasrudin about the goal of goals in a utilization-focused approach to evaluation? Consider the following famous Sufi story.

> A king who enjoyed Nasrudin's company, and also liked to hunt, commanded him to accompany him on a bear hunt. Nasrudin was terrified.
>   When Nasrudin returned to his village, someone asked him: "How did the hunt go?"
>   "Marvelously!"
>   "How many bears did you see?"
>   "None."
>   "How could it have gone marvelously, then?"
>   "When you are hunting bears, and you are me, seeing no bears at all *is* a marvelous experience" (Shah, 1964: 61).

If this tale were updated by means of an evaluation report, it might read something like this:

EVALUATION OF THE BEAR PROJECT

This is a study undertaken for His Majesty's Ministry of the Interior, under the auspices of the Department of Natural Resources, for the Division of Parks, Section on Hunting, Office of Bears. This is a study of the relationship between the number of bears sighted on a hunt and the number of bears shot on a hunt. Our hypothesis is that there is a direct, linear relationship between the sighting of bears and killing of bears. That data was collected on a recent royal hunting expedition. The sample size is therefore somewhat small and generalizations cannot be made with confidence. In effect this is an exploratory case study, Campbell and Stanley (1963) Research Design No. 1.
    The data support the hypothesis at the 0.001 level of statistical significance. Indeed, the correlation is perfect. The number of bears sighted was zero, and the number of bears killed was zero. In no case was a bear killed without first being sighted. We therefore recommend that in future projects new Royal regulations be implemented requiring that bears first be sighted before they are killed.

Respectfully submitted,

The Incomparable Mulla Nasrudin
Royal Evaluator

While this evaluation report may be statistically somewhat less rigorous than the average evaluation study, it shares one major characteristic with almost all other reports of this genre, namely, it is impossible to tell whether or not it answers anyone's question. Who decided that the goal evaluated should be the number of bears killed? Perhaps the project staff simply used the hunt as a format for getting royal (federal) money to conduct field trips and the real good is a heightened sensitivity to nature, a closer relationship between Nasrudin and the king, a reduction of Nasrudin's fear of bears, or an increase in the king's power over Nasrudin. It may even be possible (likely!) that different characters in the situation have different objectives and would like different outcome measures. If so, it seems unlikely that all characters will be interested in the same evaluation data. Who will decide what it all means? For Nasrudin, the data indicated a "marvelous" outcome. Other decisionmakers might read the data differently.

This question of who will decide what it all means takes us back to the first step in a utilization-focused approach to evaluation: identifying and organizing relevant decisionmakers and information users. *Identification* of relevant decisionmakers is necessary to permit direct evaluator-decisionmaker interaction to focus evaluation questions. Relevant decisionmakers and information users are identified and organized so that they can make decisions about the nature and content of the evaluation. As the Sufi story on hunting bears illustrates, it is impossible to separate the issue of goals clarification from the issue of specific decisionmakers, i.e., whose goals are serving as evaluation criteria.

In utilization-focused evaluation, framing the evaluation question in the context of program goals is one option in efforts to identify and focus the relevant evaluation questions. *Clarifying goals, however, is neither necessary nor appropriate in every evaluation.* Moreover, there are a variety of ways of conceptualizing goal attainment for evaluation purposes, depending on the nature of the program's organizational structure. For evaluators to understand when a goals clarification process is appropriate in utilization-focused evaluation, it is helpful to consider program variations in organizational characteristics, decisionmaking structures, and problem solving strategies. This chapter begins by exploring alternatives to the highly rational goal model of organizations described in Chapter 6. Those alternatives lead to a proposal for a decision-making strategy that evaluators can use to help determine the goal of goals in any particular evaluation. Drawing on recent theory from the sociology of organizations and from the results of our study of the utilization of federal health evaluations, this chapter discusses one major option in efforts to focus the evaluation question, i.e., the option of framing the evaluation question in the context of program goals. In so doing, the role of the evaluator in utilization-focused evaluation will also be elaborated.

The Rational Goal Attainment Model

Under the classical closed system, rational view of organizations (Weber, 1947), organizations were expected to try to maximize attainment of their major goal, e.g., profit. A central goal is assumed to be the basic focus of organizational activity. In evaluation, this model is represented by the traditional question, "to what extent did the program achieve its major goal?" Etzioni (1964: 16) has suggested that the reason the evaluation literature is characterized by negative findings is that evaluation studies are based on this inappropriate rational model of goal attainment:

> Since most organizations most of the time do not attain their goals in any final sense, organizational monographs are frequently detoured into lengthy discussions about this lack of success to the exclusion of more penetrating types of analysis. Since goals, as symbolic units, are ideals which are more attractive than the reality which the organization attains, the organization can almost always be reported to be a failure. While this approach is valid, it is only valid from the particular viewpoint chosen by the researcher. This *goal-model* approach defines success as a complete or at least a substantial realization of the organizational goal.

The Systems Model: From Maximizing to Optimizing

The first major step away from the purely closed system, rational view of organizations represented by the goal model was systems theory. Etzioni (1964: 17), for example, proposed replacing the goal-model with a systems model where the criterion of success becomes optimization rather than maximization:

> Using a systems model we are able to see a basic distortion in the analysis of organizations that is not visible or explicable from the perspective of goal-model evaluation. . . . The systems model explicitly recognizes that the organization solves certain problems other than those directly involved in the achievement of the goal, and the excessive concern with the latter may result in insufficient attention to other necessary organizational activities, and to a lack of coordination between the inflated goal activities and the de-emphasized non-goal activities.

One of Etzioni's important contributions to our understanding of goals was his critique of the goal model for its assumption of a static organization. Viewed as dynamic entities, organizations and programs change constantly as they adapt to their environments. Goals change as well;

existing goals may be supplanted or supplemented by new goals; goals may be modified, de-emphasized, reprioritized, and so on, depending upon a variety of organizational processes and contingencies. In addition, the systems view introduces the notion of organizations having different kinds of goals that play varying roles in programs and organizations. Perrow (1970: 173-174) distinguished five categories of goals: (1) societal goals, (2) output goals, (3) system goals, (4) product goals, and (5) derived goals. He concludes that these goals

> are the product of a variety of influences, some of them enduring and some fairly transient. . . . Finally, it is clear that goals are multiple and conflicting, and thus the "character" of an organization is never stable . . . [because] organizations pursue a variety of goals, sometimes in sequence, sometimes simultaneously.

Viewed as dynamic entities, then, goals and other organizational characteristics (structure, technology) change depending upon what is necessary to *optimize* the use of organizational resources in the attempt to guarantee organizational survival. From a systems perspective, the appropriate evaluation question is: "how close does the organizational allocation of resources approach an optimum distribution?" (Champion, 1975: 43).

The systems approach to evaluation involves the measurement of a variety of indicators of effectiveness (e.g., productivity, morale, adaptiveness, growth, quality) in a comparative framework. These indicators of effectiveness are considered to be interdependent and to vary with other organizational characteristics. Price (1968) compiled an inventory of propositions concerning effectiveness using systems assumptions with particular emphasis on operative goals. The comparative framework means that "rather than comparing existing organizations to ideals of what they might be, we may assess their performances relative to one another" (Etzioni, 1964: 17).

The problem with the systems model is how to decide what is optimal. While one may agree that optimizing is a better term than maximizing for describing what really happens in program decisionmaking, from an evaluation perspective someone still has to decide what is optimal and how "optimality" will be measured. Evaluators may be concerned with a variety of effectiveness indicators, but Becker and Neuhauser (1975: 45-46) argue that for practical purposes, systems evaluators simply look at the degree of attainment of the *primary* goal of the governing body of a program or organization—an approach that is actually little different from the maximizing approach of the rational goal model. In other cases, systems evaluators look at attainment of a series of goals, but lack a clear method for determining the *optimal* relationship among goals.

Recently a third view of organizations, decisionmaking, and goals has emerged. This third view, the open systems perspective, is an alternative to the overrationalistic goal model of maximization and the overrelativistic systems model of optimization. The goal of goals in a utilization-focused approach to evaluation is derived from this third perspective.

The Open Systems Perspective: Satisficing in the Face of Uncertainty

Chapter 3 discussed at length the emergent view among several organizational sociologists that "the central problem for complex organizations is one of coping with uncertainty" (Thompson, 1967: 13). Both organizations and individuals within organizations are faced with numerous uncertainties. Social action programs are particularly vulnerable to environmental uncertainties. Will funding be continued? Will programs be enlarged or retrenched? Can staff be maintained? How will clients react to the program? What effects will the program have on clients? How will changes in the political climate affect the program? The degree of uncertainty varies from organization to organization, program to program, but there always is uncertainty.

Terreberry (1971) has reviewed recent work in economics, business, management, sociology, and social psychology concerning the effects of uncertainty on organizations. She pulled together a substantial literature indicating that the kind, extent, and sheer rapidity of social change requires greater organizational adaptability and makes the future less predictable. Classical models of rational organizational decisionmaking are substantially undermined by this uncertainty: "increasingly, the rational strategies of planned innovation and long-range planning are being undermined by unpredictable changes" (Terreberry, 1971: 60). She argued that the complexity of modern society has increased the degree to which organizations face multiple uncertainties. Modern organizations have become "open systems" subject to a variety of environmental influences and contingencies.

There is a growing literature based on the open system approach to organizations (cf. Maurer, 1971). This emergent view of organization processes has substantial implications for evaluation, particularly the place of goals in evaluation. To understand the implications of open systems for evaluation, it is necessary to understand how decisionmaking is changed in open system programs.

When decisionmakers are struggling to reduce uncertainty under highly turbulent conditions, the nature of the decisionmaking process changes. Cyert and March (1963: 100) found in their studies of business organizations that "so long as the environment of the firm is unstable—and predictably unstable—the heart of the theory [of organizational behavior] must be the process of short-run adaptive reactions." Short-run adaptive reactions are not aimed at maximizing attainment of a central goal; nor do such reactions lead necessarily to optimal goal attainment. Short-run adaptive reactions involve "*satisficing*" (Simon, 1957) rather than maximizing or optimizing. Under the criterion of satisficing, decisionmakers search for *satisfactory* solutions. In situations of great complexity and multiple uncertainties, rational decisionmaking gives way to "heuristic" problem solving (Taylor, 1965: 73, 80).

This shift in perspective is based on two crucial assumptions. First, a decisionmaker never has all the information needed to meet the conditions necessary for rational action. Rationality requires making the best choice from among all possible alternatives, taking into account the consequences of each alternative. In reality, all possible alternatives are seldom known and knowledge of consequences is always incomplete. Secondly, even if all the necessary knowledge were available, the human mind could not manage the complexity of dealing with all the possible permutations and combinations.

> The capacity of the human mind for formulating and solving complex problems is very small compared with the size of the problems whose solution is required for objectively rational behavior in the real world—or even for a reasonable approximation to such objective rationality (Simon, 1957: 198).

Despite incomplete information, great complexity, and multiple uncertainties, the decisionmaker is still required to act. He or she therefore simplifies the situation and exhibits what Simon (1957: 204) calls "subjective rationality" or "bounded rationality:" "the key to the simplification of the choice process . . . is the replacement of the goal of *maximizing* with the goal of *satisficing*, of finding a course of action that is 'good enough.'"

Donald Taylor (1965: 62-63), in his extensive review of decisionmaking and problem solving literatures, relates the idea of satisficing both to the concept of search and to that of level of aspiration. By doing so, he illustrates the active-reactive nature of organizational behavior:

Administrative man, confronted with a situation in which he must make a decision, is assumed to begin by searching for possible alternative courses of action and for information concerning the consequences of each alternative. He is assumed to select the first alternative he encounters which meets some minimum standard of satisfaction with respect to each of the values he is seeking to attain—in other words, he satisfices. . . . The concept of satisficing should not be misinterpreted to imply that an individual confronted simultaneously with several alternatives will fail to pick the optimal one. . . . The concept of satisficing is closely linked to the concept of search. The essential idea is that the individual searches until he finds an alternative that is "good enough. . . . "

It is expected that satisficing administrative man will as a result of experience modify the minimum standards he seeks to attain. If *search* for a satisficing alternative proves unsuccessful for an extended period, then the decision-maker is expected to reduce his minimum standards. If, on the other hand, a satisficing alternative is easily found on one occasion, then upon subsequent occasions of the some general character, the decision-maker may well increase his expectations. . . .

The concept of satisficing is closely related to the concept of *level of aspiration*, a concept which has been the subject of considerable research in psychology. . . . That research, among other things, shows clearly the effect of success and failure upon changes in level of aspiration over time.

This view of decisionmaking fits well with the data presented in Chapter 3 on how federal health evaluations were used. Utilization of evaluation research occurs as decisionmakers try to reduce uncertainty as part of the process of short-run adaptive reactions. Evaluations provide important information to decisionmakers, but information is also sought from other sources—and is never complete. Program development is a process of facing problems and solving them. It is a process of "muddling through" or of "disjointed incrementalism" (Lindblom, 1959; Braybrooke and Lindblom, 1963). The incrementalist notion refers to a coping strategy for satisficing where decisonmakers consider only those activities and outcomes which differ incrementally (i.e., to a small extent) from existing highly focused issues or "focus-elements" (Shackle, 1961: 122). In this action-reaction-adaptation process, decisionmakers do not simply adjust means to ends as would be done under conditions of "rational" decisionmaking; rather "ends are chosen that are appropriate to available or nearly available means" (Hirschman and Lindblom, 1962: 215). Reviewing contemporary work in several fields, Hirschman and Lindblom (1962) concluded that there is considerable convergence of evidence supporting the incrementalism view.

The open systems perspective emphasizes disjointed incrementalism, muddling through, and satisficing in contrast to the rational goal-maximization perspective. But the open systems perspective does not describe an "irrational" process in the colloquial sense of the term. Rather, it is a pragmatic perspective. It is not a matter of organizational Horatio Algers struggling singlemindedly to accomplish a single goal, but rather one of program decisionmakers doing their best to solve specific problems in the face of great complexity and multiple uncertainties. It is not a romantic picture, but the evidence is that for many programs it is a highly realistic one. The task now is to examine the implications of this perspective for the goal of goals in a utilization-focused approach to evaluation.

Active-Reactive-Adaptive Decisionmakers and Evaluators

There is no single term that fully describes the nature of decisionmaking under open system conditions, but to call this emergent view the "active-reactive-adaptive" approach to decisionmaking is both descriptive and perscriptive. It is descriptive in that it attempts to describe how decisionmakers in many organizations actually function; it is prescriptive in that this strategy is a process whereby evaluators can determine the focus, content, and methods of specific evaluation studies.

The active-reactive-adaptive approach to decisionmaking is very similar to what Etzioni calls a "mixed-scanning" strategy. Under this decisionmaking strategy, policymakers move back and forth between contextuating" information (which is the goals-oriented overview of policy) and "bit" information (which provides the details about immediate, incremental needs and alternatives): "together they make for a third approach which is more realistic *and* more transforming than each of its elements" (Etzioni, 1968: 283). Etzioni's definition of mixed-scanning is aimed primarily at national policymaking for the "active society." What is missing in the imagery of mixed-scanning is the highly reactive-adaptive side of much decisionmaking. Etzioni stressed the active aspects of decisionmaking, but much of what passes for action in decisionmaking is really reaction and adaptation—i.e., trying to make the best of things until uncertainty is sufficiently reduced or external constraints have been sufficiently removed to permit a reassertion of activism.

It is the paradox of decisionmaking that effective action is born of reaction. Only when organizations as open systems take in information from the environment and react to changing conditions can they act on that same environment to reduce uncertainty and increase discretionary flexibility (cf. Thompson, 1967). The same is true for the individual decisionmaker or for a problem solving group. Action emerges through reaction and leads to adaptation. The imagery is familiar: thesis-antithesis-synthesis, stimulus-response-change. But what does all this have to do with the goal of goals in a utilization-focused approach to evaluation?

The active-reactive-adaptive evaluator in utilization-focused evaluation moves back and forth between overall program goals and specific evaluation questions in order to establish the relevance of various information options to decisionmakers and information users in a particular situation. The evaluator need not attempt to construct a written-in-stone set of goals for the evaluation because it is assumed that goals are changeable in uncertain environments, fluid in the face of different contingencies, and abstractions that are only semireal. This follows in part the incrementalist strategy: "one need not try to organize all possible values into a coherent scheme, but instead can evaluate only what is relevant in actual policy choices" (Lindblom, 1965: 145).

One departs from incrementalist strategy in giving any credence at all to goals and to the appearance of rationality. The reasons for doing so are threefold. First, as noted at the close of the preceding chapter, the language of goals is widely used and commonly accepted as the best way currently available for talking about hopes, ideals, and future intended outcomes. Second, goals provide a context within which specific evaluation questions can be framed, understood, and communicated. Third, the notion of goals is highly relevant under certain conditions, namely, (a) when decisionmakers and information users operate in relatively closed systems with routine technology and a relatively high degree of environmental stability and certainty, and (b) when decisionmakers believe in and operate on a model of instrumental rationality.

The crux of the matter is that effective evaluators trying to enhance utilization decide how to act with regard to goals by reacting and adapting to particular situations and specific decisonmakers or information users. Under certain conditions maximizing criteria may be applied; at other times optimizing criteria are called for; at still other times the evaluator will focus on satisficing criteria through highly specific, non-goal-oriented evaluation questions.

In other words, there is no *one* effective strategy of decision-making in the abstract, apart from the societal context in which it is introduced and from the control capacities of the actors introducing it. The most effective strategy is the one that is most well-suited to the specific situation and to the actor's capacities (Etzioni, 1968: 293).

A mixed-scanning, active-reactive-adaptive approach to goals clarification is a demanding process, but it gives the evaluator flexibility to work with decisionmakers and information users to design an evaluation that is both meaningful in terms of their own setting and useful.

Framing the Evaluation Question in the Context of Program Goals and Objectives

Knowing when to exercise the option of framing the evaluation questions in the context of program goals and objectives depends on the evaluator's understanding of the organizational dynamics of a particular program. The difficulty is in determining the organizational dynamics so as to match the goals clarification process to the nature of the decision-making process in a specific program. The reason for reviewing and critiquing maximizing (goal model), optimizing (systems model), and satisficing (incremental model) strategies of decisionmaking was to provide the evaluator with a framework for understanding variations in organizational dynamics and possible belief systems of different decision-makers. The next section relates more directly evaluation options to variations in program dynamics.

Organizational Dynamics and Program Goals: Theory and Practice

The power of evaluation resides in its potential for reducing uncertainty (Chapter 3). Uncertainty is not, however, a dichotomous variable. The degree of uncertainty varies for different decisionmakers, for different parts of an organization, and for different organizations (cf. Thompson, 1967). Emery and Trist (1965) identify four types of environments characterized by varying degrees of uncertainty based on the degree of system connectedness that exists among the components of the environment. What is important about their work from an evaluation perspective is their presentation of evidence that the degree of uncertainty facing an organization directly affects the degree to which goals and strategies for attaining goals can be concretized and stabilized. The less certain the environment, the less stable and the less concrete the organization's goals.

This theoretical perspective has very practical implications for evaluators. It means that the more unstable and turbulent the environment of a program, the less likely it is that the evaluator will be able to generate concrete and stable goals. Secondly, few evaluations can investigate and assess all the many program components and special projects of an agency, organization, or program. The clarity, specificity, and measurability of goals will vary throughout a program depending upon the environmental turbulence faced by specific projects and program subparts. As the evaluator works with decisionmakers and information users to focus the evaluation, the degree to which it is useful to labor over writing a goals statement will vary for different parts of the program. Since some parts of a program may have highly unstable goals, it may not be efficient or useful to try to force such programs into a static and rigid goals model. *The evaluation issue is what information is needed not whether or not goals are clear, specific, and measurable. Clear, specific and measurable goals are only one means to the end of conducting a useful evaluation.*

An example may help clarify the options involved. The Minnesota State Department of Education funded a "human liberation" program in the Minneapolis Public Schools, using federal funds. The program was an innovative high school course aimed at enhancing communication skills around the issues of sexism and racism. Initial funding was to be for three years, but a renewal application would have to be filed each year. Program staff were not at all sure how the program would fit into the local high school where it was located, much less how it would fit into the total school system. An external, out of state evaluator was hired to assist the program. The evaluator's idea of assistance was to force staff to articulate clear, specific, and measurable goals in behavioral terms. The staff had no previous experience in writing behavioral objectives, nor was program conceptualization sufficiently advanced to concretize goals. Virtually everything about the program was uncertain: curriculum content, student reaction, staffing, funding, relationship to the school system, public support—none of these things were known with any degree of certainty.

For an evaluator operating within a rational goals model framework such a program is chaos. How can a program operate if it does not know where it is going? How can it be evaluated if there are no operational objectives? Yet, the evidence is that thousands of programs operate with highly fluid structures and changing goals. Moreover, the research literature on organizations clearly points to the "appropriateness" of dynamic goals and flexible structures under conditions of great uncertainty (cf. Burns and Stalker, 1961; Lawrence and Lorsch, 1967; Hage and Aiken, 1970). Evaluators who view such programs from the perspective of the rational goals model see chaos and confusion; organizational sociologists who view such programs from the perspective of organizational dynamics in open systems see adaptation and environmental-organizational interdependence. *From a utilization-focused approach to evaluation the burden rests with the evaluator to understand what kind of evaluation is appropriate for different types of programs rather than forcing all programs into a single evaluation mold.*

In the Minneapolis Human Liberation Program, the first year evaluation based on behavioral objectives was quite negative—and disastrous. It was dismissed by program staff as irrelevant and ignored by school officials who understood the problems of first year programs. The program staff refused to work with the same evaluator the second year and faced the prospect of a new evaluator with suspicion and hostility. When we were asked for help during the second year, it was immediately clear that the new program staff wanted nothing to do with writing behavioral goal statements. The funders and school officials agreed to a formative evaluation with program staff as decisonmakers and information users. The evaluation focused on *staff information needs* for short-run, adaptive decisions aimed at immediate program improvement. This meant confidential interviews with students about strengths and weaknesses of the course; observations of classes to describe interracial dynamics and student reactions; and beginning work on trying to develop measures of racism and sexism. On this latter point, program staff were undecided as to whether they were really trying to change student attitudes and behaviors, or just make students more "aware." They needed time and information to work out satisfactory approaches to the problems of racism and sexism.

By the third year, the program had begun to take more concrete shape. Uncertainties about student reaction and school system support had been reduced by the evaluation. Initial findings indicated support for the program. Program staff were more confident and experienced. They decided that for the third year they wanted to develop more concrete, quantitative instruments to measure student changes. They were ready to deal with program outcomes, though it was clear that such goals and objectives were to be viewed as experimental and flexible. By working back and forth between specific information needs, contextual goals, and focused evaluation questions, it was possible to conduct an evaluation that was used to improve the program, which was the purpose of the evaluation agreed to by decisionmakers and evaluators. The key to utilization was matching the evaluation to program conditions and decisionmaker needs.

Variations in Goal Specificity in Complex Programs

Just as different programs experience variations in environmental uncertainty, so too do *different parts of programs* have to cope with varying degrees of uncertainty. Lawrence and Lorsch (1967) studied the relationship between environmental uncertainty and the nature of differentiation and integration in complex organizations. They were particularly interested in how different parts of an organization developed special interdependencies with those elements in the environment that affect only that subsystem in the organization. For example, the simplest community corrections department usually has several subsystems. There is a probation officer subsystem, one or more residence subsystems for placement of offenders, a documents and records subsystem, and a central administrative subsystem. These subsystems have different functions and, to some extent, deal with different environments; therefore each subsystem experiences uncertainty in different ways and to varying degrees.

> It is readily apparent that each of these environments can range from highly dynamic to extremely stable. The importance of this variability can easily be obscured by the usual approach of thinking of an organization's environment as a single entity. Here, each major subsystem was seen as coping with its respective segment of the total environment (Lawrence and Lorsch, 1972: 334-335).

Two of the hypotheses tested and confirmed by Lawrence and Lorsch (1972: 336-337) are of particular relevance to evaluators. First, "the time orientations of subsystem members will vary directly with the modal time required to get definitive feedback from the relevant subenvironments," and secondly, "the members of a subsystem will develop a primary concern with the goals of coping with their particular subenvironment."

This means that evaluators have to be very clear about which part of a complex organization or program is the focus of an evaluation and how subparts of programs relate to the whole. One way of doing this is to chart the goals of programs and subprograms. Mapping the program's goals in this way can serve as a basis for active-reactive-adaptive discussion about which subprogram will be the focus of an evaluation effort.

To facilitate the framing of evaluation questions in complex programs, it is often helpful to approach goals clarification at three levels: the overall mission of the program, the goals of specific programmatic units (or subsystems), and the specific objectives that specify client outcomes. The mission statement describes the general direction of the overall program or organization in long-range terms. Mission statements function to carve out the territory within which a program will operate. The statement may specify nothing more than a minimal target population and a basic problem to be attacked. For example, the mission of the Minnesota

Comprehensive Epilepsy Program is to improve the lives of people with epilepsy through research, education, and treatment. This tells us that the program is concerned with much more than just medical treatment for individual epileptics. There are also research and educational thrusts to the program. Moreover, research is listed before treatment and, in this case, accurately reflects program priorities. But clearly the general mission of "improving the lives of people with epilepsy" is too vague to serve as an indicator for evaluation purposes.

Goals and objectives can be established for the various thrusts of the program. The terms "goals" and "objectives" have been used interchangeably up to this point, but it is useful to distinguish between them as representing different levels of generality. Goals are more general than objectives and encompass the purposes and aims of program subsystems (i.e., research, education, and treatment in the epilepsy example). Objectives are narrow and specific, stating what will be different as a result of program activities. Objectives specify the concrete outcomes of a program. To illustrate these differences a simplified version of the mission statement, goals, and objectives for the Minnesota Comprehensive Epilepsy Program is presented below. This outline was developed after an initial discussion with the program director. The purpose of the outline was to establish a context for later discussions aimed at more clearly framing specific evaluation questions. In other words, this goals clarification and objectives mapping exercise was used as a means of focusing the evaluation question rather than as an end in itself.

MINNESOTA COMPREHENSIVE EPILEPSY PROGRAM: MISSION STATEMENT, GOALS, AND OBJECTIVES

Program Mission: To improve the lives of people with epilepsy through research, education, and treatment.

Research Component

Goal 1: To produce high quality, *scholarly research* on epilepsy.
    Objective 1: To *publish* research findings in high quality, refereed journals.
    Objective 2: To conduct research on . . .
        a. neurological aspects of epilepsy,
        b. pharmacological aspects of epilepsy,
        c. epidemiology of epilepsy, and
        d. social and psychological aspects of epilepsy

Goal 2: To produce interdisciplinary research.
    Objective 1: To propose, fund, and conduct research projects that *integrate* principal investigators from different disciplines.

Objective 2: To increase *interaction* among researchers from different disciplines.

Education Component

Goal 3: To educate health professionals about the nature and conditions of epilepsy so as to change knowledge, attitudes, and behaviors.

Objective 1: To increase the *knowledge* of health professionals who serve people with epilepsy so that they know . . .

    a. what to do if a person has a seizure,

    b. the incidence and prevalence of epilepsy,

    c. etc.

Objective 2: To change the attitudes of health professionals so that they

    a. are sympathetic to the needs of epileptics, and

    b. believe in the importance of identifying the special needs of epileptics.

Objective 3: To change the *behaviors* of health professionals so that they

    a. identify whether or not the person they are serving is epileptic, and

    b. match their services to the specific needs of epileptic persons they serve.

Goal 4: To educate persons with epilepsy about their disorder.

Goal 5: To educate the general public about the nature and incidence of epilepsy.

Treatment Component

Goal 6: To diagnose, treat, and rehabilitate persons with severe, chronic, and disabling seizures.

Objective 1: To increase seizure control in treated patients.

Objective 2: To increase the functional independence of treated patients.

Administrative Component

Goal 7: To integrate the separate program components into a comprehensive whole that is greater than the sum of its parts.

Objective 1: To demonstrate that funding many researchers, clinicians, and educators from different disciplines at one site results in spin-offs and break-throughs that would not occur if components were funded in isolation from each other.

Objective 2: To facilitate interaction among participants in different program components.

This outline of goals and objectives is illustrative of several points. First, the only dimension that consistently differentiates goals and objectives is the relative degree of specificity of each: objectives narrow the focus of goals. There is no absolute criterion for distinguishing goals from objectives; the distinction is always a relative one.

Secondly, the purpose of constructing this outline must be understood. The purpose was not to fully describe the Comprehensive Epilepsy Program. This outline was generated after a single session with the program director. Its purpose was to facilitate discussion as we attempted to focus on evaluation questions of interest to core staff. It was clear at the outset that there were not sufficient resources to fully evaluate all four component parts of the program. Moreover, different component parts faced different contingencies. The treatment and research components have more concrete outcomes than the education and administrative components. The differences in the specificity of the objectives for the four program components reflect real differences in the degree to which the content and functions of those program subsystems were known at the beginning of the evaluation. Thus, with limited resources and variations in goal specificity, it was necessary to decide which aspects of the program could best be served by evaluation research.

Third, this outline of goals and objectives for the Comprehensive Epilepsy Program is not particularly well written. I have extracted the outline directly from rough notes written during the first meeting with the director. The language in several cases could be more concise; some goals and objectives contain two or more ideas that should be separated so that each ideal is singular and unitary; and there are gaps in the logical ordering of goals and objectives where intervening steps need to be specified. But such inadequacies are of little consequence for the purpose at hand. Once the focus of the evaluation is sharpened and the important evaluation questions have been identified, relevant goals and objectives can be more carefully written. Goals and objectives not relevant to the evaluation can be ignored. At this early point in the evaluation process the outline of program mission statement, goals, and objectives is a tool for sharpening the focus on the central issues about which the decisionmakers most need information. *Which program components and which goals should be evaluated to produce the most useful information for decisionmakers?* That is the question. To answer it one does not need technically perfect goal statements. Once the evaluation question is focused, relevant goals and objectives can be phrased in technically impeccable language—if such rephrasing improves the evaluation.

The point here is to avoid wasting time in the construction of grandiose, complex models of program goals and objectives just because the folklore of evaluation prescribes that the first step in evaluation is traditionally identification and clarification of program goals in clear, specific, and measurable terms. In complex programs evaluators can spend so much of their time writing goals that they lose sight of whether or not full elaborations of goals and objectives serve a useful purpose. To further develop the distinction between writing goals for the sake of writing goals and writing them to use as tools in sharpening relevant evaluation questions, it is necessary to consider the issue of prioritization. In utilization-focused evaluation research goals are prioritized in a manner quite different from that usually prescribed.

Establishing Priorities:
The Importance Criterion and a Usefulness Criterion

The basic solution to the problems of multiple and conflicting goals is establishing priorities. The usual criterion for prioritizing goals is a ranking or rating in terms of *importance*. Multiattribute-utility measurement (Gardiner and Edwards, 1975) and the decision-theoretic approach to evaluation (Edwards et al., 1975) employ both rankings and ratings of importance. The rating approach works as follows:

Rate dimensions [goals] in importance, preserving ratios. To do this, start by assigning the least important dimension an importance of 10. (We use 10 rather than 1 to permit subsequent judgments to be finely graded and nevertheless made in integers.) Now consider the next-least-important dimension. How much more important (if at all) is it than the least important? Assign it a number that reflects that ratio. Continue on up the list, checking each set of implied ratios as each new judgment is made. Thus, if a dimension is assigned a weight of 20 while another is assigned a weight of 80, it means that the 20 dimension is one-fourth as important as the 80 dimension (Gardiner and Edwards, 1975: 16).

The reason for prioritizing goals is clear: evaluations ought to focus on important goals. Thus, with limited resources the evaluator would choose to focus the evaluation on the most important program goals, i.e., the goal ranked first on the list. Data might also be gathered on other goals, but the primary focus of the evaluation is measurement of the degree to which the most important goal is being attained. This is the classical model of outcomes evaluation. But from a utilization perspective this model is inadequate.

The fact that a goal is ranked first in importance does not necessarily mean that decisionmakers and information users need information about attainment of that goal more than they need information about a less important goal. In a utilization-focused approach to evaluation program goals are also prioritized by applying the criterion of usefulness of evaluative information. That goal about which evaluation information would be least useful to decisionmakers and information users is ranked last; that goal about which evaluative information would be most useful is ranked first. The ranking of goals by the importance criterion is often quite different from the ranking of goals by the usefulness of evaluation information criterion. Consider the following example from the Minnesota Comprehensive Epilepsy Program:

Ranking of Goals By Importance	Ranking of Goals by Usefulness of Evaluative Information
1. To produce high quality, scholarly research on epilepsy.	1. To integrate the separate program components into a comprehensive whole that is greater than the sum of its parts.
2. To produce interdisciplinary research.	2. To educate health professionals about the nature and conditions of epilepsy.
3. To integrate the separate program components into a comprehensive whole that is greater than the sum of its parts.	3. To diagnose, treat, and rehabilitate persons with severe, chronic, and disabling seizures.
4. To diagnose, treat, and rehabilitate persons with severe, chronic, and disabling seizures.	4. To produce interdisciplinary research.

Why the discrepancy? The core program staff did not feel they needed a formal evaluation to monitor attainment of the most important program goal. The publishing of scholarly research in refereed journals was so important that the program director intended to personally monitor performance in that area. Moreover, he was relatively certain about how to facilitate achievement of that goal. There was no specific evaluation question related to that goal that he needed answered. By contrast, the issue of "comprehensiveness" was quite difficult to get at. It was not at all clear how comprehensiveness could be facilitated, though it is third on the importance list. The core program staff were anxious to evaluate the development of comprehensiveness. Such data had high utilization potential.

The education goal, second on the usefulness list, does not even appear among the top four goals on the importance list. Yet, information about educational impact was ranked high on the usefulness list because it was a goal area about which the program staff had many questions. The education component was expected to be a difficult, long-term effort. Information about how to increase the educational impact of the Comprehensive Epilepsy Program had high utilization potential.

There are several reasons why a ranking of goals according to the usefulness of evaluative information criterion is likely to differ from the ranking by importance. Sometimes goals ranked first in importance have a long-range time frame; program staff may find it more useful to focus on evaluation of goals with a shorter time span. Second, top priority goals (in terms of importance) may be subject to multiple, nonprogram influences to a greater extent than more immediate goals; thus data about performance on a lower priority goal may be a more useful indicator to staff of their effectiveness than data on a goal the achievement of which could not be attributed solely to program efforts. For example, in programs, where the long-range goal of greatest importance is behavioral change, the evaluation may focus on the more immediate but less important goal of attitude change. Behavior is subject to multiple influences, not many of which are amenable to direct or short-run intervention. Attitudes are more subject to short-term intervention and may be one link in the chain to behavioral change. If resources or design problems do not permit measuring both attitude change and behavioral change, the criterion of generating useful information about attitude change may take precedence over the criterion of evaluating the more important goal of behavioral change.

Another reason for the differences in rankings may be the likelihood of getting definitive findings. It is sometimes difficult to obtain measurable differences on important outcomes such as reduced racism and sexism. Thus decisionmakers may opt for evaluation of something about which they can expect to find measurable differences. The choice may be between the likelihood of ambiguous findings about attainment of the most important goal, or clearer findings about the attainment of a less important goal. Evaluators can estimate the probabilities in both cases;

in a utilization-focused approach the decisionmakers and information users make the final decision about which way to go.

In my experience, the most frequent reason for differences in importance and usefulness rankings is variation in the degree to which decisionmakers already have what they consider good information about performance on the most important goal. At the program level, staff members may be so involved in trying to achieve their most important goal that they are relatively well informed about performance on that goal. Performance on less important goals may involve less certainty for staff; information about performance in that goal area is therefore more useful because it tells staff members something they do not already know.

Earlier, I cited the experience of working with individual school teachers whose primary goal was high student achievement on basic skills. They expected any evaluation to measure such achievement. When asked why they needed information on student achievement, they responded that it was important for the school principal and parents: "of course, we already know how well our students are achieving because we're with them every day. Testing achievement won't tell us anything new." Once it was clarified that the teachers themselves were the decisionmakers for the evaluation and they could ask questions that they were interested in, the suggested focus of the evaluation changed: "well, if the information is for us, we wouldn't measure achievement. Those standardized test don't tell us anything anyway. What we really need is help in how to increase students' self esteem, how to stimulate their affective development. The cognitive domain will probably always be most important in public schools, but we have a handle on that. The problem is how to figure out what's happening in the affective domain. That would be really useful information!"

What I hope is emerging through these examples is an image of the evaluator as an active-reactive-adaptive problem solver. The evaluator actively solicits information about program contingencies, organizational dynamics, environmental uncertainties, and decisionmaker goals in order to focus the evaluation on questions of real interest to identified decisionmakers and information users. The evaluator works with decisionmakers and information users to determine what useful information can be generated in the context of decisionmaker needs and program realities.

Evaluation of Central or Peripheral Goals?

Prioritization of program goals on the basis of usefulness of evaluation information means that an evaluation might focus on goals of apparent peripheral importance rather than more central program goals. The consequences of evaluating central versus peripheral goals is a matter of some controversy. Those who view evaluation as part of a rational decisionmaking process (the goal model) stress the importance of evaluating central goals. In her early work Carol Weiss (1972b: 30-31) offered the following advice to evaluators about how to handle the prioritization process:

> The evaluator will have to press to find out priorities—which goals the staff sees as critical to its mission and which are subsidiary. But since the evaluator is not a mere technician for the translation of a program's stated aims into measurement instruments, he has a responsibility to express his own interpretation of the relative importance of goals. *He doesn't want to do an elaborate study on the attainment of minor and innocuous goals*, while vital goals go unexplored.

One primary reason for focusing on central goals is to provide data for major decisions about a program. But, as demonstrated in Chapter 2, major decisions are rare. Incremental, day-to-day, piecemeal decisions are the basis for most program activity. Taken as a whole, over a long period of time, these bit decisions accumulate to establish basic program direction. Thus, from an incrementalist (satisficing) perspective it is appropriate to focus an evaluation on peripheral program goals because they may be more amenable to immediate action. Incremental decisions tend to be small steps, and evaluation of peripheral objectives may focus on the taking of such small steps. As one evaluator in our utilization of federal health evaluations said:

> Although I wouldn't necessarily want to choose between major or minor evaluation studies, the point about minor evaluation studies is well taken. If you have an energetic, conscientious program manager, he's always interested in improving his program around the periphery, because that's where he usually can. And an evlauation study of some minor aspect of his program will enable him to significantly improve (EV52: 17).

In our study of the utilization of federal health evaluations we put the issue to decisionmakers and evaluators as follows:

> Another factor sometimes affecting utilization has to do with whether or not the central objectives of a program are evaluated. Some writers argue that evaluations can have the greatest impact if they focus on major program objectives. What happened in your case?

Only one of 38 respondents felt that utilization was likely to be enhanced by evaluating peripheral goals. The overwhelming consensus was that, at the very least, central goals ought to be evaluated and, where possible, both central and peripheral goals should be studied. As they elaborated, nine decisionmakers and eight evaluators said that utilization had probably been helped by the concentration on central issues. This last sentence, however, reflects an important shift in emphasis. As decision-makers talked in their own words about the central versus peripheral question in terms of utilization, they switched from talking about goals to talking about "issues." Utilization is increased by focusing on central issues. *And what is a central issue? It is an evaluation question that someone really cares about.* The subtle distinction here is critical. Evaluations are useful to decisionmakers if they focus on central issues—which may or may not include achievement of central goals.

A Case Example of Utilization-Focused Evaluation

The best example of the subtle shift from goals to issues in our interviews concerns a highly utilized evaluation of the Hill-Burton Hospital Construction Program by their Office of Program Planning and Analysis. This evaluation is worth looking at in detail because it illustrates the key aspects of utilization-focused evaluation. The evaluation was conducted with one percent funds specifically mandated for evaluation in federal legislation. The director of that office established a permanent committee on evaluation projects to make decisions about how to spend one percent monies for evaluation. The evaluation committee was made up of representatives from all the other branches and services in the division: people from the state Hill-Burton agencies, from the Comprehensive Health Planning agencies, from the health care industry, and regional Hill-Burton people. The committee met at regular intervals

> just [to] kick around ideas for things we thought ought to be looked at in the program. Every member was free to make suggestions. If the committee thought a suggestion was worthwhile we would usually give the person that suggested it an opportunity to work it up in a little more detail (DM159: 3).

During the interview with the project officer, two of the permanent evaluation committee staff were present. One of them noted that the report reads like a rational goal-model evaluation but was actually developed incrementally.

You'll get the idea that somebody had systematically studied the objectives of the program saying these are the objectives we want to find out: whether or not state agency planning and operating accomplishes these objectives. But I don't think that's the kind of thinking we were actually doing at that time, because . . . none of them knew what they were doing.

So we got started: "Well, we can look at one thing and evaluate it, the formula." And we said, "Well, we can also see what state agencies are doing." See? And it was this kind of seat-of-the-pants approach to the whole situation. That's the way you got into it (PO159: 4).

The evaluation committee members were carefully selected on the basis of their knowledge of central program issues. While this was essentially an internal evaluation, the committee also made use of outside consultants: "we tried to get people who had a knowledge of how the Hill-Burton program functioned" (PO159: 9). As another committee member explained:

In our kind of program, with the long history and complexity of Hill-Burton, there was no lack of things to evaluate. But we felt that there was enough expertise in the program, that this should be the way to proceed and not just the scattering of contracts. . . . Even if you do that, to get some real meat and real meaning and be worth the money requires considerable attention . . . We thought it better to do a few things well than anything sloppily. . . . It's not a scientific process by any means . . . The form of it evolved from the process (PO159: 5).

Looking back on the study the decisionmaker reported that this committee was the key to the utilization process:

I think that the makeup of the committee and the makeup of the interview teams, and so forth, was such that it helped this study command quite a deal of attention from the state agencies and among the federal people involved in the program . . . Well, I guess I had as much to do with the selection of the members as anybody. I asked a lot of people's advice, of course, and they had to be approved by the division chief, but my attempt was to have some cross-fertilization between the two organizations and also from the health care industry as well, and I don't think maybe we got quite as much variety in there as I'd like in terms of the background of people, but I think we did pretty well (DM159:18).

There is no better example in our sample of the first step in a utilization-focused approach to evaluation: identification and organization of relevant decisionmakers and information users. And how do you keep a group like this working together? The answer emerged when we asked the decisionmaker about the evaluation of central versus peripheral goals.

> *Decisionmaker:* "Well, I think this was heavily focused toward the major aspects of the program . . . "
> *Interviewer:* "Do you think the fact that you did focus on major—some of the larger, more important aspects of this program—did that make a difference in how the study was used?"
> *Decisionmaker:* "Well, I think it probably made a difference in the interest with which it was viewed by people. . . . I think if we hadn't done that . . . if the committee hadn't been told to go ahead and proceed in that order, and given the freedom to do that, the committee itself would have lost interest. The fact that they felt that they were going to be allowed to pretty well free-wheel and probe into the most important things *as they saw them* I think had a lot to do with the enthusiasm with which they approached the task (DM159: 22)."

The Hill-Burton case allows us to draw together the points made thus far throughout this book. The study began under conditions of considerable uncertainty. Funding was uncertain, the program faced possible termination, and there was no systematic information about what the 50 state Hill-Burton agencies were doing. A group of relevant decisionmakers and information users were assembled to identify and focus the evaluation question. They began using an incrementalist strategy ("seat-of-the-pants approach") but eventually framed the evaluation question in the context of program goals and objectives. The project officer reported: "what, of course, they got into fairly early in the game was they were going to have to think about criteria. What do state agencies do and what should they be doing?" (PO159: 5). There was always this moving back and forth—action, reaction, adaptation—until the evaluation finally focused on central issues of relevance to the identified and organized decisionmakers and information users.

Central Objectives and the Personal Factor

In the Sufi story about hunting bears that opens this chapter, the point was made that different participants in the hunt had different goals. Goals and objectives embody personal and collective values. *The evaluation question of what goals and objectives will be evaluated cannot be answered until a prior issue is settled: WHOSE goals and objectives for*

the program will be evaluated? Several respondents in our study commented on the subjective and personal nature of the idea of "central"
program goals, particularly where a program operates at several levels.
Consider the response of a decisionmaker for one of many Neighborhood
Health Center Programs.

> *Interviewer:* "To what extend did this evaluation study look at the major
> aspects of the study?"
>
> *Decisionmaker:* "Well, now, you have a controversy because of different
> audiences with different real or hypothesized objectives in mind. I mean,
> the central OEO office when it started said the only value to the program is its
> antipoverty consequences. I'm sure the OMB people thought the major
> program objective was impact on health status. The evaluation clearly did
> not address either of those and could not have at the time. So you have a
> great difference in perception of program objectives. . . . Now if one takes
> the narrower legislative objectives and says, well, did you provide services
> that were comprehensive and continuous in community-based settings,
> emphasizing preventive care and all that junk, then this study did focus on
> those objectives. And, if not the data, then at least the findings suggest
> that it met those objectives. I don't think OMB was ever satisfied with
> those narrow objectives, with the objectives stated in the legislation. You
> know, but that was the way the world is (DM51: 13).

Different people have different perceptions of central program goals.
Yet, evaluators often have a hard time accepting the implications of
this relativism, because they have been taught to evaluate central goals
or else their work is not important. But whether it is the evaluator's
opinion about centrality, the funder's, the client's, some special interest
group perspective, or the viewpoint of program staff, the question of
what constitutes central program goals and objectives remains an intrinsically subjective one. It cannot be otherwise. There is no Jungian collective
conscience or consciousness that the evaluator can tap to determine the
centrality, appropriateness, or morality of program goals. At some point
the issue of whose goals will be evaluated must be addressed. Thus, the
question of central versus peripheral goals cannot really be answered in
the abstract. The question thus becomes, "central from whose point of
view?" The personal factor interacts with the goals clarification process to
focus the evaluation question in a utilization-focused approach.

The personal factor, or what Thompson (1967) called "the variable
human," is also important because individuals vary both in their aptitude
for handling uncertainty and in their ability to exercise discretion.

Information is power only for people who know how to use it and are open to using it. There is no one effective strategy of evaluation in the abstract, separate from the organizational context in which it is introduced or the information using capabilities of the people using it. The capacities of those involved make a major difference in which strategies of decisionmaking and evaluation are used. Thus, the challenge for utilization is at least partly one of matching: getting information about the right questions, issues, and goals to the right people.

The focus, use, and power of evaluation will vary, then, depending on who is identified as the relevant decisionmaker(s) and information user(s). To emphasize this point one final time, think back to the goals clarification game described in Chapter 6. That chapter began by comparing the goals clarification process to the game of "twenty questions" sometimes played at parties. The evaluator thinks of an object (a clear, specific, and measurable goal) and program staff get successive chances to try to guess what he or she has in mind (i.e., staff keep trying to write something that approximates a clear, specific, and measurable goal). The purpose of the present chapter has been to suggest ways of adapting the goals clarification game to the particular circumstances, needs, and persons in a specific program. The active-reactive-adaptive approach to framing evaluation questions in the context of program goals means that there is no definitive set of rules for playing the goals clarification game— with one notable exception: *the players whose goals serve to help focus the evaluation should also be the primary intended users of the evaluation.*

There is a substantial body of research indicating that different individuals behave quite differently in the twenty questions game (and by extension, in any decisionmaking process). Worley (1960), for example, studied subjects' information-seeking endurance in the game under experimental conditions. Initially, each subject was presented with a single clue and given the option of guessing what object the experimenter had in mind or of asking for another clue. This option was available after each new clue, but a wrong guess would end the game. Worley found large and consistent individual differences in the amount of information sought. Donald Taylor (1965) cites the research of Worley and others as evidence that decisionmaking and problem solving behavior is dynamic, highly variable, and contingent upon both situational and individual characteristics. This does not make the evaluator's job any easier. It does mean that the first step in a utilization-focused approach to evaluation— identification and organization of relevant decisionmakers and information users—remains the key to the utilization process. As evidenced in the case of the Hill-Burton permanent committee on evaluation, careful selection of knowledgeable, committed, and information-valuing persons can make a significant difference. The selection process for that committee can serve as a model of how to identify and organize decisionmakers for evaluation purposes. The goals clarification game is most useful when played by people who are searching for information because it helps them focus on central issues without letting the game become an end in itself and without turning the process into a contest between staff and evaluators.

The Goals Paradox: Review and Conclusion

In this chapter we began by looking at theories on decisionmaking in organizations. The rational goal model approach (maximizing), the systems approach (optimizing), and the incrementalist strategy (satisficing) were reviewed. Out of these approaches the active-reactive-adaptive approach to decisionmaking emerged. This strategy gives the evaluator flexibility to work with decisionmakers and information users to design an evaluation that is meaningful in terms of their own setting and useful in terms of their own perspective on program goals.

The active-reactive-adaptive approach is a strategy for exercising the utilization-focused evaluation option of framing the evaluation question in the context of program goals. By understanding the organizational dynamics and multiple uncertainties of a particular program, the evaluator tries to match the degree of goal specificity to particular decisionmaker needs. It is also important in complex programs to know which part of the program is the focus on the evaluation and how subparts of a program relate to the whole.

To facilitate the framing of evaluation questions in complex programs, it is sometimes helpful to approach goals clarification at three levels: the overall mission of the program, the goals of specific programmatic units (or subsystems), and the specific objectives that specify client outcomes. Then comes the issue of prioritization. In programs with multiple or conflicting goals and limited evaluation resources, some kind of prioritization is necessary to focus an evaluation. The usual criterion is the relative importance of each goal. However, the fact that a goal is ranked first in importance does not necessarily mean that decisionmakers and information users need information about attainment of that goal more than they need information about a less important goal. Thus, in a utilization-focused approach to evaluation goals are also prioritized by applying the criterion of evaluative usefulness. Applying the criterion of evaluative usefulness means that an evaluation might focus on goals of apparent peripheral importance rather than more central program goals.

Using data from our utilization of federal health evaluation research study, the central versus peripheral goals debate was recast as a question of determining central evaluation issues. A central issue is an evaluation question that someone really cares about. The evaluation of the Hill-Burton program provided a model for framing an evaluation in the context of program goals so as to focus on central issues identified by relevant decisionmakers and information users. This led to reaffirmation of the importance of the personal factor in the utilization process. The personal factor interacts with the goals clarification process to focus the evaluation question. Thus, the active-reactive-adaptive approach to framing evaluation questions in the context of program goals means that there is no definitive set of rules for playing the goals clarification game— with one exception: the players whose goals serve to help focus the evaluation should also be the primary intended users of the evaluation. The goals clarification game is most likely to result in evaluations with high utilization potential when played by people who are actively searching for information.

Nasrudin's hunting trip in search of bears ended with the "marvelous" outcome of seeing no bears. Our hunting trip in search of the goal of goals has no conclusive ending, because the goal will vary from evaluation to evaluation, situation to situation. The process of framing an evaluation question in the context of program goals and objectives is clearly not the straightforward, logical exercise depicted by the classical literature on rational decisionmaking. Decisionmaking processes in the real world of open systems and environmental uncertainty are not purely deductive maximizing or optimizing exercises. This is the paradox of goals. Goals are rational abstractions in nonrational systems; they are the rational expression of a highly subjective process. Statements of goals emerge at the interface between the ideals of human rationality and the reality of human values. Therein lies their strength and their weakness. Goals provide direction for action and evaluation, but only for those who share in the values expressed by the goals. Evaluators live inside that paradox.

Chapter 8

EVALUATION OF PROGRAM IMPLEMENTATION

A Setting

In conducting interviews for our study of the utilization of federal health evaluations, we were told of one quite dramatic instance of research utilization. It concerned an evaluation of a program established by a state legislature as a demonstration program to teach welfare recipients the basic rudiments of parenting and household management. The state welfare department was charged with the responsibility for conducting workshops, distributing brochures, showing films, and training case workers on how low income people could better manage their meager resources and how they could become better parents. A single major city was selected for pilot testing the program, and a highly respected independent research institute was contracted to evaluate the program. Both the state legislature and the state welfare department were publicly committed to using the evaluation findings for decisionmaking.

The evaluators selected a sample of welfare recipients to interview before the program began. They collected considerable data about parenting, household management, and budgetary practices. Eighteen months later, the same welfare recipients were interviewed a second time. The results showed no measureable change in parenting or household management behavior. In brief, the program was found to be ineffective. These results were reported to the state legislators, some of whom found it appropriate to make sure the public learned about their accountability efforts through the newspapers. As a result of this adverse publicity, the legislature terminated funding for the program—a clear instance of utilization of evaluation findings for decisionmaking.

Now, suppose we wanted to know why the program was ineffective. That question could not be answered by the evaluation as conducted because it focused entirely upon measuring the attainment of intended program outcomes, i.e., the extent to which the program was effective in changing the parenting and household management behaviors of welfare recipients. As it turned out, there is a very good reason why the program was ineffective. When the funds were initially allocated from the state to the city, the program became immediately embroiled in the politics of urban welfare. Welfare rights organizations questioned the right of government to tell poor people how to spend their money or rear their children: "you have no right to tell us to manage our households according to white, middle class values. And who is this Frenchman named Piaget who's going to tell us how to raise our American kids?"

As a result of these and other political battles the program was delayed and further delayed. Procrastination being the better part of valor, the first parenting brochure was never printed, no household management films were ever shown, no workshops were held, and no case workers were ever trained. In short, *the program was never implemented—but it was evaluated*! It was then found to be ineffective and was killed.

The Importance of Implementation Analysis

It is important to know whether or not a program is effective after it is properly implemented, but to answer that question it is first necessary to know whether or not the program was indeed properly implemented. This chapter considers the meaning and purpose of implementation evaluation from a utilization perspective.

In the spring of 1974, the entire issue of the periodical *Evaluation* was devoted to a consideration of "the human services shortfall." Lynn and Salasin (1974: 4) defined this shortfall as "a large and growing gap between what we expect from government-supported human service systems, and what these systems in fact deliver." The human services shortfall is made up of two parts: (1) failure of implemented programs to attain desired outcomes and (2) failure to actually implement policy in the form of operating programs. Evaluators have directed most of their attention to the first problem by conducting outcomes evaluations, but there is growing evidence that the second problem is equally, if not even more critical. In a recent book on social program implementation, editor Walter Williams concludes: "the underlying theme of this book is that the lack of concern for implementation is currently *the* crucial impediment to improving complex operating programs, policy analysis, and experimentation in social policy areas" (Williams and Elmore, 1976: 267; italics in original). The preface to the book states the problem quite succinctly.

> The fundamental implementation question remains whether or not what has been decided actually can be carried out in a manner consonant with that underlying decision. More and more, we are finding, the answer is no. So it is crucial that we attend to implementation (Williams and Elmore, 1976: xi).

The problem of making policy operative is fundamental in all realms of government intervention. At the international level, studies collected and edited by John C. de Wilde (1967) demonstrate that program implementation and administration are the critical problems in Third World development plans. Organizational sociologists have documented the particular problem of implementing programs that are new and innovative alongside or into existing programs (e.g., Corwin, 1973; Hage and Aiken, 1970). Diffusion of innovation theorists have thoroughly documented the problems of implementing new ideas in new settings (e.g., Guba, 1968; Rogers et al., 1969, 1971; Havelock, 1973). Provus (1971) pointed to the importance of evaluating implementation of educational programs before outcomes could be usefully evaluated. Yet, Williams and Elmore (1976: xii) find that implementation analysis has seldom been taken seriously, much to the detriment of research utilization:

> The failure to focus on implementation has blighted not only program administration but also policy research and analysis. In the former case, policy ideas that seemed reasonable and compelling when decisions were made often have become badly flawed and ineffective programs as they drifted down the bureaucratic process. It is not just that the programs fall short of the early rhetoric that described them; they often barely work at all. Ignoring implementation has been equally disastrous for research

and analysis. *Indeed, it is possible that past analysis and research that ignored implementation issues may have asked the wrong questions, thereby producing information of little or no use to policy-making* (italics in original).

The notion that asking the wrong questions leads to useless information is fundamental to everything we have discussed. To avoid gathering useless information *it is important to frame evaluation questions in the context of program implementation*. Framing evaluation questions in the context of program implementation is a major approach in identifying and focusing relevant evaluation questions. Implementation evaluation is one of the options available to active-reactive-adaptive evaluators in conducting utilization-focused research.

Both an implementation framework and a goals framework are important; the one that is clarified first in a given evaluation process varies. Implementation evaluation is distinguished as a separate element in order to call attention to its importance and to deal with the unique considerations that affect the conceptualization of an implementation analysis. A utilization-focused approach to evaluation is not, however, a linear process easily represented by a series of logical steps. Both implementation evaluation and outcomes evaluation are important elements in a comprehensive evaluation. The inclusion of both elements can be critical; their ordering is situational.

Outcomes Evaluation Versus Implementation Evaluation

It is perhaps easiest to understand implementation evaluation in contrast to outcomes evaluation. While the ideal evaluation includes both, few evaluations have made this ideal operational. Evaluation research has been dominated by an emphasis on measuring outcomes. Outcomes evaluation is the comparison of actual program outcomes with desired outcomes (goals). One of the major reasons goals clarification has received so much attention from evaluators is because applied social science research has been preoccupied with outcomes evaluation. This has been especially true in education. Provus (1971: 10-11) has cogently described the predominance of outcomes evaluation in the field of educational assessment:

Evaluation of program outcomes establishes performance criteria for program recipients. This approach is represented by all that is most current and "scientific" in educational evaluation. Starting with the work of Tyler and the perfection of standardized instruments with norms for various populations, and continuing with the present interest in group criterion referenced tests, individual situational testing, and unobtrusive measures of performance, the preoccupation of the present generation of evaluators has been and continues to be with microanalysis of a learner's behavior at various times before and after exposure to a lesson, program, treatment, or institution.

In educational research, outcomes evaluation is represented by pretest versus posttest performance on standardized achievement tests; in criminal justice programs, outcomes evaluation measures comparative recidivism rates; in health programs, the outcomes are changes in incidence and prevalence rates; in manpower programs, the outcomes are employment rates; in drug abuse treatment programs, the outcomes are rates of repeated addiction; and so it goes for each area in the human service delivery system. The problem with pure outcomes evaluation is that the results give decisionmakers very little information upon which to act. Simply knowing that outcomes are high, low or different does not tell decisionmakers very much about what to do. What is missing is information about the actual nature of the program being evaluated. In the example which provided the setting for this chapter, the decisionmakers knew only that the welfare parent training program had no measureable effects; they did not even known whether or not a program actually existed that could be expected to have effects. Based only on erroneous outcomes information they terminated a policy approach that had never actually been tried. Unfortunately, such inappropriate decisions based only on outcomes evaluations are not uncommon.

A serious look at the actual substance of the program being evaluated car prevent some of the obvious but oft repeated evaluation failures of the past.

For example, although it seems obvious to mention, it is important to know whether a program actually exists. Federal agencies are often inclined to assume that, once a cash transfer has taken place from a government agency to a program in the field, a program exists and can be evaluated. Experienced evaluation researchers know that the very existence of a program cannot be taken for granted even after large cash transfers have taken place. Early evaluation of Title I programs in New York City provide an illustration of this problem. . . . Obvious though it may seem, evaluations continue without either raising or answering the primary quesion: "Does the program exist?" This error could not arise if evaluation researchers looked carefully and seriously at program content before decisions about evaluation research methods were made (Guttentag and Struening, 1975b: 3-4).

While terminating a policy inappropriately is one possible error when cnly outcomes data are used, enlarging a program inappropriately is also possible when decisionmakers have no real information about program operations and implementation. In one instance a number of drug addiction treatment programs in a county were evaluated, collecting nothing but outcomes data on rates of readdiction for treated patients. All programs had relatively mediocre success rates, except one program which had had 100 percent success for two years. The county board immediately voted to triple the budget of that program. Within a year, the readdiction rates for that program had fallen to the same mediocre level as other programs. By enlarging the program based on outcomes data the county board had eliminated the key elements in the program's success—its small size and dedicated staff. The highly successful program had been a six patient halfway house with one primary staff counselor who ate, slept, and lived that program. He established such a close relationship with each addict that he knew exactly how to keep each one straight. When the program was enlarged, he became administrator of three houses and lost personal contact with the clients. The successful program became only mediocre. Thus, a highly effective program was lost because the county board acted without any information about actual program operations and without an assessment of the basis for the program's success.

If one had to choose between implementation information and outcomes information because of limited evaluation resources, there are many instances in which implementation information would be of greater value. A decisionmaker can use implementation information to make sure that a policy is being put into operation according to design—or to test the very feasibility of the policy. Unless one knows that a program is operating according to design, there may be little reason to expect it to produce the desired outcomes. Furthermore, until the program is implemented and a "treatment" is believed to be in operation, there is little reason to evaluate outcomes. The decisionmaker on the Hill-Burton evaluation from our utilization of federal health studies made this point quite emphatically:

When we called the committee together and began to discuss the question of evaluating state agency performance there was no decision at that point that there was going to actually be interviews with the state agencies. That's something that grew naturally out of the discussion of the committee members. They concluded fairly early in their discussions that they were groping in the dark to try and evaluate agencies when they weren't really sure what the agencies were doing. And so the idea to interview them and gather all this information relative to what's going on in the state agencies grew out of the committee's feeling that they needed to know what was going on before they could even attempt an evaluation of whether what was going on was good, bad, or indifferent (DM159: 6).

Where outcomes are evaluated without knowledge of implementation, the results seldom provide a direction for action because the decisionmaker lacks information about what produced the observed outcomes (or lack of outcomes). This is the "black box" approach to evaluation: clients are tested before entering the program and after completing the program, while what happens inbetween is a black box. Carol Weiss (1972b: 43) describes this approach and its dangers.

Why should the evaluator be concerned with program input? Haven't we noted earlier that his job is to find out whether the program (whatever it is) is achieving its goals? Does it make any difference to his work whether the program is using rote drill, psychoanalysis, or black magic? There are evaluators who are sympathetic to such an approach. They see the program as a "black box," the contents of which do not concern them; they are charged with discovering effects. But if the evaluator has no idea of what the program really is, he may fail to ask the right questions.

Most black box evaluations that study outcomes alone do so because of tradition and routine; no thoughtful decision has been made about what kind of evaluative information would be most useful. Nowhere is this better illustrated than in the use of standardized achievement tests in educational evaluation.

The Black Box Approach to Evaluation: The Case of Standardized Tests

The most widespread example of the routine collection of outcomes data with no corresponding program implementation information is the yearly administration of standardized, norm-referenced achievement tests in public schools. Testing is a multimillion dollar business. Thousands of school districts routinely administer tests. Vito Perrone, in a review of the abuses of standardized tests as instruments for school evaluation, notes that since the Depression testing has become "a part of the conventional wisdom of schools." He goes on to explain that since the educational crisis following the Soviet launch of Sputnik I, there has been increased demand for school evaluations: "evaluation in most instances became synonymous, unfortunately, with outcome data produced by standardized tests" (Perrone, 1977: 18). Yet as evaluation instruments, such tests provide minimal useful information: the results are of little use to teachers or parents and the tests cannot be reliably used for evaluating individual students (cf. Perrone, 1977; Perrone et al., 1976; Patton, 1975b). They may tell the public and school board members how schools rank on achievement, but these rankings do not tell school officials what to do to improve the educational experience for students. To improve schools, officials need information about what actually happens in classrooms— and that they do not have. Standardized tests have little relationship to the actual objectives of instruction at any given time and place (Skager, 1971; Sax, 1974: 258-259), and are likely to have even less relationship to actual educational practice in a particular district. Furthermore, the ranking of schools by achievement is relatively stable from year to year for most school systems. Knowledgeable people in a district already know which schools will rank high and which will rank low; they also know that rankings have more to do with student and community characteristics than with curriculum and actual teaching practices.

Why, then, do communities spend thousands of dollars year after year to collect information that is not used and only tells people what they already know? The school board says it is for parents, parents hope teachers use the tests, teachers just file them with the principal, and principals suppose that school board members want the tests. Clearly no relevant decisionmakers and information users have been identified. On the whole, it is a useless system and a gigantic accountability hoax.

A utilization-focused approach to evaluation carries no simple, ready-made instruments or standardized approaches, but does frame the evaluation question in the context of program implementation, not just program outcomes.

> Unless there is some reasonably accurate and coherent definition of the program, the evaluator does not know to what to attribute the outcomes he observes. Let's remember that evaluation is designed to help with decision making. Decision makers need to know what it was that worked or didn't work, what it was that should be adopted throughout the system or modified. Unless the evaluation can provide evidence on the nature of the program as it existed . . . there is little basis for decision (Weiss, 1972b: 44).

Evaluations that collect only data on student achievement with standardized tests cannot provide evidence on the nature of the educational program as it actually exists; thus, such evaluations have low utilization potential and high potential for abuse and misinterpretation. Educational evaluations that rely entirely on outcomes from standardized achievement tests represent the epitomy of the black box approach. Hidden inside that black box can be quite important information that makes a world of difference in understanding a program.

Unlocking the Black Box of Program Implementation

The first step in unlocking the black box of program implementation is finding out whether or not the program actually moved from an idea to initial implementation. The evaluator asks: "Does the program exist?" According to Williams, the number of programs that fail to ever become operational may be quite high because "the major problem for policy analysis is not in developing relatively sound policy alternatives but in failing to consider the feasibility of implementing these alternatives" (Williams and Elmore, 1976: 268). The crucial implementation stage for Williams occurs between the decision and operation stages, when new programs are being tried for the first time. The weaknesses of the planning process suddenly become quite glaring:

> Surely policymakers at the time of choice ought to have reasonable estimates of the organizational capacity to carry out alternative proposals. But however obvious that may be, few people have ever thought in terms of analyzing implementation during the decision-making stages! (Williams, 1976: 270).

This makes the evaluator's job all the more difficult because it means there are seldom clear criteria for even conceptualizing implementation processes, much less evaluating them.

The further one delves into implementation analysis, the more complex the alternatives become. The black box in pure outcomes evaluations quickly becomes a Pandora's box in more comprehensive evaluation designs with an implementation analysis component. Consider, for example, the Pandorian question of how close an actual program has to be in comparison to its initial proposal or plan before it can be said to be implemented. One decisionmaker interviewed in our utilization of federal health evaluations study felt that policymakers had been misled into thinking that the evaluation report on his program concerned the ideal program as planned, when in fact only partial implementation had occurred. The report was thus discredited in this decisionmaker's eyes because he felt its use in congressional hearings had done the program a disservice.

> When you start reading your hearings, for instance, and find them using it as a resource in some ways, frankly, it concerns me a little bit, because I felt like portions of this did not have substantive enough data to be making determinations. That is, how can you judge the effect of the cancellation provision when it wasn't fully implemented at the point in time that the study was using? How could you put any reliance upon a study when the repayment provision wasn't fully implemented? Do you see what I Mean? So I didn't put credence in the thing (DM145: 25).

But just how close to the ideal must the program be before it can be said to be fully implemented? The next section discusses this and related issues within the black box of program implementation.

Ideal Program Plans and Actual Implementation

Once the evaluator has determined that at least some activity actually exists, i.e., that there is indeed a program to be evaluated, the next question is: what should the program look like before it can be said to be fully implemented and operational? This question is difficult to answer because programs are not implemented in the classical, rational fashion of single-mindedly adopting a set of means to achieve a predetermined end. From an incrementalist, satisficing perspective (see Chapter 7) organizations and decisionmakers do not methodically implement a program as if they had found the best means to achieve top priority goals. Programs take shape slowly as decisionmakers react to multiple uncertainties and emerging complexities. Jerome Murphy makes this point quite emphatically in his study of the implementation of Title V of the Elementary and Secondary Education Act. He found great variation in implementation in the various states. He describes evaluations of those programs as exercises in blaming and scapegoating instead of attempts to understand educational change in the context of organizational dynamics, concluding that the widespread assumption that competently led bureaucracies operate like goal-directed, unitary decision-makers may well be a major barrier to dealing with problems of bureaucratic change. Both program evaluations and reform efforts must come to grips explicitly with the enduring attributes of organizations (Murphy, 1976: 96).

Sociologists who study formal organizations, social change, and diffusion of innovations have carefully documented the substantial slippage in organizations between plans and actual operations. For Rogers (1962) it is the difference between trial and adoption; for Smelser (1959) it is the difference between specification, implementation, and routinization; for Mann and Neff (1961) it is the slippage between planning change, taking steps to make change, and stabilizing change; and for Hage and Aiken (1970) it is the difference between initiation, implementation, and routinization of change. In each case, regardless of how these sociologists conceptualize the stages of organizational change and innovations adoption, they emphasize two points: (1) *routinization or final acceptance is never certain at the beginning; and (2) the implementation process always contains unknowns that change the ideal so that it looks different when and if it actually becomes operational.*

Hage and Aiken (1970: 100) found that organizational conflict and disequilibrium are greatest during the implementation stage of organizational change. No matter how much planning takes place,

> the human element is seldom adequately considered in the implementation of a new product or service. There will be mistakes that will have to be corrected. Alteration of the existing structure will also create conflicts and tensions among members of the organization.

As programs take shape power struggles develop:

> The stage of implementation is thus the stage of conflict, especially over power. It is the time when the new program results in the greatest disequilibirium in the organization because it is the stage when the program becomes a reality and the members of the organization must actually live with it . . . tempers flare, interpersonal animosities develop, and the power structure is shaken (Hage and Aiken, 1970: 104).

The difference between the ideal, rational model of program implementation and the day-to-day, incrementalist, and conflict-laden realities of program implementation is explained with a minimum of jargon in the following notice found by Jerome Murphy (1976: 92) in the office of a state education agency:

Notice

The objective of all dedicated department employees should be to thoroughly analyze all situations, anticipate all problems prior to their occurrence, have answers for these problems, and move swiftly to solve these problems when called upon. . . .

However . . .

When you are up to your ass in alligators, it is difficult to remind yourself that your initial objective was to drain the swamp.

Programs are implemented incrementally by adapting to local conditions, organizational dynamics, and programmatic uncertainties. In reporting the findings of RAND's large-scale Change Agent Study, Milbrey McLaughlin (1976: 169) wrote:

> Specifically, the Change Agent Study concluded that *successful implementation is characterized by a process of mutual adaptation.* . . . Implementation did not involve merely the direct and straighforward application of an educational technology or plan. Implementation was a dynamic organizational process that was shaped over time by interactions between project goals and methods and the institutional setting. As such, it was neither automatic nor certain (italics in the original).

Evaluation disasters can result from failing to recognize that implementation of program ideals is neither automatic nor certain. The national evaluation of Follow Through is a prime example of such a disaster. Follow Through was introduced as an extension of Head Start for primary-age children. It was a planned variation "experiment" in compensatory education featuring 22 different models of education to be tested in 158 school districts on 70,000 children throughout the nation. The evaluation alone employed 3,000 people to collect data on program effectiveness. However, as Alkin (1970: 2) has observed, the evaluation lacked focus from the beginning:

> The greatest deficiency of the evaluation project is its failure to provide adequate specification of the kind of study it is intended to be and the functions which it proposes to serve. . . . If they [the evaluators] accepted four million dollars in evaluation funds, it should be expected that they would have been more aggressive in demanding clarification of the objectives and the decision-making purposes.

It was assumed in the evaluation plan that models could and would be implemented in some systematic, uniform fashion. Elmore, however, has rightly pointed out the folly of this assumption.

Each sponsor developed a large organization, in some instances larger than the entire federal program staff, to deal with problems of model implementation. Each local school system developed a program organization consisting of a local director, a team of teachers and specialists, and a parent advisory group. The more the scale and complexity of the program increased, the less plausible it became for Follow Through administrators to control the details of program variations, and the more difficult it became to determine whether the array of districts and sponsors represented "systematic" variations in program content (Williams and Elmore, 1976: 108).

The Follow Through data analysis showed greater variation within groups than between them, i.e., the 22 models did not show systematic treatment effects as such. Most effects were null, some were negative, but "of all our findings, the most pervasive, consistent, and suggestive is probably this: *The effectiveness of each Follow Through model depended more on local circumstances than on the nature of the model*" (Anderson, 1977: 13; italics in original). In reviewing these findings, Eugene Tucker of the U.S. Office of Education suggests that, in retrospect, the Follow Through evaluation should have begun as a formative effort with greater focus on implementation strategies:

It is safe to say that evaluators did not know what was implemented in the various sites. Without knowing what was implemented it is virtually impossible to select valid effectiveness measures. . . . Hindsight is a marvelous teacher and in large scale experimentations an expensive one (Tucker, 1977: 11-12).

Yet the importance of framing evaluation questions in the context of program implementation appears to be a hard lesson to learn. Provus (1971: 27-29) clearly warned against precisely the kind of design used in the Follow Through evaluation at a 1966 conference on educational evaluation of national programs, a conference which included U.S. Office of Education officials. By 1971, he had fully developed and published his "discrepancy evaluation" model, which places heavy emphasis on implementation evaluation:

An evaluation that begins with an experimental design denies to program staff what it needs most: information that can be used to make judgments about the program while it is in its dynamic stages of growth. . . . Evaluation must provide administrators and program staff with the information they need and the freedom to act on that information. . . .
We will not use the antiseptic assumptions of the research laboratory to compare children receiving new program assistance with those not re-

ceiving such aid. We recognize that the comparisons have never been productive, nor have they facilitated corrective action. The overwhelming number of evaluations conducted in this way show no significant differences between "experimental" and "control" groups (Provus, 1971: 11-12).

Provus argued that evaluations had to begin by establishing the degree to which programs were actually operating as desired. Discrepancy evaluation is a comparison of the actual program with the ideal program. These ideals "may arise from any source, but under the Discrepancy Evaluation Model they are derived from the values of the program staff and the client population it serves" (Provus, 1971: 12). Evaluation of programs, even national programs, must begin at the local level because

> it follows that if there are types of programs with different developmental characteristics, the development standards for these program types will vary also. . . . This local work is usually of the process assessment type in which evaluators systematically collect and weigh data descriptive of ongoing program activity (Provus, 1971: 13).

Provus essentially argued that the nature of the evaluation should be adapted to fit the organizational realities of program development and implementation. *The reality is that actual programs look different from ideal program plans. The evaluation challenge is to assist identified decisionmakers in determining how far from the ideal plan the program can deviate, and in what ways it can deviate, while still meeting fundamental criteria.* How different can an actual program be from its ideal and still be said to have been implemented? The answer must be clarified between decisionmakers and evaluators as they conceptualize the evaluation and focus the evaluation question. It depends on decisionmaker needs and the particular organizational dynamics of the program being evaluated. Williams outlines the issues for negotiation and clarification as follows:

> At some point there should be a determination of the degree to which an innovation has been implemented successfully. What should the implemented activity be expected to look like in terms of the underlying decision? For a complex treatment package put in different local settings, decisionmakers usually will not expect—or more importantly, *not want*—a precise reproduction of every detail of the package. The objective is performance, not conformance. To enhance the probability of achieving the basic program or policy objectives, the implementation should consist of a realistic de-

velopment of the underlying decision in terms of the local setting. In the ideal situation, those responsible for implementation would take the basic idea and modify it to meet special local conditions. There should be a reasonable resemblance to the basic idea, as measured by inputs and expected outputs, incorporating the best of the decision and the best of the local ideas (Williams and Elmore, 1976: 277-278).

I would not belabor these points if it were not so painfully clear that implementation processes are so frequently ignored in evaluation research. Edwards et al., (1975: 142) note in their introduction to the decision-theoretic approach to evaluation that "we have frequently encountered the idea that a [national] program is a fixed, unchanging object, observable at various times and places." Because this idea seems so firmly lodged in so many minds and continues to spawn so many evaluation disasters, I feel compelled to prolong this section with one more piece of evidence to the contrary.

RAND Corporation, under contract to the U.S. Office of Education, studied 293 federal programs supporting educational change. It is one of the largest and most comprehensive studies of educational change ever conducted. RAND's Change Agency Study concluded that implementation "dominates the innovative process and its outcomes:"

> In short, where implementation was successful, and where significant change in participant attitudes, skills, and behavior occurred, implementation was characterized by a process of mutual adaptation in which project goals and methods were modified to suit the needs and interests of the local staff and in which the staff changed to meet the requirements of the project. This finding was true even for highly technological and initially well-specified projects; unless adaptations were made in the original plans or technologies, implementation tended to be superficial or symbolic, and significant change in participants did not occur (McLaughlin, 1976: 169).

The Change Agent Study found that the usual emphasis in federal programs on the *delivery system* is inappropriate. McLaughlin recommended

> a shift in change agent policies from a primary focus on the *delivery system* to an emphasis on the *deliverer*. An important lesson that can be derived from the Change Agent Study is that unless the developmental needs of the users are addressed, and unless projects are modified to suit the needs of the user and the institutional setting, the promise of new technologies is likely to be unfulfilled (McLaughlin, 1976: 180).

In the context of the examples of evaluation absurdities cited in this chapter, and combined with the works of Provus, Williams, Murphy and others, the Rand Change Agent Study has enormous implications for the utilization of evaluation. The conclusion of the RAND study means that *implementation evaluation is critical because program implementation is neither automatic nor certain. It means that implementation evaluation must also be adaptive and focused on users if the evaluation is to be relevant, meaningful, and useful. It means that judging program implementation according to some written-in-stone blueprint is inappropriate and dysfunctional. It means that criteria for evaluating implementation must be developed through a process of interaction with identified and organized decisionmakers and information users in order to determine how they view implementation. It means that evaluators will have to be active-reactive-adaptive in framing evaluation questions in the context of program implementation.*

Types of Implementation Evaluation

In order to be active-reactive-adaptive in framing evaluation questions, evaluators need to understand implementation evaluation alternatives. There are three evaluation options with respect to studying implementation: (1) the effort approach, (2) the process approach, and (3) the treatment specification approach. These are not mutually exclusive approaches; a comprehensive evaluation may include all three types of implementation evaluations.

EFFORT EVALUATION

Effort evaluations focus on documenting "the quantity and quality of activity that takes place. This represents an assessment of input or energy regardless of output. It is intended to answer the questions 'What did you do' and 'How well did you do it?' " (Suchman, 1967: 61). Effort evaluation moves up a step from asking if the program exists to asking how active the program is. If relatively inactive, it is unlikely to be very effective.

> Evaluation of program effort refers to an assessment of the amounts and kinds of program activities considered necessary for the accomplishment of program goals within a particular stage of development. It refers not only to staff time, activity, and commitment, but also to the allocation and use of material resources—funds, space, equipment, etc. . . . information

such as the following might be obtained about program effort: what techniques for recruiting potential clientele have been employed; how much staff time, effort, funds, etc., have been expended; what ancillary resources have been used, e.g., outside consultation, media, public relations, etc.? (Tripodi et al., 1971: 45).

An effort evaluation establishes the level of program activity by observing the degree to which inputs are available and operational at desired levels. Have sufficient staff been hired with the proper qualifications? Are staff-client ratios at desired levels? How many clients with what characteristics are being served by the program? Are necessary materials available? An effort evaluation involves making an inventory of program operations.

PROCESS EVALUATION

The second option in implementation analysis is process evaluation. This approach focuses on the internal dynamics and actual operations of a program in an attempt to understand its strengths and weaknesses. Process evaluations focus on why certain things are happening, how the parts of the program fit together, and how people perceive the program. This approach takes its name from an emphasis on looking at how a product or outcome is produced rather than looking at the product itself, i.e., it is an analysis of the processes whereby a program produces the results it does. Process evaluation is developmental, descriptive, continuous, flexible, and inductive.

Process evaluations search for explanations of the successes, failures, and changes in a program. Under field conditions in the real world, people and unforeseen circumstances shape programs and modify initial plans in ways that are rarely trivial. The process evaluator sets out to understand and document the day-to-day reality of the setting or settings under study. He tries to unravel what is actually happening in a program by searching for the major patterns and important nuances that give the program its character. A process evaluation requires sensitivity to both qualitiative and quantitative changes in programs throughout their development; it means becoming intimately acquainted with the details of the program. Process evaluations look not only at formal activities and anticipated outcomes, but also investigate informal patterns and unanticipated consequences in the full context of program implementation and development.

Finally, process evaluations usually include perceptions of people close to the program about how things are going. A variety of perspectives may be sought from people inside and outside the program. For example, Hayman and Napier (1975: 84) describe a variety of ways process data can be collected at the classroom level in educational evaluations: "it is now possible to gather reliable process data in numerous ways—from peers, outside resource people, students, and, of course, the teacher's own observations." These differing perspectives can provide unique insights into program processes as experienced by different people.

A process evaluation can provide useful feedback during the developmental phase of a program. It can also be used to collect implementation data for use in diffusion and dissemination processes. One evaluator in our utilization of federal health evaluations reported that process information had been particularly useful to federal officials in expanding a program nationwide.

> We used as our sample those centers which had been in existence for a year. This was to allow for the start-up problems and, you know, gearing up and getting under speed and all that stuff. The reason they wanted it done when it was done was so that it would be able to affect subsequent centers. . . .
>
> I like to think in terms of programmatic issues, in terms of making a difference in the next center that opened, or in the whole series of things that were required in order for a center to get on the way. . . . *The process evaluations that we did for the centers one by one, one at a time, each of those were affected by the results.* And so, the timing was very critical for that, and I think it was the appropriate time (EV51: 22).

Suchman (1967: 67) suggests that

> the analysis of process may be made according to four main dimensions dealing with: (1) the attributes of the program itself; (2) the population exposed to the program: (3) the situational context within which the program takes place; and (4) the different kinds of effects produced by the program.

However, he considers process evaluation an ancillary component in that

> this analysis of the process whereby a program produces the results it does, is not an inherent part of evaluative research. An evaluation study may limit its data collection and analysis to determining whether or not a program is successful . . . without examining the why's and wherefor's (sic) of this success or failure (Suchman, 1967: 66).

Scriven (1967: 49-50) concurs that process analysis has only a limited role to play in evaluation:

It is not inappropriate to regard some kinds of process investigation as evaluation. But the range of process research only overlaps with and is never subsumed by nor equivalent to that of evalution.

Other evaluators, however, think that process evaluation ought to be taken more seriously. Process evaluation is one of the four major components of the CIPP (context, input, process, product) model of evaluation developed by Stufflebeam et al. (1970, 1971). They consider process evaluation to be an integral part of "a total evaluation model." They see process evaluation in a broad sense, as (1) gathering data to detect or predict defects in the procedural design or its implementation during the implementation stages, (2) providing information for program decision, and (3) establishing a record of program development as it occurs.

In a utilization-focused approach to evaluation research process analysis is neither inherently ancillary nor inherently integral to evaluation research. Process evaluation is one of the optional approaches available to decisionmakers, information users, and evaluators as they attempt to frame evaluation research questions in the context of program implementation.

TREATMENT SPECIFICATION

The treatment specification approach to implementation evaluation involves identifying and measuring precisely what it is about a program that is supposed to have an effect. What is going to happen in the program that is expected to make a difference? How are program goals supposed to be attained? What theory do program staff hold about what they have to do in order to accomplish the results they want? In technical terms, this means identifying independent variables that are expected to affect outcomes (the dependent variables). Treatment specification reveals the causal assumptions undergirding program activity. The treatment specification approach to implementation evaluation means measuring the degree to which specified treatments actually occur. This can be a tricky and difficult task laden with methodological and conceptual pitfalls.

Social programs are complex undertakings. Social program evaluators look with something akin to jealously at evaluators in agriculture who evaluate a new strain of wheat or evaluators in medicine who evaluate the effects of a new drug. . . . The same stimulus can be produced again, and other researchers can study its consequences—under the same or different conditions, with similar or different subjects, but with some assurance that they are looking at the effects of the same *thing.*

Social programs are not nearly so specific. They incorporate a range of components, styles, people, and procedures ... the content of the program, what actually goes on, is much harder to describe. There are often marked internal variations in operation from day to day and from staff member to staff member. When you consider a program as large and amorphous as the poverty program or the model cities program, it takes a major effort to just describe and analyze the program input (Weiss, 1972b: 43).

Yet unless there is basic information about program intervention activities, the evaluator does not know to what to attribute the outcomes observed. This is the classic problem of treatment specification in social science research and, of course, takes us into the arena of trying to establish causality.

Any new program or project may be though of as representing a theory or hypothesis in that—to use experimental terminology—the decision-maker wants to put in place a treatment expected to *cause* certain predicted effects or outcomes (Williams and Elmore, 1976: 274; italics in original).

From this perspective, one task of implementation evaluation is to identify and operationalize the program treatment.

Many evaluations, especially experimental design evaluations, equate program treatment specification with comparing programs bearing different labels. Because this practice is so prevalent—and so distorting— the next section is a critique of the labeling approach to tr atment specifications, followed by a more extensive explanation of how treatments ought to be specified when this approach is used in utilization-focused evaluation.

Program Implementation and Treatment Identification: The Problem of Labeling the Black Box

This section is a simple sermon on the Pandorian folly attendant upon those who would unlock the black box of program implementation through the reification of program labels. There may be no more widespread contravention of basic research principles in evaluation than the practice of using program labels as a substitute for actual data on program implementation. Labels are not treatments. Program labels give no clues about causal relationships. Attaching the same label to a set of projects in programs like Head Start, Community Corrections, Community Mental Health Centes, or Job Corps neither makes the projects that bear those labels comparable nor tells you anything about what a given project actually does.

My own suspicion is that the reification of program labels is a major source of null findings in evaluation research. Labels lead to the aggregation of effective with ineffective programs that have nothing in common except their label. A 1976 evaluation of Residential Community Corrections Programs in Minnesota is a case in point. The report was prepared by the Evaluation Unit of the Governor's Commission on Crime Prevention and Control. The evaluation report compares recidivism rates for three types of programs: (1) halfway houses, (2) PORT (Probationed Offenders Rehabilitation and Training) projects, and (3) juvenile residences.

The term "halfway house" refers to a "residential facility designed to facilitate the transition of paroled adult exoffenders who are returning to society from institutional confinement." The limitation to adults serves to distinquish halfway houses from juvenile residence which serve juveniles. The identification of paroled ex-offenders as the target population of halfway houses distinguishes the *primary* intervention stage of these projects from the PORT projects in which the primary intervention stage is probation (GCCPC, 1976: 8).

The report presents aggregated outcome data for each type of community corrections program. The evaluators take pride in not analyzing differences among individual projects: "efforts have been made to avoid leading the reader to the conclusion that any given residential community corrections program is 'better' or 'worse' than another" (GCCPC, 1976: 4). The evaluators recognize the design problems of attributing causality to individual project outcomes, but they have no problem aggregating projects about which they have no systematic implementation data. In effect they are comparing the outcomes of three labels: halfway houses, PORT projects, and juvenile residences. The evaluators' idea of dealing with the implementation issue is contained in one sentence: "the projects included in this study are in various stages of implementation, but all are at least in their second or third year of funding from the Commission" (GCCPC, 1976: 6). Nowhere in the several hundred pages of the report is there any systematic data presented about the actual nature of the treatment experiences provided in these programs. People go in and people come out; what happens in between is a black box of no interest to the evaluators.

The evaluation concludes that "the evidence presented in this report indicates that residential community corrections programs have had little, if any, impact on the recidivism of program clients" (GCCPC, 1976: 289). These preliminary findings resulted in a moratorium on funding of new residential community corrections, and the final report recommended maintaining that moratorium. With no attention to the meaningfulness of their analytical labels and with no treatment specifications, the evaluators passed judgment on the effectiveness of an $11 million program.

The irony of this travesty is that the Evaluation Unit of the Minnesota Crime Commission prides itself on the scientific rigor of its work because it requires experimental designs in all program evaluations. In the name of Science, the black box lives on—and prospers. Treatments are never specified beyond amorphous program labels. Just what is it about a halfway house that leads one to expect reduced recidividism? The evaluators never tell us; nor do they document the presence of the supposed treatment.

The problem with the aggregated comparisons was that they were meaningless. In talking with staff in a few of these community corrections projects it rapidly became clear that the separate efforts vary tremendously in treatment modality, clientele, and stage of implementation. The comparisons were based on averages, but the averages disguise important differences. There was no such thing as the average project among those settings; yet they were combined for comparative purposes. The report obscured both individual sites that are doing excellent work and those of dubious quality. It included no careful descriptions of individual residences and no data from clients, staff, or others about the actual nature of these programs. The evaluation revealed nothing about what these facilities do; it only stated that, in the aggregate, the facilities were not effective.[1]

Unfortunately, this example is not an exceptional case. One has only to read the journals in any of the disciplines to find comparisons based on aggregations of programs with similar labels, but lacking any implementation or treatment specification data. There are comparisons between "open" schools and "traditional" schools which present no data on relative openness. There are comparisons of individual therapy with group therapy where no attention is paid to the homogeneity of either category of treatment. The list could be expanded ad infinitum. Edwards et al. (1976: 142) confirm the widespread nature of the labeling approach to treatment specification:

A common administrative fiction, especially in Washington, is that because some money associated with an administrative label (e.g., Head Start) has been spent at several places and over a period of time, that the entities spending the money are comparable from time to time and from place to place. Such assumptions can easily lead to evaluation-research disasters.

Treatment Specification: An Alternative to Labeling

A recent newspaper cartoon showed several federal bureaucrats assembled around a table in a conference room. The chair of the group was saying, "of course the welfare program has a few obvious flaws . . . but if we can just think of a catchy enough name for it, it just might work!" (Dunagin, 1977). In black box evaluations the program labels, catchy or not, are the only thing that can be given credit for program success or blame for program failure. In cases like the Minnesota Community Corrections evaluation, simply knowing the project label was of little help in figuring out what the program actually did.

Treatment specification for implementation evaluation purposes means being able to state what is going to happen in the program that is expected to make a difference. How are program goals supposed to be attained? What theory do program staff hold about what they have to do in order to accomplish the results they want? In technical terms, this means identifying independent variables that are expected to affect outcomes. It is what Provus (1971: 50) called "a program design. The design tells us what we're evaluating, what we can expect to find out in the field. Our first task is to gather information on the design."

Treatment specification reveals the causal assumptions undergirding program activity. For example, one theory undergirding community corrections is that integration of criminal offenders into local communities is the best way to rehabilitate those offenders and thereby reduce recidivism. It is therefore important to gather information about the degree to which each project actually integrates offenders into the community. Halfway houses and juvenile residences can be run like small-scale prisons, completely isolated from the environment. Treatment specification tells us what to look for in each project to find out if the program's causal theory is actually being put to the test. At this point we are not dealing with the question of how to measure the relevant independent variables in a program theory, but only attempting to specify the intended treatment in nominal terms.

In 1976, the Ramsey County Community Corrections Department in Minnesota wanted to evaluate their foster group home program for juvenile offenders. In discussions with the identified and organized decisionmakers and information users, it became clear that there was no systematic data about what Ramsey County foster group homes were actually like. The theory undergirding the program was that juvenile offenders would be more likely to be rehabilitated if they were placed in warm, supportive, and nonauthoritarian environments where they were valued by others and could therefore learn to value themselves. The goals of the program were to make juveniles happy and capable of exercising independent judgment, and to reduce recidivism.

The evaluation question was framed in the context of both program goals and program implementation. A major priority of the evaluation effort was to describe and analyze the Ramsey County Group Home "treatment environment." This priority derived from the fact that at the beginning of the study there was no systematic knowledge about what the homes were actually like. What happens in a group home? What does a juvenile experience? What kind of "treatment" is a youth exposed to in a group home? What are the variations in group homes? Are there certain types that seem to be more successful in terms of the outcomes of (1) providing positive experiences for youth and (2) reducing recidivism?

The data analysis showed that group homes in Ramsey County could be placed along a continuum where one end represented homes that were highly supportive and participatory and the other represented homes that were nonsupportive and authoritarian. Homes were about evenly distributed along the continua of support versus nonsupport and participatory versus authoritarian patterns, i.e., about half the juveniles experienced homes that tended to be more supportive-participatory and about half tended to be more nonsupportive-authoritarian. Juveniles from supportive-participatory group homes showed significantly lower recidivism rates than juveniles from nonsupportive-authoritarian ones ($r = .33$, p   .01). Variations in type of group home environment were also found to be significantly related to other outcome variables (Patton et al., 1977b).

In terms of treatment specification, these data demonstrated two things: (1) in about half of the county's 55 group homes, juveniles were not experiencing the kind of treatment that the program design called for; and (2) outcomes varied directly with nature and degree of program implementation. Clearly it would make no sense to conceptualize these 55 group homes as a homogenous treatment. We found homes that were run like prisons, homes where juveniles were physically abused. We also found homes where young offenders were loved and treated as though they were members of the family. Aggregation of recidivism data from all of these homes into a single average rate would produce null findings in most comparisons with other aggregated programs. But when the treatment is specified and degrees of implementation are measured, it is possible to evaluate quite reasonably the program theory both in terms of feasibility and effectiveness.

Evaluating Treatment Environments:
A Social Ecological Approach

Thus far, most evaluation research has been purely outcomes-oriented, with little or no treatment specification. An important exception is Rudolf Moos, who has drawn upon a large body of social science research on business organizations, prisons, families, schools, hospitals, factories, and a broad range of bureaucratic settings, gradually conceptualizing certain key dimensions of the environment in organizations, families, and treatment programs. The work of Moos is a model for treatment specifications; the group home evaluation just discussed drew heavily on it. Moos (1975: 4) explains his approach as follows:

> The social climate perspective assumes that environments have unique "personalities," just like people. Personality tests assess personality traits or needs and provide information about the characteristic ways in which people behave. Social environments can be similarly portrayed with a great deal of accuracy and detail. Some people are more supportive than others. Likewise, some social environments are more supportive than others. Some people feel a strong need to control others. Similarly, some social environments are extremely rigid, autocratic, and controlling. Order, clarity, and structure are important to many people. Correspondingly, many social environments strongly emphasize order, clarity and control.

Different social scientists use different terms to describe these dimensions of the environment, but there are many similarities in what they are describing (e.g., Hage and Aiken, 1970; Burns and Stalker, 1961; Anderson and Walberg, 1968). Below are some of the terms that are used to specify and distinguish different treatment environments:

Formal	Informal
Centralized	Decentralized
Authoritarian	Participatory (Democratic)
Divisive	Cohesive
Standardized	Individualized
Hierarchical	Egalitarian

Controlled	Expressive
Partitioned	Integrated
Independent Parts	Interdependent Parts
Routinized	Individualized
Isolated	Community-Oriented
Low Communications	High Communications
Interactions	Interactions

It is important to understand that *these terms are meant to be descriptive* rather than pejorative, prejudicial, or prescriptive. These terms or dimensions are ways of thinking about the differences among organizations, families, and treatment programs. Under certain conditions one type of organization or program environment may be desirable, while under other circumstances a different type may be desirable.

Rudolf Moos (1974, 1975) has done the most comprehensive work in conceptualizing and operationalizing the treatment environment for purposes of program evaluation. Moos calls his work "a social ecological approach" to evaluation research. He has developed concepts and scales to describe and measure variations in treatment environments for mental health institutions, correctional institutions, family environments, military units, and classrooms. He is working toward a taxonomy of social environments and has already developed nine "social climate scales" in his work at the Social Ecology Laboratory and Psychiatry Research Training Program at Stanford University.

Moos has related his treatment environment variables to a variety of program outcome variables in criminal justice, education, and health settings, with statistically significant and meaningful results. His work takes on added significance because deinstitutionalization is currently the dominant theoretical direction in social intervention. He has developed a set of variables in a well-constructed theoretical framework to evaluate the implementation and effects of deinstitutionalization.

Moos' work constitutes an exemplary model of the contribution evaluation research can make to social science theory. However, from a utilization-focused perspective any theoretical model, including the sophisticated and comprehensive social ecological approach, must be adapted to the specific evaluation needs of identified decisionmakers and information users. Moos' variables ought not be adopted wholesale; careful consideration must be given to their relevance in representing the nascent theoretical notions of relevant decisionmakers and information users. In the Ramsey County foster group home evaluation described in the previous section, we did just that. Once evaluation task force members identified the relevant treatment dimensions as "warmth, support, involvement, and participatory family decisionmaking," we showed them some of Moos' factors to see if they were representative and descriptive of the program's intervention theory. With additions, deletions, and adaptations, the Moos conceptual and operational scheme proved very helpful. *But the theoretical formulation process began with identified evaluation task force decisionmakers—not with a scholarly search of the literature.* The theory tested was the theory held by relevant decisionmakers and information users.

Evaluators may want to test their own particular theories based on what their disciplinary literature specifies as important independent variables. Where resources are adequate and the design can be managed, the evaluators may prevail upon decisionmakers to include tests of those theories the evaluators hold dear. But first priority goes to providing identified decisionmakers with information about the degree to which their own implementation ideals and treatment specifications have actually been realized in program operations. Causal models are often forced on program staff when they bear no similarity to the models on which that staff bases its program activities. The evaluators' research interests are secondary to the information needs of identified decisionmakers and information users in utilization-focused evaluation.

Implementation Overview: Framing the Evaluation Question In the Context of Program Implementation

There is considerable evidence that failure at the implementation stage is a major reason for the human services shortfall and ineffective social programs. Evaluations that have ignored implementation issues (and such evaluations are abundant) may have asked the wrong questions. Thus, to avoid gathering useless or erroneous information *it is important to understand the option of framing evaluation questions in the context of program implementation.* This can be a major element in utilization-focused evaluation, particularly in comprehensive evaluations that also include framing the evaluation question in the context of program goals.

Evaluatiion research has been dominated by outcomes evaluation. Evaluating outcomes without knowledge of implementation is the "black box" approach to evaluation. Unlocking the black box means studying program implementation. The difference between the ideal, rational model of program implementation and the day-to-day, incrementalist, and conflict-laden realities of program implementation has enormous implications for a utilization-focused approach to evaluation. Successful implementation is characterized as a process of adaptation of the ideal to local conditions, organizational dynamics, and programmatic uncertainties. Active-reactive-adaptive evaluators will work with identified decisionmakers and information users to determine how far from and in what ways the program can deviate from the ideal plan while still meeting fundamental implementation criteria.

Once the evaluator has determined that the program in question actually exists (the first implementation issue in an evaluation), there are three evaluation options with respect to studying implementation: (1) effort evaluation, (2) process evaluation, and (3) the treatment specification approach. Effort evaluations focus on documenting the quantity and quality of program activity; if the program is relatively inactive, it is unlikely to be very effective. Process evaluation focuses on the internal dynamics of a program in an attempt to understand its strengths and weaknesses; this approach takes its name from looking at how a product or outcome is produced, i.e., it is an analysis of the processes whereby a program produces the results it does. The treatment specification approach involves identifying and measuring precisely what it is about a program that is supposed to have an effect; in technical terms, this means identifying independent variables that are expected to affect outcomes (the dependent variables).

Depending on the nature of the issues involved and the information needed, any one, two, or all three of the approaches to implementation evaluation might be employed. The point is that without information about actual program operations, decisionmakers are extremely limited in their ability to interpret performance data or to improve program functioning. *Effort evaluations, the treatment specification approach, and process evaluations answer different questions and focus on different aspects of program implementation. The key is to match the type(s) of evaluation to the information needs of relevant decisionmakers and information users.* One of the decisionmakers we interviewed in our utilization study was emphatic on this point:

> Different types of evaluations are appropriate and useful at different times. . . . HEW tends to talk about evaluation as if it's a single thing. Whereas the important thing is a better understanding within HEW that there are different types of evaluation. That it should not be used as EVALUATION! Using the word generically, as a generic word, is harmful. . . . We ought to stop using evaluation as if it's a single homogenous thing (DM111: 29).

Implementation evaluation is one of the options from which decision-makers and information users can choose as the evaluator works with them to frame the evaluation question. Not all final evaluation designs will include implementation data. Variations in implementation may already be known to decisionmakers, or information other than implementation may be more important, relevant, and useful to them given the uncertainties they face. Thus, whether implementation evaluation is part of the final design depends on the particular evaluation question that emerges as the focus of study. *What is crucial is that during the process of framing the evaluation question the issue of implementation analysis is raised.* Evaluators have a responsibility in their active-reactive-adaptive interactions with decisionmakers and information users to explore evaluation options. Decisionmakers and evaluators both need to know what can be learned through implementation analysis, effort studies, process evaluations, and treatment specification so that they can decide what information is most useful in the particular circumstances at hand.

NOTE

1. I am indebted to two colleagues for their critiques of this evaluation: Malcolm Bush, Urban Affairs and Education, Northwestern University; and Thomas Dewar, School of Public Affairs, University of Minnesota.

Chapter 9

THE PROGRAM'S THEORY OF ACTION:

EVALUATING CAUSAL LINKAGES

A Setting

The difficulty of making causal inferences has been thoroughly documented by philosophers of science (e.g., Bunge, 1957; Nagel, 1961). When reading on the subject as a graduate student, I marveled at the multitude of mathematical and logical proofs necessary to demonstrate that the world is a complex place. I offer instead a simple Sufi story to establish a framework for this chapter's discussion of the relationship between means and ends.

The incomparable Mulla Nasrudin was visited by a would-be disciple. The man, after many vicissitudes, arrived at the hut on the mountain where the Mulla was sitting. Knowing that every single action of the illuminated Sufi was meaningful, the newcomer asked Nasrudin why he was blowing on his hands. "To warm myself in the cold, of course," Nasrudin replied.

Shortly afterward, Nasrudin poured out two bowls of soup, and blew on his own. "Why are you doing that, Master?" asked the disciple. "To cool it, of course," said the teacher.

At that point the disciple left Nasrudin, unable to trust any longer a man who used the same process to cause different effects—heat and cold (adapted from Shah, 1964: 79-80).

Reflections on Causality in Evaluation Research

In some cases, different programs use divergent processes to arrive at the same outcome; in others, various programs use similar means to achieve different outcomes. Sometimes competing treatments aimed at the same goal operate side by side in a single program. The task of sorting out causal linkages is seldom an easy one.

Stated quite simply, the causal question in evaluation research is: does the implemented program lead to the desired outcomes? However, in previous chapters it has become clear that delineating either program implementation or program outcomes is a complex task, and establishing the linkages between implementation and outcomes is even more difficult. Do the processes, activities, and treatments of the program cause or effect the behaviors, attitudes, skills, knowledge, and feelings of the target population? One need know very little about research to know that it is impossible to establish causality in any final sense when dealing with the complexities of real programs where treatments and outcomes are never pure, single, and uncontaminated.

It is easy to become frustrated with the difficulty of establishing the relationship between program activities and program outcomes because we cannot answer such questions definitively. But that is no reason not to ask the questions. We cannot provide definitive answers but we can arrive at some reasonable estimation of the likelihood that particular activities have had an effect:

> One admits that causal thinking belongs completely on the theoretical level and that causal laws can never be demonstrated empirically. But this does not mean that it is not helpful to *think* causally and to develop causal models that have implications that are indirectly testable (Blalock, 1964: 6; italics in original).

This is important because it tells us what we can expect from evaluation research. Evaluation data are never clearcut and absolute: studies are always flawed in some way, and there are always questions of reliability and validity. Error-free instruments do not and cannot exist in the measurement of complex human, social, behavioral, and psychological phenomena. Then of what good is all this?

Evaluation research is only of use if one believes that some systematic information is better than none. Evaluation research has meaning only if one believes that a rough idea of the relationship between program activities and outcomes is preferable to relying entirely upon hope and good intentions. Evaluation research does not provide final answers, but *it can provide direction.* Thus, evaluation research does not lead to final statements about causal linkages, but can reduce uncertainty about such linkages. Therein lies its potential for utilization.

To venture into the arena of causality is to undertake the task of theory construction. As Blalock (1964: 5) explained:

> The problem of causality is part of the much larger question of the nature of the scientific method and, in particular, the problem of the relationship between theory and research. *There appears to be an inherent gap between the languages of theory and research* which can never be bridged in a completely satisfactory way. One *thinks* in terms of a theoretical language that contains notions such as causes, forces, systems, and properties. But one's *tests* are made in terms of covariations, operations, and pointer readings (italics in original).

This chapter suggests some simple conceptual approaches to theory construction in evaluation research. The next chapter considers operational, measurement, and design questions.

Deductive and Inductive Approaches to Theory Construction

Evaluation research often ignores theoretical issues altogether. Evaluators are accused of being technicians who simply collect data without regard to the theoretical relevance of possible empirical generalizations. Certainly pure outcomes evaluations are nontheoretical. Moreover, in many cases what decisionmakers need and want is quite specific data relevant to narrow, technical issues that are helpful in monitoring or fine-tuning program operations.

However, evaluation research is by no means inherently nontheoretical. It can be theoretical in the usual scientific sense of deductive, logical systems constructed to model causal linkages among general variables (cf. Hage, 1972). Specific program operations are then modeled after the theory and monitored to test it. The deductive approach usually draws on dominant theoretical traditions in specific scholarly disciplines to construct models of the relationship between program treatments and outcomes. In practice, the formality, complexity, and abstraction of most academic theories have little relevance for practitioners caught up in the day-to-day realities of program functioning.

By way of contrast to logical, deductive theory construction, a utilization-focused approach to theory construction is inductive, pragmatic, and highly concrete. *The evaluator's task is to delineate and test the theory or theories held by identified decisionmakers and information users. The causal model to be tested is the causal model upon which program activities are based.* First priority goes to providing identified decisionmakers with information about the degree to which their own implementation ideals and treatment specifications actually achieve the desired outcomes through program operations. The evaluator's own theories and academic traditions can be helpful in clarifying the program's theory of action, but reality-testing the decisionmakers' theory of programmatic action is primary; the evaluator's scholarly interests are secondary.

The inductive approach to evaluation theory construction presented here is simple and straightforward. It is neither elegant nor esoteric. Its purposes are twofold: (1) to fill in the conceptual gaps in formulation of program action and aims so as (2) to identify initial information gaps that can be used to focus evaluation questions.

Delineating the Program's Theory of Action: The Means-Ends Hierarchical Chain of Objectives

Outcomes evaluations generally focus on goal attainment, while implementation evaluations focus on the means of attaining goals. The final element in the conceptualization of the evaluation question is the linking together of means and ends. The construction of a means-ends hierarchy for a program constitutes a comprehensive description of the program's theory of action. The notion of a programmatic theory of action is derived from James Thompson's (1967: 2) conceptualizations of organizational action as "rooted on the one hand in *desired outcomes* and on the other hand in beliefs about *cause/effect relationships*" (italics in original). Understanding and delineating the program's theory of action can be an extremely important conceptual technique for assisting decisionmakers in focusing evaluation questions.

Suchman recommended beginning the construction of a "chain of objectives" by trichotomizing objectives into immediate, itermediate, and ultimate goals. The linkages between these levels actually comprise a continuous series of actions wherein immediate objectives logically precede intermediate goals and therefore must be accomplished before higher level objectives. Taken together, the program's goals constitute a chain. Any given objective in the chain is the outcome of the successful attainment of the preceding objective and, in turn, is a precondition to attainment of the next higher objective.

> Immediate goals refer to the results of the specific act with which one is momentarily concerned, such as the formation of an obesity club; the intermediate goals push ahead toward the accomplishment of the specific act, such as the actual reduction in weight of club members; the ultimate

goal then examines the effect of achieving the intermediate goal upon the health status of the members, such as reduction in the incidence of heart disease (Suchmann, 1967: 51-52).

In practice, the chain of objectives for a program has more than three links. In Chapter 7, the Minnesota Comprehensive Epilepsy Program mission statement, goals, and objectives were described. This three-tier division was useful to get an overview of the program as an initial step in focusing on that aspect where evaluation information would be most useful. Once that initial focus is selected, a more detailed, multitier chain of objectives can be constructed. For example, the epilepsy program had educational, research, treatment, and administrative goals. Once the research goal was selected by decisionmakers as most in need of evaluation, a more thorough chain of objectives was constructed. Figure 9-1 illustrates the difference between the initial three-tier conceptualization and the more refined multitier chain of objectives. To have constructed such a detailed, multitier chain of objectives for all seven epilepsy goals would have taken a great deal of time and effort. By using the simple, three-tier approach initially, it was possible to then focus on those goal areas where a full chain of objectives or hierarchy of means and ends were to be developed.

The full chain of objectives constitutes a program's theory of action. Any particular paired linkage in the theory of action, however, represents an outcome and its means of implementation. As one constructs a hierarchical chain of objectives, it becomes clear that there is only a relative distinction between ends and means: "any end or goal can be seen as a means to another goal, [and] one is free to enter the 'hierarchy of means and ends' at any point" (Perrow, 1968: 307). *In a utilization-focused approach to evaluation research, the decision about where to enter the means-ends hierarchy is made on the basis of what information would be most useful to identified decisionmakers and information users.*

Identifying Critical Validity Assumptions

The purpose of thoroughly delineating a program's theory of action is to assist decisionmakers in making explicit their assumptions about all of the linkages and activities necessary for the accomplishment of ultimate outcomes; they can focus the evaluation on those critical linkages where information is most needed at that particular point in the life of the program. This is what Suchman (1967) called making explicit the program's "validity assumptions," i.e. beliefs about cause-effect rela-

Table 9.1: Initial and Refined Epilepsy Program Theory of Action

Initial Conceptualization of Epilespy Program

Program Mission: To improve the lives of people with epilepsy through research.

Program Goal: To publish high quality, scholarly research on epilepsy.

Program Objective: To conduct research on neurological, pharmachological, epidemiological and social psychological aspects of epilepsy.

Refined Conceptualization of Epilepsy Chain of Objectives

1. Reduce epilepsy incidence and prevalence.
2. Provide better medical treatment for people with epilepsy.
3. Increase physicians' knowledge of better medical treatment for epileptics.
4. Disseminate findings to medical practitioners.
5. Publish findings in scholarly journals.
6. Produce high quality research findings on epilepsy.
7. Establish a program of high quality research on epilepsy.
8. Assemble necessary resources (personnel, finances, facilities) to establish a research program.
9. Identify and generate research designs to close knowledge gaps.
10. Identify major gaps in knowledge concerning causes of and treatment of epilepsy.

tionships. The epilepsy decisionmakers assume that publications in scholarly journals get new knowledge to medical practitioners. Validity assumptioins are, however, subject to empirical tests. Does the assumed cause-effect relationship hold? For example, many intervention or social change programs are built on the validity assumptions that new information leads to attitude change and that attitude change affects behavior. These assumptions are testable. Does new knowledge change attitudes? Do changed attitudes lead to changed behavior?

It is not possible to test all the validity assumptions or evaluate all the means-ends linkages in a program's theory of action.

> It is impossible to secure proof of the effectiveness of everything one wishes to do. Nor is it desirable. Operating personnel must proceed on the basis of the best available knowledge at the time. The question is one of how freely such validity assumptions are made and how much is at stake (Suchman, 1967: 43).

In a utilization-focused approach to evaluation research the evaluator works with the decisionmakers and information users to identify the

*critical validity assumptions where reduction of uncertainty about causal
linkages could make the most difference.*

Delineating a full set of validity assumptions in constructing a program's
theory of action can reveal both major information gaps and major conceptual gaps in program planning. Leonard Rutman (1977) has argued
that unless the program plan makes conceptual sense and there is substantial reason to believe in its validity assumptions, there is no reason
to waste resources on an evaluation; in brief, he considered a reasonably
defensible theory of action, or set of validity assumptions, to be one of
the criteria for establishing the "evaluability" of a program. Unless a
program meets minimal evaluability criteria, it cannot usefully be evaluated (Rutman, 1976).

The problem with relying on the evaluator's assessment of the reason-
ableness of programmatic validity assumptions is that what the evaluator
believes is less important than what program staff and decisionmakers
believe. The usefulness of the evaluation process is in helping program
staff and decisionmakers delineate and test their validity assumptions.
If identified decisionmakers and information users hold a set of validity
assumptions to be true, evaluation can be a mechanism for reality-testing
those assumptions. An evaluator can have greater impact by helping
program staff and decisionmakers empirically test their causal hypotheses
than by telling them such causal hypotheses are nonsense. The wheel
not only has to be recreated from time to time; its efficacy has to be re-
studied and reevaluated to demonstrate its usefulness. Likewise, the
evaluator's *certain belief* that square wheels are less efficacious than
round ones may have little impact on those who believe square wheels
are effective. The evaluator's task is to delineate the belief in the square
wheel and then assist the believers in constructing an evaluation that
will permit them to test for themselves their own causal hypotheses.
This does not mean that the evaluator ought not suggest that alternative
hypotheses be considered as well, but first priority goes to evaluation
of validity assumptions in the theory of action held by identified decisionmakers and information users.

Filling in the Conceptual Gaps

Helping decisionmakers identify conceptual gaps in a theory of action
is quite different from telling them that their validity assumptions are
unreasonable. Thus, in a utilization-focused approach to evaluation
research, the evaluator's task is not to pass judgment on the viability
of program validity assumptions, but rather to help identify and fill gaps

in the theory of action. The means-ends relationships delineated ought to be reasonable in the sense that there are no conceptual leaps of such magnitude that critical intervening actions are ignored.

The difference between passing judgment on the viability or validity of a theory of action and filling in the gaps may be illustrated as follows. Rutman (1977) has argued that programs to use prison guards as counselors to inmates ought never have been evaluated (e.g., Ward et al., 1971) because, on the face of it, the idea is nonsense. Why would anyone ever believe that such a program could work? But clearly, whether they should have or not, many people did believe that the program would work. The evaluator's task is to fill in the conceptual gaps in this theory of action so that critical evaluative information needs can be identified. For example, are there initial selection processes and training programs for guards? Are guards supposed to be changed during such training? The first critical evaluation issue may be whether prison guards can be trained to exhibit desired counselor attitudes and behaviors. The trainability of prison guards in human relations skills can be evaluated without even implementing the full contact program.

Filling in the gaps in the program's theory of action goes to the heart of the implementation question. What series of activities must take place before there is reason to even hope that impact could be demonstrated? If intervening activities and objectives will not be or cannot be implemented, then evaluation of ultimate outcomes is not very useful.

> There are only two ways one can move up the scale of objectives in an evaluation: (a) by proving the intervening assumptions through research, that is, changing an assumption to a fact, or (b) by assuming their validity without full research proof. When the former is possible, we can then interpret our success in meeting a lower-level objective as automatic progress toward a higher one. . . .
>
> When an assumption cannot be proved . . . we go forward at our peril. To a great extent the ultimate worth of evaluation for public service programs will depend upon research proof of the validity of assumptions involved in the establishment of key objectives (Suchman, 1967: 57).

The National Clean Air Act is a good example of legislation where policy and planning activity have focused only on initial objectives and ultimate goals, with little delineation of crucial intervening objectives. The ultimate goal is cleaner air; the target of the legislation is a handful of engines that each auto manufacturer tests before going to mass production. Authorization for mass production is given if these prototypes operate under carefully controlled conditions for 50,000 miles. Cars that fail pollution tests as they leave the assembly line are not withheld from dealers. Cars on the road are not inspected to make sure that pollution control equipment is still in place and functioning properly. Prototypes are tested for 50,000 miles, but most cars are eventually used for 100,000 miles, with pollution in older cars being much worse than that in new ones. In short, there are many intervening steps between testing prototype automobiles for pollution control compliance and increasing air quality. As Bruce Ackerman (1977: 4) explains:

> Over a period of time the manufacturers will build cleaner and cleaner prototypes. Billions of dollars will be spent on the assembly line to build devices that *look* like these prototypes. But until Congress, the EPA and the states require regular inspections of all cars on the road, very little will come of all this glittering machinery.
>
> Indeed, we could save billions if we contented ourselves with dirtier prototypes, but insisted on cleaner cars. . . . Congressmen themselves woefully exaggerate the importance of their votes for cleaner prototypes. They simply have no idea of the distance between prototype and reality. They somehow imagine that the hard job is technological innovation and that the easy job is human implementation.

Delineating the full theory of action identifies both major conceptual gaps and major information gaps. The conceptual gaps are filled by logic, discussion, and policy analysis. The information gaps are filled by evaluation research.

Filling in the Information Gaps: The New School Case

Once the conceptual gaps in the theory of action are delineated, the issue of evaluation focus remains. Determining the evaluation question is not simply a process of mechanically beginning by evaluating lower order validity assumptions and then moving up the hierarchy. Not all linkages in the hierarchy are amenable to testing; different validity assumptions require different resources for evaluation; data gathering strategies vary for different objectives. All of these considerations are important, but most important is determining what information would be most useful at a particular point in time. This means selecting what Murphy (1976: 98) calls "targets of opportunity" where additional information could make a difference to the direction of incremental, problem-oriented program decisionmaking:

> In selecting problems for analysis, targets of opportunity need to be identified, with political considerations specifically built into final choices. Plan-

ning activity in a certain area might be opportune because of expiring legislation, a hot political issue, a breakdown in standard operation procedures,
or new research findings. At any time, certain policies are more susceptible
to change than others.

Targets of opportunity are simply those evaluation questions about
which identified decisionmakers and information users care. Having
information about and answers to those selected questions can make
a difference in what is done in the program. Those validity assumptions
in a theory of action about which there is already a high degree of certainty
are not good targets of opportunity; those program activities to which
decisionmakers are fully committed for political, moral, or other value
reasons are likely to be poor targets of opportunity; but those validity
assumptions about which there is uncertainty and for which reduction
in that uncertainty is a matter of concern to decisionmakers make excellent
targets of opportunity. An example from an evaluation of the New School
of Behavioral Studies in Education, University of North Dakota, illustrates this.

The New School of Behavioral Studies in Education was established
as a result of a statewide study of education conducted between 1965
and 1967. The New School was to provide leadership in educational
innovations with an emphasis on individualized instruction, better teacher-
pupil relationships, an interdisciplinary approach, and better use of
a wide range of learning resources (Statewide Study, 1967: 11-15). In
1970, the New School gained national recognition when Charles Silberman
described the North Dakota Experiment as a program that was resolving
the "crisis in the classroom" in favor of open education.

The New School provided undergraduate training for juniors and
seniors, began a small doctoral program, and established a Master's
degree teaching intern program. Operations began in the summer of
1968, with the Master's intern program. After a summer of instruction
at the New School, these fully certified interns replaced teachers without
degrees so that the latter could return to the university to complete their
baccalaureates at the New School. The cooperating school districts released those teachers without degrees who volunteered to return to college
and accepted the Master's degree interns in their place. During the four
years the New School operated as a relatively autonomous experimental
college, it placed 293 interns in 48 school districts and 75 elementary
schools, both public and parochial. The school districts that cooperated
with the New School in the intern program contained nearly one third
of the state's elementary school children.

A task force of teachers, professors, students, parents, and administrators was formed by the Dean of the New School to evaluate its programs. In working with that task force, I constructed the theory of action shown in Table 9-2. The objectives stated in the first column are a far cry from being clear, specific, and measurable, but they were quite adequate for discussions aimed at focusing the evaluation question. The second column lists validity assumptions underlying each linkage in the theory of action. The third column shows that there are measures that can be used to evaluate objectives at any level in the hierarchy. Ultimate objectives are not inherently more difficult to operationalize. Operationalization and measurement are separate issues to be determined after the focus of the evaluation has been decided.

When the New School Evaluation Task Force discussed Table 9-2, they decided they had already had sufficient contact with the summer program to assess the degree to which its immediate objectives were being met. They also felt that they had sufficient experience with the program to be comfortable with the validity assumption linking objectives six and seven. With regard to the ultimate objectives, the task force members said that they needed no further data at that time in order to document the outcomes of open education (objectives one and two), nor could they do much with information about the growth of the open education movement (objective three). However, a number of critical uncertainties surfaced at the level of intermediate objectives. Once students left the summer program for the one year internships, program staff were unable to carefully and regularly monitor intern classrooms. It was not certain what variations existed in the openness of the classrooms, nor was it at all certain how local parents and administrators were reacting to intern classrooms. These were issues about which information was wanted and needed. Indeed, for a variety of personal, political, and scholarly reasons, these issues made quite good evaluation targets of opportunity. The evaluation therefore focused on three questions: (1) to what extent are summer trainees conducting open classrooms during the regular year? (2) what factors are related to variations in openness? (3) what is the relationship between variations in classroom openness and parent and administrator reactions to intern classrooms?

At the onset, nothing precluded evaluation at any of the seven levels in the hierarchy of objectives. There was serious discussion of all levels and alternative foci. In terms of the educational literature, the issue of the outcomes of open education could be considered most important; in terms of university operations, the summer program would have been the appropriate focus; but in terms of the information needs of the identi-

TABLE 9.2: The New School Theory of Action: A Hierarchy of Goals, Validity Assumption Linkages, and Evaluative Criteria

Hierarchy of Objectives	Validity Assumption Linkages	Evaluative Criteria
I. Ultimate Objectives 1. Prepare children to live full, rich, satisfying lives as adults.		1. Longitudinal measures of child and adult satisfaction, happiness and success.
	Children whose affective and cognitive needs are met will lead fuller, richer, more satisfying lives as adults.	
2. Meet the affective and cognitive needs of individual children in North Dakota and the United States.		2. Measures of student affective and cognitive growth in open and traditional schools.
	More open classrooms will better meet the affective and cognitive needs of individual children.	
3. Facilitate and legitimize the establishment and maintenance of a larger number of more open classrooms in North Dakota and the United States.		3. Measures of increases in the number of open classrooms in North Dakota and the United States over time and measures of the influence of the New School on the number of open classrooms.
	Parents and administrators will favor and expand open education once they have experienced it firsthand.	
II. Intermediate Objectives 4. Provide parents and administrators in North Dakota with a firsthand demonstration of the advantages of open education.		4. Measures of parent and administrator attitudes towards New School classrooms and open education, and measures and analysis of the factors affecting their attitudes.
	Teachers who have experienced the New School summer program can and will conduct open classrooms during the following intern year that are visible to local parents and administrators.	
5. Provide teachers and teachers-in-training with a one year classroom experience in conducting an open classroom.		5. Measures of the degree of openness of New School teaching intern classrooms and the factors affecting the degree of openness of these classrooms.
	Teachers who have experienced the summer program can and will conduct open classrooms.	
III. Immediate Objectives 6. Provide teachers and teachers-in-training with a summer program in how to conduct an open classroom.		6. Measures of teacher attitudes, teacher understanding, and teacher competency before and after the New School Program.
	In order to learn about open education it is best to experience it. Teachers teach the they are taught.	
7. Provide teachers and teachers-in-training with a personalized and individualized learning experience in an open learning environment.		7. Measures of the degree to which the New School training program is individualized and personalized, and measures of the cognitive and affective growth of teachers in the New School Program.

fied and organized decisionmakers and information users on the task force, evaluation of the immediate objectives had the highest potential for generating information useful in reducing program uncertainty. Indeed, in order to obtain the resources necessary to conduct this evaluation, Vito Perrone, Dean of the New School, had to make unusual demands on the U.S. Office of Education. The outcomes of the New School teaching program were supposed to be evaluated as part of a national Office of Education (OE) study. Perrone argued that the national study, as designed, would be useless to the New School. He talked the OE people into allowing him to spend the New School's portion of the national evaluation money on a study designed and conducted locally. The subsequent evaluation was entirely the creation of the local task force described above, and produced instruments and data that have become an integral part of the North Dakota program (cf. Pederson, 1977). The national study produced large volumes of numbers (with blanks entered on the lines for North Dakota), and as far as I can tell, was of no particular use to anyone.

Temporal Sequences and Evaluation Questions: The Timing of Evaluation

The theory of action is at least partially temporal in conceptualization because it progresses from immediate objectives to ultimate goals. Part of the test of a theory of action is the temporal logic of the hierarchy. In causal language, it is impossible for an effect or outcome to precede its cause. It is important, however, that temporal sequence not be exaggerated. Once a program is in operation, the relationships between links in the causal hierarchy are likely to be recursive rather than unidirectional. The implementation and attainment of higher level objectives interact with the implementation and attainment of lower order objectives through feedback mechanisms, interactive configurations, and cybernetic systems. Program components may be conceptually distinct in the formal version of a theory of action, but in practice these analytically distinct components, links, and stages are highly interdependent and dynamically interrelated. In short, the cause-effect relationships are mutual, multi-directional, and multilateral. Open classrooms affect the opinions and actions of parents, but parent reactions also affect the degree of openness of classrooms; classroom climate and school curriculum affect student achievement, but variations in student achievement also affect school climate and curriculum. Once again, the means-ends distinction proves to be somewhat arbitrary and simplified, but there is no avoiding such simplification: "put simply, the basic dilemma faced in all sciences is that of how much to oversimplify reality" (Blalock, 1964: 8). The challenge is to construct simplifications that pass the dual tests of usefulness and accuracy.

Identifying the temporal sequence represented by a theory of action does not mean that evaluation automatically or necessarily begins by focusing on lower order objectives and relationships. The focus of the evaluation may, however, depend to some extent on the point in the developmental life of the program at which the evaluation takes place. In our study of the utilization of federal health evaluations, we asked evaluators and decisionmakers about this issue. For the 20 federal health evaluations in our study, eight were done early in the life of new programs, eight were conducted on established programs that had been operating for a number of years, and two evaluations occurred as part of the program's swan song, i.e., the program was already in the process of being terminated; in the two remaining cases, the evaluator and decisionmaker gave different information about the timing of the study in question. None of our respondents thought that the timing of the evaluation as an isolated factor had much direct effect on utilization. Timing does, however, become important in the context of other factors, particularly as it affects the particular information that decisionmakers need and want.

Just as there are no clear criteria about how close actual program implementation should come to ideal program plans, so there are no fixed criteria about when in the life of a program it is appropriate for an evaluation to occur. In several of our case studies, there were conflicts between evaluators and decisionmakers over this issue. An example of the long-term perspective is as follows:

> Unfortunately we did not have enough background experience even at the time of this evaluation to really identify all the problems within the program, but it was very difficult to support these data-wise, statistically, and quantitatively. So it was hard to make a decision as to what questions and answers should and could come of an evaluation of this sort that would be helpful. What we felt—we being those of us closely associated with the program—what we felt all along was that this was too soon to try to evaluate the program. There just was not enough experience. Now would be a much better time, after the program has been in operation for 6 to 7 years (DM40: 9).

One short-term perspective on evaluation timing, on the other hand, went something like this:

> *Interviewer:* "Would you say that this point in the life of the program that the evaluation was done, did that have any effect on how the study was used?"
> *Evaluator:* "Yeah, I think so. I think it allowed the government to get off the hook before it had established massive and well-developed constituencies out there. I mean, that's a very important point. Typically when you go out to do an experimental or quasi-experimental design on a program that's been operating for a long time, you're dealing with programs that have built up a constituency. It's damn tough for the feds to cancel it. In this case I was out there from the very beginning and so we were able to kind of nip in the bud what could have been otherwise a bummer idea (EV148: 14)."

When the program's complete theory of action has been formulated and is taken into consideration, it becomes possible to consider the question of evaluation timing in the context of how far the program has progressed through its hierarchical chain of objectives. From this point of view *evaluation is an on-going process examining different questions at different times.* As one decisionmaker put it:

> I think the whole evaluation process is . . . a dynamic part of the planning and implementation of the program and as long as there is a program it has to continue. Like, you know, you don't do an early evaluation and say, "fine, this confirms what we're doing. We'll just keep on doing it"—and never take another look at it. Nor do you wait until you say, "well, we've reached the half life, or whatever radioactivity there is in the program, and now we'll do an evaluation" (DM119: 18).

Another decisionmaker expressed a firm belief in the importance of matching the focus of the evaluation to the stage of program development.

> Now it takes three to five years to build a new, you know, a new multimillion dollar anything, let alone a health delivery institution. . . .
>
> There are different evaluation objectives at different points in the development of a program. There are different levels of evaluation. . . . In the early years you do what I call operational and management analysis/ evaluation. You know, are they operating the way they said? They said they're gonna provide services to 10,000 people in two years. . . . Well, that can be monitored in the early years.
>
> Now if one then wants to hypothesize that there are other impacts, well, that takes much longer. If one wants to even hypothesize health impact, which I am not prepared to do, or antipoverty impact, then that is probably a much longer range kind of thing. It may even be a generational study! (DM51: 14).

This decisionmaker emphasized the point that different questions emerge at different points in the life of a program, just as different questions are relevant at different levels in a program's theory of action. Tripodi et al. (1971: 40) have formalized this idea in an evaluation they call

> *differential evaluation,* which means simply that an evaluation of a social program should be geared primarily to the present stage of program development. In this context, different evaluation questions are suggested for different program stages.

They outline different questions for studying program effort, program effectiveness, and program efficiency at three different program stages—initiation, contact, and implementation.

Edwards et al. (1975: 145) warn against such attempts to routinely match a type of evaluation to a stage of evaluation. They believe the *decision problems are the same at all stages:* "is this program a good idea? If so, what can we do to make it work as well as possible? If not, how can we devise something better, given our constraints?" They believe that the ideal evaluation technique would be aimed at assessing program merit on a continuous basis:

> In short, we cannot see any hard-and-fast lines to distinguish program evaluation at different stages in its life span. We therefore squirm about language or methods that imply such distinctions, or suggest that different techniques are appropriate for different states of program evaluation (Edwards, et al., 1975: 146).

This caution is useful in reminding us that *there are no automatic decisions in evaluation.* Knowing the stage of program development does not automatically define the appropriate evaluation question. Yet, it can be helpful to the active-reactive-adaptive evaluator to be aware that evaluation questions differ greatly at different points in the life of the program and at different levels in a program's theory of action. Different information is useful to different decisionmakers at different times. Sensitivity to theory of action linkages and decisionmakers perspectives increases the possibility of timing a particular type of evaluation to mesh with the decisionmakers' information needs and capabilities. *The right time to conduct a particular type of evalution is when it will provide relevant and useful information to identified and organized decisionmakers and information users.*

Comparing Theories of Action

There is much emphasis in evaluation research on comparing different programs to see which is more effective or efficient. Comparisons are basic to social scientific methods. Etzioni (1964: 17) suggests that comparative frameworks are fundamental to evaluation research so that "rather than comparing existing organizations to ideals of what might be, we may assess their performances relative to one another."

Evaluations can be designed to compare the effectiveness of programs with the same goal, but if those goals do not bear the same importance in the two programs' theories of action, the comparisons may be misleading. Before undertaking a comparative evaluation, it is useful to compare programmatic theories of action in order to understand the extent to which apparently identical or similarly labeled programs are in fact comparable.

Programs with different goals simply cannot be fairly compared to each other on a unidimensional basis. Teacher centers provide an example. The U.S. Office of Education has suggested that teacher centers should be evaluated according to a single set of universal outcomes. But Sharon Feiman (1977) has shown that teacher centers throughout the country vary substantially in both program activities and goals.

Feiman described three types of teacher centers: "behavioral," "humanistic," and "developmental." Table 9-3 summarizes the variations among these types of centers.

It would seem that, at least to some extent, different teacher centers are trying to accomplish different outcomes. The three models cannot be compared to determine which one is most effective because they are trying to do different things. Evaluation can help determine whether or not each of the outcomes have been attained for each specific program, but it cannot determine which outcome is most desirable—that is a values question (see Chapter 5). Because each theory of action is different, evaluation of each program type will be different.

On the other hand, Feiman has conceptually created only three models of operational teacher centers. Each is characterized by a specific process linked to a specific set of desired outcomes. But theoretically there are nine models, one model for each combination of process and outcome. In practice there are a nearly endless variety of mixes, with some teacher centers undoubtedly using all three processes. To make comparisons, general variables that cut across program types must be identified and operationalized. Careful treatment specification (Chapter 8) linked to relevant program outcomes can provide useful evaluation information that permits meaningful comparisons of different programs' theories of action. For example, several variables derived from the work of Hage (1965), Patton (1973), and Moos (1974), might be constructed to describe and compare teacher centers.

1. *Centralization-Decentralization:* the degree to which teachers share in center decisionmaking.

2. *Formality-Informality:* the degree to which the interaction between the teachers and the center staff is based on their respective status positions and standard role expectations.

TABLE 9.3: Variations in Types of Teacher Centers

Type of Center	Primary Process of Affecting Teachers	Primary Outcomes of the Process
1. Behavioral Centers	Curriculum specialists directly and formally instruct administrators and teachers.	Adoption of comprehensive curriculum systems, methods, and packages by teachers.
2. Humanistic Centers	Informal, nondirected teacher exploration; "teachers select their own treatment."	Teachers feel supported and important; pick up concrete and practical ideas and materials for immediate use in their classroom.
3. Developmental Centers	Advisors establish warm, interpersonal, and directive relationship with teachers working with them over time.	Teachers' thinking about what they do and why they do it is changed over time; teacher personal development.

3. *Individualization-Standardization:* the degree to which different teachers can do different things in different ways at different speeds with different criteria for success.

4. *Diversification-Homogeneity of Learning Resources:* the range of forms of learning stimuli and resources incorporated into the activities, curriculum, and experiences of the center.

5. *Peer Interaction:* the degree to which the activities, curriculum, physical arrangement, and organization of the classroom contribute to peer interaction as an experiential basis for teachers to learn from.

6. *Integration-Segmentation:* the degree to which the activities of the center are integrated into a relatively integrated whole.

These treatment specification variables can be linked to changes in teachers' feelings, attitudes, behaviors, and skills to test both program-specific and more general theories of action, depending upon the information needs of identified decisionmakers and information users. While such cross-sectional analyses of different programs cannot establish firm causal relationships, multivariate techniques can facilitate the creation of quite useful and valid causal inferences for theory testing (Blalock, 1964).

Causal Theorizing in Perspective

While causal linkages may never be established with certainty, the delineation of assumed causal relationships in a chain of hierarchical objectives can be a useful exercise in the process of focusing the evaluation question. While it may not be appropriate to construct a detailed theory of program action for every evaluation situation, it is important to understand and consider the option. Framing the evalution question in the context of the program's theory of action is another alternative available to active-reactive-adaptive evaluators in utilization-focused evaluation research. This approach includes the construction of a means-ends hierarchy, the specification of validity assumptions linking means and ends, consideration of comparative criteria across different programs, and attention to the temporal sequence in the hierarchy of objectives so as to time a particular type of evaluation with the decisionmakers' information needs at a particular point in the life of a program.

Attention to theoretical issues can provide useful information to decisionmakers when their theories are formulated and reality-tested through the evaluation research process. Theory construction is also a mechanism by which evaluators can link particular program evaluation questions to larger social scientific issues for the purpose of contributing to scientific knowledge through empirical generalizations. But in a utilization-focused approach to evaluation research, the initial theoretical formulations originate with identified decisionmakers and information users; scholarly interests are adapted to the evaluation needs of relevant decisionmakers, not vice versa.

It is important, then, to ask causal questions, even though evaluation data can only provide an approximate picture of what is really happening. It is also important to interpret the results with prudence and care. Consider the wisdom of Buddhism:

> One day an old man approached Zen master Hyakujo. The old man said, "I am not a human being. In ancient times I lived on this mountain. A student of the Way asked me if the enlightened were still affected by causality. I replied saying that they were not affected. Because of that I was degraded to lead the life of a wild fox for five hundred years. I now request you to answer one thing for me. Are the enlightened still affected by causality?"
>
> Master Hyakujo replied, "They are not deluded by causality."
>
> At that the old man was enlightened (adapted from Hoffman, 1975: 138).

Causal evaluation questions can be enlightening; they can also lead to delusions. Unfortunately, there is no clear way of telling the difference. It is nevertheless important to consider causal questions, especially when others are not doing so. But never force the issue—you might be degraded to lead the life of a wild fox for five hundred years!

Chapter 10

THE METHODOLOGY DRAGON:

ALTERNATIVE PARADIGMS OF EVALUATION

MEASUREMENT AND DESIGN

A Setting

A children's story tells of a boy named Han who was the poor gatesweeper of an ancient Chinese city. One day a messenger brought word that the wild horsemen of the north were coming to destroy the city. The Mandarin called together his councilors: the leader of the merchants, the captain of the army, the wisest of the wise men, and the chief of the workmen. The council decided that the only hope of saving the city was to pray to the Great Cloud Dragon for help. The next morning a small fat man arrived at the gate where the boy Han was sweeping. The old man had a long white beard, a shiny bald head, and he leaned on a long staff. He told Han that he was the Great Cloud Dragon come to save the city.

Han was quite surprised. "You don't look like a dragon," he said.

"How do you know?" asked the little old man. "Have you ever seen one?"

"No, I guess not. I will take you to the Mandarin, Honorable Dragon."

The Mandarin was busy meeting with his councilors. He was not happy about being disturbed. When Han humbly introduced the little old man as the Great Cloud Dragon, the Mandarin became very angry. "Don't be ridiculous. He's a fat man who is tracking dirt on my fine carpets. Away with him."

"I have come to help you," said the little fat man. "But if you want a dragon to help you, you must treat him with courtesy. I have come a long way. Give me something to eat and something to drink and speak to me politely, and I will save the city."

The Mandarin was unimpressed. "Everybody knows what dragons look like. They are proud lords of th sky. They wear gold and purple silk. They look like Mandarins."

"This is no dragon," said the captain of the army. "Everyone knows that dragons are fierce and brave, like warriors. The sight of them is like the sound of trumpets. They look like captains of the army."

"Nonsense!" interrupted the leader of the merchants. "Dragons are rich and splendid. They are as comfortable as a pocketful of money. They look like merchants. Everyone knows that."

"You are all wrong," said the chief of the workmen. "Everyone knows that dragons are strong and tough. Nothing is too hard for them to do. They look like workmen."

It remained only for the wisest of the wise men to speak. "The one thing that is known—and indeed I can show it to you in 47 books—is that dragons are the wisest of all creatures. Therefore they must look like wise men."

At that moment screams and yells were heard outside. On the horizon the dark mass of wild horsemen could be seen. The councilors pushed the little old man aside and ran away to hide.

"Well," said Han. "I don't think we have much time. The enemy will be here soon. I don't know whether you are a dragon or not, but if you are hungry and thirsty, please do me the honor of coming into my humble house."

The old man ate and drank, then he said to Han, "for your sake I will save the city." The wild horsemen were nearly to the gate. The little man blew a great breath. A huge storm arose which caught the horsemen and drove them away. As the storm subsided the little fat man said to Han, "now I will show you what a dragon looks like." As he sprang up into the air his changed form filled the sky. According to the story, "he grew taller than the tallest tree, greater than the greatest tower. He was the color of sunset shining through rain. Scales covered him, scattering light. His claws and teeth glittered like diamonds. His eyes were noble like those of a proud horse. He was more beautiful and more frightening than anything Han had ever seen. He flew high, roaring, and vanished into the deep sky."

Han went through the city telling the hiding people that the dragon had saved them. The Mandarin rewarded Han and named him the Honorable

Defender of the city. "We are saved," said the Mandarin. "But best of all we know what a dragon looks like. He looks like a small, fat, bald old man" (adapted from Williams, 1976).

Everyone Knows What a Dragon Looks Like

Science begins with definitions and classification systems. The awesome complexity of reality is simplified and ordered by defining and classifying selected elements within that reality. What we sometimes lose sight of is that *all scientific systems of definition and classification are perceptual, artificial, and arbitrary. Whose definitions prevail at any given time and place is a matter of politics, persuasion, and preference.* It is in the nature of things that there can never be an absolute definition of what a dragon looks like.

Every stage in evaluation research involves the processes of definition and classification. One first has to decide what a decisionmaker looks like. Then we classify goals according to whether they are vague or clear, general or specific, measurable or immune to measurement. Program implementation is defined and programs are classified by type, size, mission, evaluability, and effectiveness. Variables are defined to describe treatment environments and program interventions. We even classify types of evaluations: formative and summative; goal-free and goal-based; outcomes evaluation and implementation evaluation; effort, process, and treatment specification approaches. Finally we come to the methodological issues. For program people, methodology is the not-so-friendly dragon of measurement and design, breathing fire and numbers, questionnaires and equations.

Occasionally I am successful in convincing students or colleagues that evaluation questions ought to stem from the information needs of relevant and identified decisionmakers and information users. They will agree that, to be useful, evaluations ought to assess decisionmakers' goals, examine their ideals of program implementation, and test their theories of program action. During the conceptual phase of the evaluation, these students and colleagues are sympathetic to the importance of an active-reactive-adaptive role for evaluators working with decisionmakers and information users to arrive at crucial definitions of the problem. Where we part company is in the role to be played by decisionmakers and information users in making measurement and design decisions. "The evaluator is nothing," they argue, "if not an expert in methods and statistics. Clearly social scientists ought to be left with full responsibility for operationalizing program goals and determining data collection procedures." Edwards and Guttentag (1975: 456) are prime examples of this perspective: "using multi-attribute utility measurement matrix, the decisionmakers' values determine on what variables data should be gathered. The researcher then decides how to collect the data."

Making Measurement and Design Decisions

In a utilization-focused approach to evaluation research, the researcher has no intrinsic rights to unilaterally make critical design and data collection decisions. Quite the contrary, it is crucial that identified decisionmakers and information users participate in the making of measurement and methods decisions so that they understand the strengths and weaknesses of the data—and so that they believe in the data. Utilization potential can be severely diminished if decisionmakers are excluded at the critical operationalization stage, which is when the evaluation comes down to actually making data choices.

Measurement and methods decisions are not simply a matter of expertly selecting the best techniques. Researchers operate within quite narrow methodological paradigms about what constitutes valid and reliable data or rigorous and scientific design. A basic theme of this chapter is that *design and data collection decisions are a far cry from being neutral, objective, or rational; such decisions are political, subjective, and satisficing.* The various scholarly disciplines have quite variable methodological standards. Most social scientists routinely apply those methods in which they have been trained, with little sensitivity to the biases introduced by a particular data collection scheme. Why? Because that is what they have been trained to do, not because their expertise necessarily generates the best information about a particular issue. Such methodological narrowness is anything but active-reactive-adaptive.

Social and behavioral scientists—experts in the ultimate subjectivity and arbitrariness of all human perception—are often least aware of their own sociomethodological biases and of how those biases affect their view of the social program world. To be sure, social scientists are not the only participants in the evaluation process operating on the basis of selective perception; decisionmakers also hold conditioned views about the nature of social reality. One of the tasks during the active-reactive-adaptive interactions between evaluators and decisionmakers is to mutually explore design and data biases so that the evaluation generates information that is useful and believable to decisionmakers and information users.

Paradigmatic Bias

In order to present measurement and design alternatives to decision-makers, it is necessary for evaluators to become aware of their own narrow paradigmatic biases. The purpose of the scientific method is to control for bias. Bias is the dragon against which scientific knights battle with methodological rigor. Scientists struggle to be value-free, objective, and neutral. But such virtues are more believable in fairy tales than in real life. The fundamental assumption of utilization-focused evaluation is that there are no value-free alternatives. The issue is not one of avoiding bias, but rather one of making biases explicit and then deciding whose values and which biases will prevail. Bias is inevitable; it is inherent in the very paradigms that undergird our theories and methods.

A paradigm is a world view, a general perspective, a way of breaking down the complexity of the real world. As such, paradigms are deeply embedded in the socialization of adherents and practitioners: paradigms tell them what is important, legitimate, and reasonable. Paradigms are also normative, telling the practitioner what to do without the necessity of long existential or epistemological consideration. But it is this aspect of paradigms that constitutes both their strength and their weakness— their strength in that it makes action possible, their weakness in that the very reason for action is hidden in the unquestioned assumptions of the paradigm.

> Scientists work from models acquired through education and through subsequent exposure to the literature often without quite knowing or needing to know what characteristics have given these models the status of community paradigms. . . . That scientists do not usually ask or debate what makes a particular problem or solution legitimate tempts us to suppose that, at least intuitively, they know the answer. But it may only indicate that neither the question nor the answer is felt to be relevant to their research. Paradigms may be prior to, more binding, and more complete than any set of rules for research that could be unequivocally abstracted from them (Kuhn, 1970: 46).

Evaluation research is dominated by the largely unquestioned, natural science paradigm of hypothetico-deductive methodology. This dominant paradigm assumes quantitative measurement, experimental design, and multivariate, parametric statistical analysis to be the epitome of "good" science. This basic model for conducting evaluation research comes from the tradition of experimentation in agriculture, which gave us many of the basic statistical and experimental techniques most widely used in evaluation research.

> The most common form of agricultural-botany type evaluation is presented as an assessment of the effectiveness of an innovation by examining whether or not it has reached required standards on prespecified criteria. Students— rather like plant crops—are given pretests (the seedlings are weighed or measured) and then submitted to different experiences (treatment conditions). Subsequently, after a period of time, their attainment (growth or yield) is measured to indicate the relative efficiency of the methods (fertilizer) used. Studies of this kind are designed to yield data of one particular type, i.e., "objective" numerical data that permit statistical analyses (Parlett and Hamilton, 1976: 142).

By way of contrast, the alternative to the dominant hypothetico-deductive paradigm is derived from the tradition of anthropological field studies. Using the techniques of in depth, openended interviewing and personal observation, the alternative paradigm relies on qualitative data, holistic analysis, and detailed description derived from close contact with the targets of study. The hypothetico-deductive, natural science paradigm aims at prediction of social phenomenon; the holistic-inductive, anthropological paradigm aims at understanding of social phenomenon. From a utilization-focused perspective on evaluation research, neither of these paradigms is intrinsically better than the other. They represent alternatives from which the active-reactive-adaptive evaluator can choose; both contain options for identified decisionmakers and information users. Issues of methodology are issues of strategy, not of morals (cf. Homans, 1949). Yet, it is not easy to approach the selection of evaluation methods in this adaptive fashion. The paradigmatic biases in each approach are quite fundamental. Great passions are aroused by advocates on each side. Kuhn (1970: 109-110) has pointed out that this is the nature of paradigm debates:

> To the extent that two scientific schools disagree about what is a problem and what is a solution, they will inevitably talk through each other when debating the relative merits of their respective paradigms. In the partially circular arguments that regularly result, each paradigm will be shown to satisfy more or less the criteria that it dictates for itself and to fall short of a few of those dictated by its opponent. . . . Since no paradigm ever solves all problems it defines and since no two paradigms leave all the same problems unsolved, paradigm questions always involve the question: Which problems is it more significant to have solved?

In utilization-focused evaluation, the answer to that question is personal and situational rather than absolute.

The Dominant Paradigm

The most explicit affirmation of the dominance of the hypothetico-deductive paradigm as *the* scientific method in evaluation research is in the meta-evaluation work of Bernstein and Freeman (1975). The purpose of the Bernstein-Freeman study, supported by the Russell Sage Foundation, was to assess the quality of evaluative research as it is currently practiced. Their population of interest included all evaluation studies initially funded directly by the agencies of the federal government in the fiscal year of 1970. They sampled all evaluations of large-scale social action programs aimed at problems in health, education, welfare, public safety (crime), income security, housing, and manpower that had a minimum research budget of $10,000. Their final analysis was based on 236 such evaluation research projects.

What is of interest to us is the way Bernstein and Freeman operationalized or measured "quality." The quality variables they identified and measured represented a fully explicit description of the dominant evaluation research paradigm—the hypothetico-deductive scientific method. Table 10-1 shows how they coded their six-major indicators of quality; a higher code number represents higher quality evaluation research. What emerges is a picture of high quality evaluation as complete quantitative data obtained through an experimental design and analyzed with sophisticated statistical techniques. Applying these criteria, Bernstein and Freeman found (not surprisingly) that "academic research" is generally of higher quality than "entrepreneurial research" (research conducted by private firms). But their definition of quality ignores whether the information collected was relevant, understandable, or useful from the point of view of decisionmakers and program participants; whether the outcomes measured were those held to be important by program funders, administrators, and participants; or even whether the methods and measurements used were appropriate to the problem under study. For Bernstein and Freeman, the quality of evaluation research is judged entirely by its conformance with the dominant, hypothetico-deductive paradigm.

Thus there can be little doubt about the current dominance of this paradigm. There is broad consensus that it is the most desirable approach to evaluation research. Bernstein and Freeman cited Suchman (1967), Caro (1971), and Rossi and Williams (1972) in support of their quality coding scheme. Weiss and Bucuvalas (1977) were less prescriptive and

TABLE 10.1: Bernstein and Freeman (1975) Codings of Evaluation Quality Variables

Variable Measuring Some Aspect of Evaluation Quality	Coding Scheme (where higher coding number represents higher quality)
Process Procedures: Sampling	1 = Systematic random 0 = Nonrandom, cluster or nonsystematic
Data analysis	2 = Quantative 1 = Qualitative and quantitative 0 = Qualitative
Statistical procedures	4 = Multivariate 3 = Descriptive 2 = Ratings from qualitative data 1 = Narrative data only 0 = No systematic material
Impact Procedures: Design	3 = Experimental or quasi-experimental with randomization and control groups 2 = Experimental or quasi-experimental without both randomization and control groups 1 = Longitudinal or cross-sectional without control or comparison 0 = Descriptive, narrative
Sampling	2 = Representative 1 = Possibly representative 0 = Haphazard
Measurement procedures	1 = Judged adequate in face validity 0 = Judged less than adequate in face validity

more inclusive in their definition of research quality when they studied utilization of 50 federal social science research reports, but their definition of quality is predominantly technical, statistical, and quantitative. Wholey et al. (1970: 93) considered evaluations conducted according to the hypothetico-deductive paradigm to be the only kind of studies worthy of federal support: "federal money generally should not be spent on evaluation of individual local projects unless they have been developed as field experiments, with equivalent treatment and control groups." Recent writings on evaluation methodology by a committee of the Social Science Research Council (Reicken and Boruch, eds., 1974) were aimed quite explicitly at extending and consolidating the dominance of the hypothetico-deductive paradigm in evaluation and policy research. Peter Rossi (1972) reported general consensus about the most desired evaluation research methods at a conference on evaluation and policy research sponsored by the American Academy of Arts and Sciences in 1969; this consensus was virtually identical to the model found most desirable by Bernstein and Freeman.

A cursory skimming of major educational and social science research journals should confirm the dominance of the hypothetico-deductive paradigm with its quantitatve, experimental bias. In their widely used methodological primer Campbell and Stanley (1966: 3) called this paradigm "the only available route to cumulative progress." It is this belief in and commitment to the natural science model on the part of the most prominent academic researchers that makes the hypothetico-deductive paradigm dominant. As Kuhn (1970: 80) explains, "a paradigm governs, in the first instance, not a subject matter but rather a group of practitioners." Those practitioners most committed to the dominant paradigm are found in universities where they not only employ *the* scientific method in their own evaluation research but where they also nurture students in a commitment to that same methodology (cf. Bernstein and Freeman, 1975).

The problem from a utilization-focused approach to evaluation is that the very dominance of the hypothetico-deductive paradigm with its quantitative, experimental emphasis appears to have cut off the great majority of its practitioners from serious consideration of any alternative evaluation research paradigm or methods. The label "research" has come to mean the equivalent of employing the "scientific method" of working within the dominant paradigm. There is, however, an alternative.

The Alternative Paradigm

The alternative methodological paradigm is derived most directly from anthropological field methods. More generally, this holistic-inductive paradigm draws on work in qualitative methodology, phenomenology, symbolic interactionism, Gestalt psychology, ethnomethodology, and the general notion or doctrine of *Verstehen* ("understanding"). Kenneth Strike (1972: 28) describes this tradition as follows:

> The basic dispute clustering around the notion of *verstehen* has typically sounded something like the following: The advocate of some version of the *verstehen* doctrine will claim that human beings can be understood in a manner that other objects of study cannot. Men have purposes and emotions, they make plans, construct cultures, and hold certain values, and their behavior is influenced by such values, plans, and purposes. In short, a human being lives in a world which has "meaning" to him, and, because his behavior has meaning, human actions are intelligible in ways that the behavior of non-

human objects is not. The opponents of this view, on the other hand, will maintain that human behavior is to be explained in the same manner as is the behavior of other objects of nature. There are laws governing human behavior. An action is explained when it can be subsumed under some such law, and, of course, such laws are confirmed by empirical evidence.

In short, the Verstehen approach assumes that the social sciences need methods different from those used in agricultural experimentation and natural science because human beings are different from plants. The alternative paradigm stresses understanding that focuses on the meaning of human behavior, the context of social interaction, an emphatic understanding of subjective (mental, not nonobjective) states, and the connections between subjective states and behavior. The tradition of Verstehen places emphasis on the human capacity to know and understand others through sympathetic introspection and reflection from detailed description and observation.

The alternative paradigm proposes an active, involved role for the social scientist or evaluation researcher:

> Hence, insight may be regarded as the core of social knowledge. It is arrived at by being on the inside of the phenomena to be observed.... It is participation in an activity that generates interest, purpose, point of view, value, meaning, and intelligibility, as well as bias (Wirth, 1949: xxii).

This is a quite different scientific process from that envisioned by the classical, experimental approach to science:

> This in no way suggests that the researcher lacks the ability to be scientific while collecting the data. On the contrary, it merely specifies that it is crucial for validity—and, consequently, for reliability—to try to picture the empirical social world as it actually exists to those under investigation, rather than as the researcher imagines it to be (Filstead, 1970: 4).

Thus the importance of field techniques from an anthropological rather than natural science tradition, techniques like participant observation, in depth interviewing, detailed description, and qualitative field notes.

Evaluation research is not without advocates for and practitioners of alternative methodological approaches. Robert Stake's "responsive approach to evaluation" is an alternative to the dominant paradigm.

> Responsive evaluation is an alternative, an old alternative, based on what people do naturally to evaluate things, they observe and react. The approach

is not new. But this alternative has been avoided in district, state, and federal planning documents and regulations because it is subjective and poorly suited to formal contracts. It is also capable of raising embarrassing questions. This chapter advocates technical steps (e.g., replication and nonverbal operationalization) to bolster the reliability of observation and opinion-gathering without sacrificing relevance (Stake, 1975: 14).

Stake recommended responsive evaluation because "it is an approach that trades off some measurement precision in order to increase the usefulness of the findings to persons in and around the program" (ibid). Also clearly embodying the alternative paradigm is the "illuminative evaluation" approach of Parlett and Hamilton (1976: 144):

Illuminative evaluation takes account of the wider contexts in which educational programs function. Its primary concern is with description and interpretation rather than measurement and prediction. It stands unambiguously within the alternative anthropological paradigm. The aims of illuminative evaluation are to study the innovatory program: how it operates; how it is influenced by the various school situations in which it is applied; what those directly concerned regard as its advantages and disadvantages; and how students' intellectual tasks and academic experiences are most affected. It aims to discover and document what it is like to be participating in the scheme, whether as teacher or pupil, and, in addition, to discern and discuss the innovation's most significant features, recurring concomitants, and critical processes. In short, it seeks to address and to illuminate a complex array of questions.

Opposing Paradigms

We now have before us the broad outlines of two contrasting evaluative research paradigms. In a very real sense these are opposing and competing paradigms. In our utilization of federal health evaluation studies, every respondent answered methodological questions by placing himself or herself with reference to these competing paradigms. Respondents would typically begin by explaining any reasons for departure of the particular study in question from the dominant paradigm ideal of quantitative measures obtained through an experimental design. Studies were described as "hard" or "soft" along a continuum where "harder" was clearly better. There were frequent stories of conflicts over methods to be employed. These were not only conflicts between evaluators and decisionmakers, but also conflicts among decisionmakers or among evaluators.

Decisionmakers and evaluators we interviewed frequently pointed out that final measurement and design decisions usually represented compromises between methodological ideas and realities. (Chapter 11 discusses the implications of these compromises for analysis and interpretation of evaluation findings.) We will therefore more fully explore the ideals among which evaluators and decisionmakers choose as they begin discussions of methods and measurement. Such an analysis, based on ideal types, will at times exaggerate differences. Tacit understandings about flexible parameters may appear as absolute rules of procedures, while areas of mutuality, common concern, and similarity of commitments are largely ignored. Contrasts will be emphasized in order to capture the underlying and fundamental elements in the two paradigms that are the basis of their opposition and competition.

The very dominance of one paradigm (the hypothetico-deductive, natural science model) and the subordination of the second (the alternative holistic-inductive paradigm) demonstrates that it is more important to attack this imbalance than to maintain neutrality. My concern here is twofold: first, that practitioners and adherents of the dominant paradigm show little awareness of the existence of an alternative paradigm; and secondly, that practitioners of the dominant paradigm seem to be insensitive to the degree to which their methodology is based upon a relatively narrow philosophical, ideological, and epistemological view of the world.

> It is important to get this point quite clear, for one would suppose that philosophical tenets would not be central to the shaping of an enterprise which is so emphatic in its claim to be Science. It is important also because the practitioners of the style do not usually seem aware that it is a philosophy upon which they stand (Mills, 1961: 56).

Thus the assets of the alternative need to be stressed and the shortcomings of the dominant paradigm seriously examined. Herbert Blumer (1969: 47) put the issue this way:

> This opposition needs to be stressed in the hope of releasing social scientists from unwitting captivity to a format of inquiry that is taken for granted as the naturally proper way in which to conduct scientific inquiry.

This heuristic technique of comparing ideal-typical methodological paradigms is aimed at making both approaches accessible to evaluators and decisionmakers. The real point is not that one approach is intrinsically better or more scientific than the other, but that evaluation methods ought to be selected to suit the type of program being evaluated and the nature of decisionmakers' evaluation questions:

> Good methodology is crucial if we are to garner sound and useful results, but it is only a means to an end rather than an end in itself. What kinds of methods are best depend on what kinds of questions we want to answer. Thus, a methodologist's role is only to assist those who pose the questions or problems for which it is his business, qua methodologist, to help them find answers (Bennett and Lumsdaine, 1975: 19).

The contrasts which follow are aimed at increasing evaluators' awareness of the options available to them in playing this creative role of methodologist.*

Qualitative versus Quantitative Methodology

Kuhn (1970: 184-185), in his discussion of science paradigms, has noted that the values scientists hold help them choose between incompatible ways of practicing their discipline: "the most deeply held values concern predictions: they should be accurate; quantitative predictions are preferable to qualitative ones." Kuhn was writing mainly about natural scientists, but it is clear that their values concerning prediction have been enthusiatically embraced by social scientists and educational researchers. Not only are quantitative predictions preferable to qualitative ones, but qualitative analyses in general have little legitimacy beyond certain limited exploratory situations.

The methodological status hierarchy in science is clear; the harder the data, the more scientific the results and the higher the status (where "hardness of data" means the degree to which one can assign numbers to what one is studying and manipulate those numbers using sophisticated statistical techniques). The danger of this methodological status hierarchy is that it denigrates those who employ qualitative methodology. Bernstein and Freeman (1975) even rank studies which gathered both quantitative and qualitative data as lower in methodological quality than studies which

---

* The contrasts which follow are adapted from Patton (1975). I am indebted to Harold Finestone, University of Minnesota, for helpful comments on an early version of the ideas presented here.

gathered only quantitative data. *The problem is the advocacy of statistics to the virtual exclusion of other types of data.* C. Wright Mills (1961: 50) observed in this regard that the dominance of statistical methodology has led to a "methodological inhibition" that he called "abstracted empiricism." The problem with abstracted empiricism is that "it seizes upon one juncture in the process of work and allows it to dominate the mind."

The dominance of quantitative methodology has acted to severely limit the kinds of questions asked and the types of problems studied. While most phenomena are not intrinsically impossible to measure quantitatively, certain types are clearly easier to measure numerically than others. It is easier to measure the number of words a child spells correctly than to measure that same child's ability to use those words in a meaningful way. Educational researchers have most often opted for the first approach. It is easier to count the number of minutes a student spends reading books in class than it is to measure what reading means to that student. We have a large number of studies of the former, but we know little about the latter.

Quantitative methodology assumes the necessity, desirability, and even the possibility of applying some underlying empirical standard to social phenomena. By way of contrast, qualitative methodology assumes that some phenomena are not amenable to numerical mediation. *The point here is that different kinds of problems require different types of research methodology.* If we only want to know the number of words a child can spell or the frequency of interaction between children of different races in desegregated schools, then statistical procedures are appropriate. However, if we want to understand the relevance of the words to that child's life situation or the meaning of interracial interactions, then some form of qualitative methodology (such as participant observation, in depth interviewing, systematic field work) that allows the researcher to obtain firsthand knowledge about the empirical social world in question may well be more appropriate.

> If the problems upon which one is at work are readily amenable to statistical procedures, one should always try to use them. . . . No one, however, need accept such procedures, when generalized, as the only procedures available. Certainly no one need accept this model as a total canon. It is not the only empirical manner.
>
> It is a choice made according to the requirements of our problems, not a "necessity" that follows from an epistemological dogma (Mills, 1961: 73-74).

One evaluator in our federal utilization study had personally struggled with this choice between qualitative and quantitative methods. He was evaluating community mental health programs, and reported that quantitative measures frequently failed to capture real differences among programs. For example, he found a case where community mental health staff cooperated closely with the state hospital. On one occasion, he observed a therapist from the community mental health center accompany a seriously disturbed client on the "traumatic, fearful, anxiety-ridden trip to the state hospital." The therapist had been working with the client on an outpatient basis. After commitment to the state facility, the therapist continued to see the client weekly and assisted that person in planning toward and getting out of the state institution and back into the normal community as soon as possible. The evaluator found it very difficult to measure this aspect of the program quantitatively.

> This actually becomes a *qualitative* aspect of how they were carrying out the mental health program, but there's a problem of measuring the impact of that qualitative change from when the sheriff used to transport the patients from that county in a locked car with a stranger in charge and the paraphenalia of the sheriff's personality and office. The qualitative difference is obvious in the possible effect on a disturbed patient, but the problem of measurement is very, very difficult. So what we get here in the report is a portrayal of some of the qualitative differences and a very limited capacity of the field at that time to measure those qualitative differences. *We can describe some of them better than we can measure them* (EV5: 3).

A more extended example may help illustrate the importance of seeking congruence between the phenomenon studied and the research methodology employed for the study. The example concerns the key issue of whether or not educational innovation makes a difference in children's achievement. After examining some four decades of educational research, John Stephens (1967) concluded that educational innovation makes little difference. "But," asked Edna Shapiro (1973: 542), "can such a judgment be made when the researcher has sampled only an extremely narrow band of measurement within a constant and equally restrictive situation?"

Shapiro asked this question after finding no achievement test differences between (1) children in an enriched Follow Through program modeled along the lines of open education and (2) children in comparison schools not involved in Follow Through or other enrichment programs. *When the children's responses in the test situation were compared, no differences of any consequence were found. However, when observations of the children in their classrooms were made, there were striking differences between the Follow Through and comparison classes.*

A satisfactory explanation of the outcomes of this study raises general questions about assessing the impact of educational programs. . . . Conventional explanations would make little of the classroom differences, stressing the absence of difference in individual test response. The conventional explanation for equivocal findings (and they are not unique—the educational research literature is replete with negative findings) is that the programs being compared do not make a difference, that the research design is inadequate, or that it is naive to expect differences since program variations do not make a noticeable difference. My contention is that such explanations do not go far enough. *While it is important to try to explain negative test results, it is far more important to account for the disparity between the negative test findings and the clear differences observed in classroom behavior* (Shapiro, 1973: 527).

Based on systematic observations the Follow Through (FT) classrooms

> were characterized as lively, vibrant, with a diversity of curricular projects and children's products, and an atmosphere of friendly, cooperative endeavor. The non-FT classrooms were characterized as relatively uneventful, with a narrow range of curriculum, uniform activity, a great deal of seat work, and less equipment; teachers as well as children were quieter and more concerned with maintaining or submitting to discipline (Shapiro, 1973: 529).

Observations also revealed that the children behaved differently in these two types of environments. Yet standardized acheivement tests failed to detect these differences. Shapiro suggests that there were factors operating against the demonstration of differences that call into question traditional ways of gauging the impact and effectiveness of different kinds of school experience. *The testing methodology, in fact, narrowed the nature of the questions that were being asked and predetermined nonsignificant statistical results.* Shapiro's analysis of how the quantitative methodological procedures determined the research results was so insightful and important that she is quoted here at length.

> Studies of the effectiveness of different kinds of educational programs share a common methodology: children of comparable background and ability are exposed to or participate in experiences which vary in certain ways and are subsequently tested on aspects of learning or performance presumed to demonstrate the impact of the differences in their experiences. . . .
> In this study, too, the child's responses in the test situation were considered critical. What children do in the classroom—the kinds of questions they ask, the kinds of activities they engage in, the kinds of stories, drawings,

poems, structures they produce, the kinds of relationships they develop with other children and the teacher—indicates not only what they are capable of doing but what they are allowed to do. Classroom data are generally down graded in attempts to study the effects of educational programs. . . . I assumed that the internalized effects of different kinds of school experience could be observed and inferred only from responses in test situations, and that the observation of teaching and learning in the classroom should be considered auxiliary information, useful chiefly to document the differences in the children's group learning experiences.

The rationale of the test, on the contrary, is that each child is removed from the classroom and treated equivalently, and differences in response are presumed to indicate differences in what has been taken in, made one's own, that survives the shift to a different situation.

The findings of this study, with the marked disparity between classroom responses and test responses, have led me to reevaluate this rationale. This requires reconsideration of the role of classroom data, individual test situation data, and the relation between them. *If we minimize the importance of the child's behavior in the classroom because it is influenced by situational variables, do we not have to apply the same logic to the child's responses in the test situation, which is also influenced by situational variables?*

The individual's responses in the test situation have conventionally been considered the primary means to truth about psychological functioning. Test behavior, whether considered as a sign or sample of underlying function, is treated as a pure measure. Yet the test situation is an unique interpersonal context in which what is permitted and encouraged, acceptable and unacceptable, is carefully defined, explicitly and implicitly. *Responses to tests are therefore made under very special circumstances. The variables that influence the outcome are different from those which operate in the classroom, but the notion that the standard test or interview provides equal treatment for all subjects is certainly open to question* (Shapiro, 1973: 532-534; emphasis added).

Shapiro elaborated and illustrated these points at considerable length. Her conclusion went to the heart of the problem posed by the dominance of a single methodological paradigm in evaluation research: *"research methodology must be suited to the particular characteristics of the situations under study. . . . An omnibus strategy will not work"* (Shapiro, 1973: 543; emphasis added).

At best, some social scientists are willing to recognize that qualitative methodology may be useful at an exploratory stage of research prefatory to quantitative research. What they deny is that qualitative methodology can be a legitimate source of either data collection, systematic evaluation, or theory construction. However, "to force all of the empirical world to fit a scheme that has been devised for a given segment of that world is philosophical doctrinizing and does not represent the approach of a genuine empirical science" (Blumer, 1969: 23).

Gathering qualitative data is an alternative that not only employs different methods but also asks different questions. As Kuhn (1970: 106) has explained, one of the functions of scientific paradigms is to provide criteria for choosing problems that can be assumed to have solutions: "changes in the standards governing permissible problems, concepts, and explanations can transform a science." It is the failure of the dominant natural science paradigm to answer important questions like those raised by Shapiro that makes serious consideration of the alternative paradigm so crucial for evaluation research.

Objectivity versus Subjectivity

Qualitative methodology and a responsive, illuminative approach to evaluation research most frequently stimulate charges of subjectivity—a label regarded as the very antithesis of scientific inquiry. Objectivity is considered the sine qua non of *the* scientific method. To be subjective means to be biased, unreliable, and nonrational. Subjective data imply opinion rather than fact, intuition rather than logic, impression rather than confirmation. Social scientists are to eschew subjectivity and make their work "objective and value-free." Of course, involvement in the arena of social action research may take one so close to questions of politics and values that it is impossible to completely eliminate subjectivity. Under these conditions,

> the task for the development of evaluative research as a "scientific" process is to "control" this intrinsic subjectivity, since it cannot be eliminated . . . to examine the principles and procedures that man has developed for controlling subjectivity—the scientific method (Suchman, 1967: 11-12).

Not surprisingly, the means for controlling subjectivity through the scientific method are the techniques of the dominat paradigm, particularly quantitative methods and an emphasis on reliability. Yet the previous section argued that quantitative methods work in practice to limit and even bias the kinds of questions that can be asked and the nature of admissible solutions. In effect, identification of objectivity as the major virtue of the dominant paradigm is an ideological statement the function of which is to legitimize, preserve, and protect the dominance of a single evaluation methodology.

Michael Scriven (1972a: 94) has insisted that quantitative methods are no more synonymous with objectivity than qualitative methods are synonomous with subjectivity:

> Errors like this are too simple to be explicit. They are inferred confusions in the ideological foundations of research, its interpretations, its application. . . . It is increasingly clear that the influence of ideology on methodology and of the latter on the training and behavior of researchers and on the identification and disbursement of support is staggeringly powerful. Ideology is to research what Marx suggested the economic factor was to politics and what Freud took sex to be for psychology.

Scriven's lengthy discussion of objectivity and subjectivity in educational research is a major contribution in the struggle to detach the notions of objectivity and subjectivity from their traditionally narrow associations with quantitative and qualitative methodology, respectively. He presents a cogent argument for recognizing not only the prediction of social phenomena but also the pursuit of understanding—Verstehen—as legitimate science. The quest for social "prediction" in the same sense as prediction operates in the classical natural science paradigm is "pipe dreaming" (Scriven, 1972: 115). The practice of science has led to a formalistic split between the mental (subjective) and the logical (objective) that keeps researchers from seeing that:

> *Understanding,* properly conceived, is in fact an "objective" state of mind or brain and can be tested quite objectively; and it is a functional and crucial state of mind, betokening the presence of skills and states that are necessary for survival in the sea of information. There is nothing wrong with saying, in this case, that we have simply developed an enlightened form of inter-subjectivism. But one might also equally well say that we have developed *an enlightened form of subjectivism—put flesh on the bones of emphathy* (Scriven, 1972a: 127; italics in original).

Scriven thus suggested two different ways of looking at the same thing. The idea of dual perspectives concerning a single phenomenon goes to the very heart of the contrasts between paradigms. Two scientists may look at the same thing, but because of different theoretical perspectives, assumptions, or ideology-based methodologies, they may literally not see the same thing (cf. Petrie, 1972: 48). Indeed, Kuhn (1970: 113) has argued that

> something like a paradigm is prerequisite to perception itself. What a man sees depends both upon what he looks at and also upon what his previous visual-conceptual experience has taught him to see. In the absence of such

training there can only be, in William James' phrase, "a bloomin' buggin' confusion.' "

As the parable of Han and the Dragon which opened this chapter illustrates, perceptions of the world (and of dragons) vary depending on how one has been trained. The Mandarin thought a dragon must look like a proud lord—a Mandarin. The captain of the army was convinced that a dragon would look like a warrior. The merchant, the chief workman, and the wise man each defined and perceived the dragon in a different way. They could each look at the same thing, but because of different ideology-based definitions, assumptions, and perspectives, they literally would not see the same thing. There may even be people whose pre-conceived definitions of the world tell them that no such things as dragons exist!

It is in this context that the dominant paradigm's assertion of objectivity can be called ideology. Such an accusation is based on the relativistic assumption that it is not possible for us to view the complexities of the real world without somehow filtering and simplifying those complexities. That filtering and simplifying affects what the observer sees because the physical act of observing necessarily brings into play the observer's past experiences of the world. The observer carries around perceptual filters based on past experiences that intervene between the real world and his or her observations of it. In the final analysis, this means that we are always dealing with perceptions, not "facts" in some absolute sense. "The very categories of things which comprise the 'facts' are theory dependent" (Petrie, 1972: 49) or, in this case, paradigm dependent. It is this recognition that the scientist inevitably operates within the constraints of a perception-based paradigm (with ideological and political underpinnings) that led Howard Becker (1970: 15) to argue that "the question is not whether we should take sides, since we inevitably will, but rather whose side we are on."

It is also in this context that the notion of subjectivity, properly con-strued, can become a positive rather than a pejorative term in evaluation research. Subjectivity in the alternative paradigm "allows the researcher to 'get close to the data,' thereby developing the analytical, conceptual, and categorical components from the data itself" (Filstead, 1970: 6), including data in the form of definitions and perceptions held by and relevant to identified decisionmakers and information users.

A positive view of subjectivity—getting close to and involved with the data (i.e., program staff and clients)—makes it possible for evaluation researchers to take into account their personal insights and behavior. As Scriven (1972: 99) lamented, "for the social sciences to refuse to treat their own behavior as data from which one can learn is really tragic." Alvin Gouldner (1970: 56) has been even more adamant on this point, suggesting that "high science methodology" creates a gap between what the researcher as scientist deals with and what that same researcher confronts as an ordinary person:

> It is a function of high science methodologies to widen the gap between what the sociologist is studying and his own personal reality. Even if one were to assume that this serves to fortify objectivity and reduce bias, it seems likely that it has been bought at the price of the dimming of the sociologist's self-awareness. In other words, it seems that at some point, the formula is: the more rigorous the methodology, the more dimwitted the sociologist; the more reliable his information about the social world, the less insightful his knowledge about himself.

To say that the evaluation researcher can learn much by getting close to the program is not to say that there is no systematic way of conducting scientific inquiry and that "anything goes." The point, rather, is to bring the mind and feelings of the human being back into the center of evaluation research—a center that has thus far been dominated by techniques and rules. Science is really nothing if it is not the application of critical intelligence to critical problems. The narrow parameters of the dominant paradigm have constrained that critical intelligence under the guise of attaining a natural science objectivity. C. Wright Mills (1961: 58) quoted Nobel Prize-winning physicist Percy Bridgman in this regard: "there is no scientific method as such, but the vital feature of the scientist's procedure has been merely to do his utmost with his mind, *no holds barred*" (italics in original).

The Verstehen or understanding approach to scientific inquiry is based on the application of critical intelligence to social phenomena without relying entirely on the abstraction of numerical representation. This alternative paradigm seeks to redraw the boundaries of legitimate scientific inquiry in order to increase the domain of what has been labeled subjective by the dominant paradigm. Thus much of what has been thought of as illegitimate in terms of subject matter and techniques can be tackled.

Space does not permit a full epistemological exploration of the arguments underlying traditional notions of objectivity and subjectivity in evaluation research. It may be helpful, however, to again use the problem of evaluating innovations in open education to illustrate the different

perspectives on objectivity and subjectivity represented by the two evaluation methodology paradigms. The dominant paradigm lauds the use of
standardized tests to measure pupil achievement in school because these
tests are highly reliable, their outcomes have been widely replicated on
varying populations, and their statistical properties are well known. In
brief, standardized tests represent an objective measure of achievement
across situations and populations. Properly administered, they minimize
the introduction of researcher bias in measuring achievement.

However, as Shapiro found in her study of innovative Follow Through
classrooms (described in Chapter 10) standardized tests can bias evaluation
results by imposing a controlled stimulus in an environment where learning
depends on spontaneity, creativity, and freedom of expression. Shapiro
found that the results of the test measured response to a stimulus (the test)
that was essentially alien to the children's experience. Because the open
classroom relies substantially less on paper-and-pencil skills and monitors
student progress on a personal basis without the use of written examina-
tions, student outcomes in the open classroom could not be "objectively"
measured by standardized tests. Such tests fail to delineate the learning
outcomes of children who make different uses of particular classroom
situations. Thus Shapiro (1973: 543) argued that

> the quest for objective control over the multiplicity of interdependent events
> occurring in a classroom had led to a concentration on ever smaller units
> of behavior, divorced from context and sampled in rigorously scheduled time
> units.

The problem is not simply one of finding a new or better standardized
test, but one of understanding the context of observed behaviors and the
meaning of specific achievement outcomes to the child in a more holistic
setting. This does not mean that standardized tests may not be useful for
certain specific questions, but they are not sufficient when the issue is
understanding, not just prediction. *Understanding in its broadest sense
requires getting close enough to the situation to gain insight into mental
states—it means subjectivity in the best scientific sense of the term.* The
alternative paradigm seeks to legitimize and incorporate this subjectivity
into evaluation research, not to the exclusion of the methodology of the
dominant paradigm, but in addition to it.

If a limited notion of subjectivity based on careful and systematic
observation by trained researchers in the best tradition of anthropological
research cannot be made a legitimate part of evaluation research, then a
host of crucial questions will be excluded from investigation:

If we cannot straighten out the situation, we are doomed to suffer from the swing of the pendulum in the other direction, a swing which it is easy to see implicit in the turn toward irrationalistic, mystical, and emotional movements thriving in or on the fringes of psychology today. There is much good in them on their own merits, but the ideology that is used to support them is likely to breed the same intolerance and repression that the positivists spread through epistemology and psychology for a quarter century (Scriven, 1972a: 97).

Distance from versus Closeness to the Data

There are several additional paradigm components that have emerged in the discussion of quantitative versus qualitative methodology and of objectivity versus subjectivity. One of these is the issue of how close the investigator should get to the data. The dominant paradigm prescribes distance in order to guarantee neutrality and objectivity. This component has become increasingly important with the professionalization of the social sciences and of the educational research establishment. Professional comportment connotes cool, calm, and detached analysis without personal involvement. But the alternative paradigm questions the necessity of distance and detachment, assuming that without empathy and sympathetic introspection derived from personal encounters the observer cannot fully understand human behavior. Understanding comes from trying to put oneself in the other person's shoes, from trying to discern how others think, act, and feel. John Lofland (1971) explains that methodologically this means (1) geting close to the people being studied through attention to the minutiae of daily life, through physical proximity over a period of time, and through development of closeness in the social sense of intimacy and confidentiality; (2) being truthful and factual about what is observed; (3) emphasizing a significant amount of pure description of action, people, and so on; and (4) including as data direct quotations from participants as they speak or from whatever they might write. "The commitment to get close, to be factual, descriptive, and quotive, constitutes a significant commitment to represent the participants *in their own terms*" (Lofland, 1971: 4).

The commitment to closeness is based upon the assumption that the inner states of people are important and can be known. From this assumption flows a concern with meaning, mental states, and world view. It is at this point that the alternative paradigm intersects with the phenomenological tradition (cf. Bussis, Chittenden, and Amarel, 1973). Attention to inner perspectives does not mean administering attitude surveys. "The inner perspective assumes that understanding can only be achieved by actively participating in the life of the observed and gaining insight by means of introspection (Bruyn, 1963: 226). Actively participating in the life of the observed means, at a minimum, being willing to get close to the program being evaluated.

A commitment to get close to the program and a willingness to view participants in their own terms implies an openness to the phenomenon under study that is relatively uncontaminated by preconceived notions and categories.

> In order to capture the participants 'in their own terms' one must learn *their* analytic ordering of the world, *their* categories for rendering explicable and coherent the flux of raw reality. That, indeed, is the first principle of qualitative analysis (Lofland, 1971: 7; italics in original).

In the Shapiro study of open Follow Through classrooms, it was her closeness to the children in those classrooms that allowed her to see that something was happening that was not captured by standardized tests. She could see differences in children, and could understand differences in the meaning of their different situations. She could feel their tension in the testing situation and their spontaneity in the more natural classroom setting. Had she worked solely with data collected by others or only at a distance, she would never have discovered the crucial differences in the classroom settings she studied—differences which actually allowed her to evaluate the innovative program in a meaningful and relevant way.

Again, it is important to note that the admonition to get close to the data is in no way meant to deny the usefulness of quantitative methodology. Rather, it means that statistical portrayals must always be interpreted and given human meaning. One evaluator in our utilization of federal health evaluations expressed frustration at trying to make sense out of data from over 80 projects when site visit funds were cut out of the evaluation: "there's no way to evaluate something that's just data. You know, you have to go look" (EV111: 3).

That many quantitative methodologists fail to ground their findings in qualitative understanding poses what Lofland (1971: 3) calls a major contradiction between their public insistence on the adequacy of statistical portrayals of other humans and their personal everyday dealings with and judgments about other human beings:

> In everyday life, statistical sociologists, like everyone else, assume that they do not know or understand very well people they do not see or associate with very much. They assume that knowing and understanding other people require that one see them reasonably often and in a variety of situations

relative to a variety of issues. Moreover, statistical sociologists, like other people, assume that in order to know or understand others one is well advised to give some conscious attention to that effort in face-to-face contacts. They assume, too, that the internal world of sociology—or any other social world—is not understandable unless one has been part of it in a face-to-face fashion for quite a period of time. How utterly paradoxical, then, for these same persons to turn around and make, by implication, precisely the opposite claim about people they have never encountered face-fo-face—those people appearing as numbers in their tables and as correlations in their matrices!

Closeness to the data is not the only legitimate way to understand human behavior, but it is a legitimate scientific alternative to the distance prescribed by the dominant scientific paradigm. For certain questions and for practical situations involving large groups, distance is inevitable, but for others face-to-face interaction is both necessary and desirable.

This returns us to the recurrent theme of matching the evaluation methodology to the problem. The highly informal, personalized environment of open education lends itself to a more personalized evaluation methodology built upon close observer-student and observer-teacher interaction. Such a personalized evaluation is important not only for the insights it can generate but because such *a personalized evaluation that takes the observer close to the data is the only evaluation research likely to be perceived as legitimate by program participants themselves.* Because a central criterion for judging the quality of evaluation research is its legitimacy and usefulness to program participants, the matching of evaluation methodology to the nature of the program being evaluated is also central.

Finally, in thinking about the issue of closeness to the data, it is useful to remember that *many major contributions to our understanding of the world have come from scientists' personal experiences.* One finds many instances where closeness to the data made key insights possible— Piaget's closeness to his children, Freud's proximity to and empathy with his patients, Darwin's closeness to nature, and even Newton's intimate encounter with an apple. The distance prescribed by the dominant paradigm makes such insights derived from personal experience an endangered species.

Holistic versus Component Analysis

As noted in Chapters 8 and 9, one of the major problems in evaluation research is clear specification of the treatment. Experimental designs depend on careful treatment specification and on control of all other possible causal variables. The experimental constraints posed by controlling the specific treatment under study necessitate simplifying and breaking down reality into small component parts. A great deal of the scientific enterprise revolves around this simplifying process which, although necessary, is also distorting. The narrowness of focus in most experiments with artificial controls and isolated treatments may lead to the preponderance of "so what?" results. Field settings are usually more complex than can be represented by single treatment specifications. Programs usually consist of a number of interactive and interdependent "treatments." To try to analyze or measure only one component of such programs for experimental purposes may seriously misrepresent the total treatment process.

There are questions of major import that do not lend themselves to experimental design or even to less rigorous quantitative methodologies that focus on a limited number of narrowly defined, preordained variables. The simplified world of variables, causes, and effects in which the scientists of the dominant pardigm operate is alien to many program staff involved in innovations. Evaluations that are relevant and meaningful to the total context in which innovations occur may need to include a holistic methodological approach that attempts to capture the Gestalt of program activities and outcomes. John Dewey (1956: 5-6) advocated a holistic approach to both teaching and research if one were to reach into and understand the world of the child.

> Again, the child's life is an integral, a total one. He passes quickly and readily from one topic to another, as from one spot to another, but is not conscious of transition or break. There is no conscious isolation, hardly conscious distinction. The things that occupy him are held together by the unity of the personal and social interests which his life carries along. . . . [His] universe is fluid and fluent; its contents dissolve and re-form with amazing rapidity. But after all, it is the child's own world. It has the unity and completeness of his own life.

Deutscher (1970: 33) adds that despite the totality of our personal experiences as living, working human beings, we have focused in our research on parts to the virtual exclusion of wholes:

> We knew that human behavior was rarely if ever directly influenced or explained by an isolated variable; we knew that it was impossible to assume that any set of such variables was additive (with or without weighting); we knew that the complex mathematics of the interaction among any set of

variables, was incomprehensible to us. In effect, although we knew they did not exist, we defined them into being.

While most scientists would view this radical critique of component analysis as extreme, I find that teachers and practitioners voice the same criticisms about the bulk of evaluation research. Narrow experimental results lack relevance for innovative teachers because they have to deal with the whole in their classrooms. The reaction of many program staff to scientific research is like the reaction of Copernicus to the astronomers of his day: "with them," he observed, "it is as though an artist were to gather the hands, feet, head, and other members for his images from diverse models, each part excellently drawn, but not related to a single body, and since they in no way match each other, the result would be monster rather than man" (from Kuhn, 1970: 83). How many program staff have complained of the evaluation research monster?

It is no simple task to undertake holistic evaluation, to search for the Gestalt in innovative programs. The challenge for the participant observer is "to seek the essence of the life of the observed, to sum up, to find a central unifying principle" (Bruyn, 1966: 316). Again Shapiro's work (1973) in evaluating innovative Follow Through classrooms in instructive. She found that test results could not be interpreted without understanding the larger cultural and institutional context in which the individual child is situated.

In utilization-focused evaluation, neither the holistic approach nor component analysis represents an omnibus strategy appropriate to all situations and problems. It is in reaction to the dominance of component analysis as *the* scientific method in evaluation research that the potential of more holistic evaluation strategies has been emphasized. As one of the most famous of all Sufi stories illustrates, touching only one part of an elephant, as each of the nine blind men did, can give a quite distorted picture of what the whole elephant looks like.

Fixed versus Dynamic Systems

The preceding chapter discussed the problem of causal analysis in evaluation research. Experimental designs are generally considered the only method permitting causal statements. In its simplest form, the scientific observer enters the picture at two points in time, pretest and posttest, and compares the treatment group to the control group on standardized measures. As already noted, such designs assume a single, identifiable, isolated, and measurable treatment. Moreover, they assume that once introduced, the treatment remains relatively constant and unchanging.

While there are some narrow, largely technical treatments that fit this description, more encompassing program innovations are anything but static treatments. By the time they are put into practice, innovations are frequently already different than they appear in program proposals. Once in operation, innovative programs are often changed as practitioners learn what works and what does not, and as they experiment, grow, and change their priorities. This, of course, creates frustration and hostility among scientific evaluators who need specifiable, unchanging treatments to relate to specifiable, predetermined outcomes. Because of a commitment to a single evaluation paradigm, evaluators may actually be prepared to do everything in their power to stop program adaptation and improvement so as not to interfere with their research design (cf. Parlett and Hamilton, 1976). The deleterious effect this may have on the program itself, discouraging as it does new developments and redefinitions in midstream, is considered to be a small sacrifice made in pursuit of higher level scientific knowledge. Moreover, there is a distinct possibility that such artificial evaluation constraints will contaminate the program treatment by affecting staff morale and participant autonomy.

Were some science of planning and policy or program development so highly evolved that initial proposals were perfect, one might be able to sympathize with the evaluator's desire to keep the initial program implementation intact. In the real world, however, people and unforeseen circumstances shape programs, and initial implementations must be modified in ways that are rarely trivial. It is not the task of program administrators and participants to shape their programs to the needs of evaluators, but rather the task of evaluators to shape their evaluation methods to fit programs.

Under field conditions where programs are subject to change and redirection, the alternative evaluation paradigm replaces the fixed treatment or outcomes emphasis of the dominant paradigm with a dynamic orientation. A dynamic evaluation is not tied to a single treatment or to predetermined goals or outcomes, but rather focuses on the actual operations of a program over a period of time. The evaluator sets out to understand and document the day-to-day reality of the setting or settings under study. He or she makes no attempt to manipulate, control, or eliminate situation variables or program develpments, but takes as a given the complexity of a changing reality. The data of the evaluation are not just outcomes but changes in treatments and patterns of action, reaction, and interaction. Under some conditions the observations of the evaluator can even serve as a source of program improvement—an impossiblity with most controlled, static experimental designs.

In short, a dynamic perspective requires sensitivity to both qualitative and quantitative changes in programs throughout their development, not just at some endpoint in time. The evaluation is process-oriented. Process evaluation is built on subjective inferences in the sense that the investigator attempts to develop empathy with program participants and understand the changing meaning of the program in the participants' own terms; process evaluation requires getting close to the data, becoming intimately acquainted with the details of the program. Thus process evaluation includes a holistic orientation to evaluation research, observing not only anticipated outcomes but also unanticipated consequences, treatment changes, and the larger context of program implementation and development. This is what Stake (1975) calls "responsive evaluation." Responsive evaluation is process-oriented, holistic, and dynamic in perspective.

Again, the issue is one of matching the evaluation design to the program, of meshing evaluation methods with decisionmaker information needs. The point of contrasting fixed, experimental designs with dynamic, process designs is to release evaluators "from unwitting captivity to a format of inquiry that is taken for granted as the naturally proper way in which to conduct scientific inquiry" (Blumer, 1969: 47). Nowhere is this unwitting captivity better illustrated than in those agencies which insist—in the name of science—that all evaluations must employ experimental designs. Two recent examples come immediately to mind. In Minnesota, the Governor's Commission on Crime Prevention and Control requires experimental evaluation designs of all funded projects. As described in Chapter 8, the designs they employ give little attention to treatment specification, but they force such designs on programs where a formal, hypothetico-deductive model is completely inappropriate. For example, a small Native American alternative school has been granted funds to run an innovative crime prevention project with parents and students. The program is highly flexible; participation is irregular and based on self-selection. The program is designed to be sensitive to Native American culture and values. It would be a perfect program for formative, responsive evaluation in the framework of the alternative paradigm. Instead, program staff have been forced to create the illusion of an experimental, pretest and posttest design. The evaluation design has interfered with the program, wasted staff time and resources, and is an example par excellence of forcing the collection of worthless information under the guise of maintaining scientific standards.

The second example is quite similar, but concerns the Minnesota State Department of Education. The project officers for an innovative arts program in a free school are insisting on quantitative, standardized test measures collected in pretest and posttest situations; a control group is also required. The arts program is being tried out in a free school as an attempt to integrate art and basic skills. Students are selfselected and participation is irregular; the program has multiple goals, all of them vague; even the target population is fuzzy; and the treatment depends on who is in attendance on a given day. The free school is a highly fluid environment for which nothing close to a reasonable control or comparison group exists. The teaching approach is highly individualized, with students designing much of their program of study. Both staff and students resent the imposition of rigid, standardized criteria which give the appearance of a structure that is not there. Yet the State Department of Education insists on a static, hypothetico-deductive evaluation approach.

On the other hand, the direction of the design error is not always the imposition of overly rigid experimental formats. Campbell and Boruch (1975) have shown that many evaluations suffer from an underutilization of more rigid designs. They made a strong case for randomized assignment to treatments by demonstrating six ways in which quasiexperimental evaluations in compensatory education tend to underestimate effects.

Matching high quality methods to programs and decisionmaker needs is a creative process that emerges from a thorough knowledge of the organizational dynamics and information uncertainties of a particular context. Regulations to the effect that all evaluations must be of a certain type serve neither the cause of increased scientific knowledge nor that of greater program effectiveness—thus the active-reactive-adaptive role of the utilization-focused evaluator.

Reliability versus Validity: Shades of Emphasis

Any consideration of paradigms in science must focus on dominant motifs and patterns. Paradigms tell scientists what to emphasize, what to look for, what questions to be concerned with, and what standards to apply. *Competing paradigms raise questions of emphasis.* It is our contention that the dominant paradigm in scientific research, with its quantitative emphasis, has been preoccupied with reliability, while the alternative paradigm emphasizes validity.

Reliability concerns the replicability and consistency of scientific findings. Of particular concern here are interrater, interitem, interviewer, observer, and instrument reliability. Validity, on the other hand, concerns the meaning and meaningfulness of the data collected and instrumentation employed. Does the instrument measure what it purports to measure? Do the data mean what we think they mean?

Merton (1957: 448), one of the most prominent theorists in sociology, has argued that the cumulative nature of science requires a high degree of consensus and therefore leads to an inevitable enchantment with problems of reliability. That scientific research has been preoccupied with questions of reliability is certainly true, but it is not necessary. Irwin Deutscher (1970: 33) has stated the problem with great cogency:

> We have been absorbed in measuring the amount of error which results from inconsistency among interviewers or inconsistency among items on our instruments. We concentrate on consistency without much concern with what it is we are being consistent about or whether we are consistently right or wrong. As a consequence we may have been learning a great deal about how to pursue an incorrect course with a maximum of precision.
>
> It is not my intent to disparage the importance of reliability per se; it is the obsession with it to which I refer. Certainly zero reliability must result in zero validity. But the relationship is not linear, since infinite perfection of reliability (zero error) may also be associated with zero validity. Whether or not one wishes to emulate the scientist and whatever methods may be applied to the quest for knowledge, we must make our estimates of, allowances for, and attempts to reduce the extent to which our methods distort our findings.

The problem with the standardized tests in Shapiro's study of open education Follow Through classrooms (1973) was not that they were unreliable, but that they were not valid measures of the learning taking place in those classrooms. Yet the suggestion that standardized tests may be an inappropriate measure of learning is met with the rejoinder that abandoning such tests means sacrificing reliability of measurement.

Validity has become a function of frequency of use of some instrument, with the result that the actual behaviors that are supposed to be associated with those instruments may be forgotten. The highly reliable instrument takes on a sanctity that places it above question: "the widespread misconceptions about the so-called IQ provide a particularly flagrant example of such a dissociation. One still hears the term "IQ" used as though it referred, not to a test score, but to a property of the organism" (Anastasi,

1973: xi). Likewise, Bernstein and Freeman (1975) seemed to consider reliability to be a sufficient indicator of validity; their example of adequate content validity in measurement procedures was the use of standardized reading comprehension, vocabulary, and arithmetic tests in an educational program aimed at increasing cognitive ability of mentally retarded children. All tests had been pretested for reliability on similar target populations; five repeated measures were taken over a two year period. Reliability was thus established, but no separate evidence for validity was offered!

When one actually looks at the operational definitions and measures of major educational and social scientific concepts, their transparency and bias are frequently astounding, though their reliability is extremely high. Many evaluators routinely use the same instruments for quite different programs, despite the fact that identical responses can mean different things in different settings and different contexts. The only way to discern such variations in shades of meaning is to directly interact with and observe respondents in the various relevant settings. Instruments prepared for evaluation in one setting are often adopted for evaluation in other settings with a facility that shows insensitivity to the issue of cross-setting validity. This does not mean that every evaluation must include development of new instrumentation. But every evaluator must include some effort to establish the validity of the instrumentation or measurement approach adopted for the setting in which it is used.

The alternative evaluation paradigm makes the issue of validity central by getting close to the data, being sensitive to qualitative distinctions, developing empathy with program participants, and attempting to establish a holistic perspective on the program. The overriding issue in the Verstehen approach to science is the meaning of the scientist's observations and data, particularly for the participants themselves. The constant focus is on a valid representation of what is happening, not at the expense of reliable measurement, but without allowing reliability to determine the nature of the data.

Discussion of varying the differential emphasis on reliability and validity in the two paradigms is particularly difficult because the ideal in both paradigms is high reliability and high validity. Nevertheless, differences in practice between the two are clearly discernible. The differences are a matter of emphasis and attention, but it it to such differences that competing paradigms owe their separate strengths and weaknesses.

Induction versus Deduction

The thrust of the dominant paradigm in evaluation research is a concern with theory verification and with the discovery of scientific laws through quantitative methods applied to uncover patterns of behavior based on comparative analysis of aggregated data. The scientist begins with hypotheses and proceeds to test these hypotheses across particular settings. The hypothetico-deductive paradigm is thus directed at producing generalizations. The assumption that this is the goal of science is so deeply ingrained that it is virtually true by definition. Science is the search for generalizations.

Yet in evaluation research, the focus on comparisons and generalizations can detract from identification and recognition of important and unique program characteristics. This contrast is once again a matter of emphasis rather than of the wholesale advocacy of one approach or the other. Dunkel (1972: 80), for example, questions the emphasis in most educational evaluation research studies on virtually nothing but norms, standards, aggregated change scores, and prediction equations:

> But this very interest perhaps unduly distracts attention from the degree to which education is idiosyncratic as well as nomothetic. Teachers rarely feel they are facing merely 3 to 300 incarnations of points on a distribution; they hope they are educating Johnny Johnson and Suzy Smith. But, to those espousing the narrow definition (of Science), dealing with the individual is usually considered an affair of art (medicine curing this patient) or technology (engineering building this bridge); the whole conceptual apparatus of science, along with its counterparts in educational philosophy and educational research, is often seen as inapplicable.

There are two ways in which an inductive approach gives attention to individual cases. Within programs, an inductive approach begins with the idiosyncratic experiences of program participants without first pigeonholing those experiences; between programs, such an approach looks for unique program characteristics that make it a case unto itself. At either level, generalizations may later emerge in the course of analyzing the content of case materials, but the initial focus is on fully understanding individual cases before combining or aggregating those unique cases.

In technical terms, evaluation researchers sometimes recognize individuality when they discuss "disordinal interactions," i.e., treatments interacting with individual variables in program experiments. This simply means that there may be some innovations that work better for certain types of clients rather than showing across-the-board effects. Both Cronbach (1966) and Kagan (1966) have expressed the belief that the discovery method works better for some students than for others; some students will perform better with inductive teaching, and some will respond better to didactic teaching. Stolurow (1965) has also suggested that learning strategies interact with individual variables.

Though such suggestions are hardly news to teachers (they know that children learn in different ways, though they do not always know how to take those differences into account in their teaching), disordinal interactions have rarely been uncovered in experimental research. Bracht and Glass (1968: 449) report that while there are convincing arguments as to why one should expect disordinal interactions, "the empirical evidence for disordinal interactions is far less convincing than the arguments." In point of fact, the actual search for disordinal interactions is rare—most researchers do not bother with the difficult statistical analyses necessary or fail to measure relevant variables:

> the *molarity* (as opposed to the *molecularity*) of both personological variables and the treatments incorporated into many experiments *may* tend to obscure disordinal interactions which *might* be observable when both the variables and the treatments are more narrowly defined . . . searching for such interactions with treatments as necessarily complex as instructional curricula may be fruitless (Bracht and Glass, 1968: 451-452).

In effect, Bracht and Glass preferred to dismiss the question rather than call into question the methodology that fails to find and predict individual differences. But for program staff, particularly staff in innovative programs aimed at individualizing treatment, the question cannot be dismissed. Indeed, for these staff, the central issue in the treatment process is how to identify and deal with individual differences in clients. Any serious and prudent observer knows that such differences exist, but experimental designs consistently fail to uncover them (e.g., Shapiro, 1973). Is it any wonder that practitioners find so much of evaluation research useless and irrelevant?

Where the emphasis is on individualization of teaching or on meeting the needs of individual clients in social action programs, an evaluation strategy is needed that can take the individual into account. A methodology that takes the individual into account must be sensitive both to unique characteristics in people and programs and to similarities among people and generalizations about treatments. This is not a call for psychological reductionism but rather an expression of what C. Wright Mills (1961) called "the sociological imagination"—i.e., a focus on the intersection of biography and history, attention to the interaction of the individual and social structure. Consider the case of teacher centers.

Feiman (1977) reports that most teacher center programs advocate individualization in that teachers are allowed to begin at their own beginnings, draw on personal strengths, and learn at their own pace. This creates special problems in evaluating the outcomes of teacher center experiences, particularly in interpreting varying levels of change in order to make interpretations about improvement. Measuring improvement for evaluation purposes turns out to be very tricky. The first problem is determining the level at which learners enter the situation. For any given knowledge area or skill, there are upper limits of competency: one cannot show improvement indefinitely. It is well-established that learning occurs most rapidly when one is just beginning to study a new subject, simply because there is more to learn at the beginning. After a time, percentage gains decline. Persons who have never driven a car can improve their skills 100 percent; those who have driven for years may only be able to show a small percentage gain after further instruction. How can the large percentage gains in a program of novices be compared to the small percentage gains in a program of experts? Teacher centers include both!

An individualized teacher center program requires an individualized set of evaluation change criteria that take into consideration where a teacher begins, what the teacher wants and needs, and what changes occur after the experience. This may mean a careful system of descriptive records for teacher center participants (or a sample thereof) not unlike the record-keeping systems developed by Carini (1975) for observing changes in students over time. Such a system permits recording some types of information about each teacher but also permits the collection of systematic data on the individual development of each teacher. Such records serve program advisors for both planning and evaluation purposes.

The point here is that *an evaluation system is worthless if it collects data about the wrong things.* Observing changes in a highly individualized program means monitoring and describing different changes for different individuals and then looking for overall patterns of participant change and learner activity in the programs. Aggregated data disguises more than it reveals about such programs. Deductive hypotheses presuppose knowledge of the relevant dimensions of change and the nature of the relationship among those dimensions. But as social science theorist Jerald Hage (1977) recently noted, the simple linear and additive equations that characterize the current state of behavioral and social science have not explained very much. The real world is made up of curvilinear, multivariate, and interactive relationships. The observable fruits of classical hypothetico-deductive social science experimentation hardly justify its domination of evaluation research.

The effects of the overriding concern with verifying deductive generalizations in the dominant paradigm include emphasis on ever larger samples, inclusion of an ever increasing number of cases in research studies, and increasing distance from and quantification of data. Case studies have fallen into disrepute in social science, although for certain types of questions, they are still very much needed in evaluation research. When the evaluation is aimed at improvement of a specific program, when the information collected is for participants and not just scientists, when the concern is for individuals rather than broad generalizations, then an inductive case study approach that identifies unique characteristics and idiosyncracies can be invaluable. Case studies can and do accumulate. Anthropologists have built up an invaluable wealth of case study data that includes both idiosyncratic information and patterns of culture. There is every reason to believe that the young discipline of evaluation research would be well served by a similar approach—and perhaps more important, that program administrators and participants would be better served by in depth case studies of their programs than by large-scale comparative studies aimed at finding similarities across program treatments. Not the least benefit of the approach we have called the alternative paradigm is that the results are readily understandable to program participants, so that their alienation from science and scientists is likely to be diminished—a humanistic consideration that has received little more than lipservice in most evaluation research.

Uniformity versus Diversity

The dominance of the hypothetico-deductive paradigm has contributed to asking overly simplified questions in the search for the one best way to conduct programs. This positivistic perspective has had an important effect on governmental policymaking and on research funding, especially for evaluation and policy research. Legislators would like to find a single solution, so they mandate research to tell them the answer—the one answer—to educational, health, welfare, human relations, bureaucratic, and other questions. Which educational model is best? What is the one best way to organize government? Which one program approach is most effective in reducing crime and rehabilitating criminals?

The truth is that there is no one best program approach across the board. There is no single factor or set of factors that can solve the mystery of human behavior, no one answer to the fundamental philosophical question: why do people do what they do? (Nor is there a single answer to that most fundamental of governmental questions: how do we get people to do what we want them to do?)

Individual people and programs are different from each other in unique ways—ways that make a difference in what people do and how they respond to programs. From the structuralist perspective that dominates social science, individual people do not make a difference. We learn in introductory sociology that the major characteristic of modern society as a rational system is the interchangeability of people in positions. According to this rationale, it does not matter who runs an educational program, the trick is to structure it effectively. Nor does it matter who uses evaluation information, the task is simply to generate quality information. But individual people and individual circumstances can make the major difference in what happens. Indeed, the personal factor (described in Chapter 4 as the key factor in determining the utilization of evaluation research) demonstrates the importance of individual people and individual cases.

This means that instead of searching for that single model of education, health, or welfare that will work everywhere, legislators and government administrators must find ways to stimulate innovation and adaptation of programs to fit unique local needs and circumstances. Evaluation of such programs must also be initially based on the unique characteristics and goals of local programs, not automatic evaluation by standardized criteria applied across the board.

The search for solutions will go on to be sure, both in science and in education. But the search ought not be for the *One* Solution. Rather, we must search for situational solutions: what is best for this program at this time in these circumstances? How can we help staff accomplish their goals? The challenge is to identify and implement alternatives, not to make universal prescriptions that treat people and projects as if they are all the same. The search for solutions to the problem of enhancing program effectiveness does not rest on any single methodological approach because no single, uniform approach will do the job in all situations. Utilization-focused evaluation is built on diversity and adaptability, not on uniformity and rigidity.

Making Paradigmatic Decisions

This chapter has outlined two paradigms of evaluation research through a set of dichotomies: qualitative versus quantitative methodology, subjectivity versus objectivity, closeness to versus distance from the data, holistic versus component analysis, fixed versus dynamic system perspectives, reliability versus validity, induction versus deduction, and uniformity versus diversity. In reality, these are not dichotomies but continua about which evaluators and scientists vary. These continua constitute *dimensions of choice* for evaluators and decisionmakers in matching methods to programs.

> [M]ethodology, whether descriptive or inferential, experimental or non-experimental, can seldom obtain valid results unless closely associated with substantive knowledge of the process being studied. Objective experimental procedures which are designed to unequivocally answer the wrong question are of little use. . . . *The problem seems to be to combine validity of the question with validity of the answer;* to combine the ability to determine causal relationships within the system with valid criteria for determining their relative importance. The issue is not resolved by claiming that "soft," subjective evaluation is inherently more sensitive to the true concerns of the people involved, or more sensitive to long-range goals and unanticipated outcomes. Rather, it becomes a question of balancing the measureable against the unmeasureable; theoretical knowledge against empirical knowledge; and the concerns of the investigator. This choice is closely related to evaluative purpose . . . and to level of evaluative feedback involved (Bennett and Lumsdaine, 1975: 20; emphasis added).

Combining validity of the question with that of the answer is partly a matter of matching decisionmaker and evaluator paradigmatic perspectives. Involving identified decisionmakers and information users in the making of measurement and design decisions is based on the assumption that utilization is enhanced if users understand, believe in, and have a stake in the data. Understanding, belief, and interest are all increased when evaluator and decisionmaker paradigms match. Nevertheless, the making of decisions about what data to collect—and how to collect it—is a painstaking process. The final design of an evaluation depends partially upon calculated paradigmatic options and considerations and partially upon opportunity, resources, time constraints, and commitment. What should be avoided is the routine selection of a design without consideration of its strengths and weaknesses. To do so is to risk being the victim of narrow paradigmatic blinders. Selective perception can lead the evaluator to miss results that are quite open and visible to those without narrow preconceptions about the nature of evaluation data.

There is no way to look at everything in an evaluation. Multiple methods are preferable, but there are always more methods possible than resources available. Selectivity and simplification are inevitable, thus the introduction of selective perception—and of bias. As noted in the opening sections of this chapter, all scientific systems of definition and classification are perceptual, artificial, and arbitrary. Whose definitions prevail at any given time and place is a matter of politics, persuasion, paradigms, and preference. When we understand the inevitable selectivity of our own paradigms, we can also understand how bias is inevitable. Bias has been considered the fire-breathing dragon of methodology, an evil to be avoided at all costs. In utilization-focused evaluation, paradigmatic bias is not hidden and feared because open and explicit paradigmatic and methodological bias can contribute to relevance and focus in framing and researching evaluation questions.

The fundamental issue is whose values will bias the question, not whether or not questions will be biased. In a very real sense all questions are biased, but biased questions can be either open or loaded. Loaded questions have predetermined answers; open questions can be answered in more than one way. Open evaluation questions reflect the values and interests of the persons asking the question, but the answers are not predetermined.

The challenge in selecting evaluation methods is to do justice to the question by providing the most valid and reliable answers possible with the resources available. This means selecting those methods that are most appropriate to answering the question within the meaning framework (bias) of decisionmakers and information users. In utilization-focused evaluation, bias becomes a friendly, helpful dragon. In the story of Han, the Great Cloud Dragon saved the city from destruction. In applied research the great dragon of bias may save evaluators not from destruction but from neglect. Utilization is enhanced when decisionmakers understand, believe in, and have a stake in evaluation data.

One evaluator in our federal utilization study interviews articulated this perspective with considerable feeling. His statement therefore provides a summary for this chapter.

Let me give you a pet bias. . . . My pet bias is that for some of these studies, people who use them get turned off by large series of numbers and sort of very sophisticated model building and this kind of stuff. They tend to think, "All right, so you've done all of this, but we don't understand a damn thing about this." What I'm pushing for, and that's why I opened my statement by saying this is a bias of mine, what I'm pushing for is really the appropriateness of the method to the setting.

We said in the beginning of our report that if we were to go into these centers at that time, with a set kind of questionnaire asking for numbers and whatnot, we'd never gain entry in the first place. Even if we did gain entry, what good is it? So my bias is to think constantly in terms of the contextual setting of these places. . . .

I guess what I'm saying is that part of the reason our study may have been as successful as it was . . . is that I think that we reported basically other people's stories to them. We tried to put a structure on it, we tried to analyze it but we were not going in with any kind of a priori kinds of assumptions. And I don't think we could have, because I don't think we understood enough about what was going on, and I think that would have gotten us into a great deal of trouble. We could have come out with a (statistical) thing probably sort of ending up very much the same as this, but I think basically we would have lost a lot of the kinds of oomph that we have in this sort of thing. So I guess what I'm arguing for is that, *depending on what one is looking for, I think one has to use an enormous range of ways of evaluating.* Just to stick to one kind of model, I think, is going to be problematic (EV4: 21).

Chapter 11

THE MEANINGS OF EVALUATION DATA:

ANALYSIS, INTERPRETATION,

DISSEMINATION, AND UTILIZATION

A Setting

"What is the sound of one hand clapping?" This question was first posed by the Japanese Zen Master Hakuin (1686-1769) as a means of facilitating enlightenment. "The disciple, given a Koan [riddle] to see through, was encouraged to put his whole strength into the singleminded search for its solution, to be 'like a thirsty rat seeking for water . . . ,' to carry the problem with him everywhere, until suddenly, if he were successful, the solution came (Hoffman, 1975: 22). The Koan is a technique originated by the Zen masters to shake their students out of routine ways of thinking and acting, open up new possibilities, and help individual students realize their full potential. The active-reactive-adaptive evaluator is engaged in some of these same processes. The utilization-focused evaluation helps decisionmakers stand outside the program and look at what is happening; evaluations can help shake staff out of routine ways of doing things, open up new possibilities, and help programs realize their full potential.

This comparison of the evaluation process to the Zen search for enlightenment is not frivolous. Religion and philosophy are ultimately personal, perceptual, and interpretive mechanisms for establishing the meaning of life; evaluation research is ultimately a personal, perceptual, and interpretive approach to establishing the meaning—and meaning-fulness—of human service activities. Leaps of faith are often involved in making sense out of research data. The Zen search through Koans consists of three basic parts: a question, an answer, and interpretation/assimilation

of the answer in terms of the student's own life; evaluation research
involves a question, an empirical answer, and interpretation/utilization
of the answer in the context of the program's own dynamics. A fundamental tenet of the Koan educational method is that *the question is as
important as the answer*; the same principle applies to utilization-focused
evaluation. The Zen Master carefully matches the Koan to the student; the
responsive evaluator focuses on questions that are relevant to specific
decisionmakers. In Zen there are many pathways to enlightenment; in
paradigm-flexible evaluation there are multiple methods available for use
in the search for information. Finally, the Zen student must struggle to
make sense out of the answer to the Koanic riddle; in evaluation the
meaning of empirical data is always a matter of interpretation, elucida-
tion, and situational application. Consider the following Koanic exchange
entitled "A Flower in Bloom."

A monk asked Master Ummon, "What is the pure body of truth?"
Master Ummon said, "A flower in bloom."
Monk: "'A flower in bloom'—what's it mean?"
Master: "Maggot in the shit hole, pus of leprosy, scab over a boil."
(Hoffman, 1975: 119).

"What's it mean?" may be a philosophical, religious, or epistemological
question. It can also be the very concrete, practical question of researchers
or program staff pouring over pages of statistical tables and reams of
computer printout generated by an evaluation study. In evaluation, the
answer one hopes for is that "it means something; it tells us something
about what to do." For any given set of data the answer depends on who is
interpreting the data.

The truism that where some people see flowers, others see maggots is
regularly and consistently ignored in the design and interpretation of
evaluation studies. Too often evaluators and decisionmakers behave as if
there is some body of data out there that has only to be collected in order
to reveal what it all means, whether or not it works, and whether or not
the program is effective. But such data simply do not exist outside the
context of a specific group of people with a particular perspective. It is
for this reason that utilization-focused evaluation begins with identification and organization of relevant decisionmakers and information users.
This is also why data analysis and interpretation processes depend on the
active participation of decisionmakers and information users, because
in the end they are the ones who must translate data into decision and
action.

Establishing Standards of Desirability:
Planning for Data Analysis before Data Collection

Evaluators and applied social scientists have traditionally limited the issue of research utilization to the question of dissemination. The social scientist determines the question, constructs a social experiment to study it, collects, analyzes, and interprets the data, and then publishes the findings so they can be used (e.g., Fairweather, 1967: 199-210). Traditionally, utilization is not an issue until there is something concrete to use. By contrast, utilization-focused evaluation plans for utilization before data are ever collected. The question that underlies the interactions between evaluators and decisionmakers is "what difference would that information make?" The evaluator asks: "what would you do if you had an answer to that question?"

During the early conceptualization phases of the evaluation, this question is fairly general, and responses are equally general or vague. But once the context has been delineated, the evaluation research question focused, and methods selected, the evaluator can pose quite specific data analysis questions—before any data are collected. Decisionmakers look at the possible variation in evaluation findings and discuss their implications for action and decision. For example, if recidivism in a community corrections program is 55 percent, is that high or low? Does it mean the program was effective or ineffective? The program had some impact, but what level of impact is desirable? What level is acceptable? What level spells trouble? These issues can be resolved, to some extent, before the data are collected, thus permitting discussions about interpretation and action in an atmosphere that is not charged with defensiveness, rationalization, and justification.

Suppose, for example, that you are evaluating a local teacher center. One of the evaluation questions concerns the extent to which teachers use the center intensively (three or more times) versus more superficial use (once or twice). Data from one such study (Feiman, 1975: 19-21) is shown in Table 11.1 below.

TABLE 11.1: Intensity of Teachers' Use of a Teacher Center*

Number of Visits Made by a Teacher to to the Center	Number of Visits	Percent of Total Visitors
1 or 2	185	80.4
3 or more	45	19.6

*Data are for visits between January 10 and February 28.

Now consider the following scenario. The staff assemble to discuss the final evaluation report.

First staff speaker: "Oh, yes, that's about what we'd anticipated.
Second staff speaker: "Plus, of course, the data don't include people who come to regular workshops and special classes."
Third staff speaker: "Then, too, since only 23 teachers noted on the background forms that they first visited the center during the period of observation, it is not likely that most of the people who came once were first-time visitors. The observation time was really too short."
Fourth staff speaker: "Then, too, January and February are bad months, you know, everyone is depressed with winter, and. . . . "

Soon it becomes apparent that either the data do not tell the staff much, at least not without other data, or that staff are not prepared to deal with what the data do suggest. This is not at all unusual as a postevaluation scenario.

Now let us try another scenario. At the outset of the evaluation study, the program staff discuss their notions of what their task is and how teacher change occurs. They decide that the kind of impact they want to have cannot occur in one or two visits to the teaching center: "if teachers don't return after one or two visits we must be doing something wrong." The period of time in question is a full twelve month period. Before the data are collected the staff complete the following table:

TABLE 11.2: Teacher Center Standards of Desirability

Interpretation of data	Percent and number of teachers who have contact with the center 3 or more times
We're doing an *outstanding job* of engaging teachers at this level	
We're doing an *adequate job* of engaging teachers at this level	
We're doing a *poor job* of engaging teachers at this level	

A recordkeeping system must then be established that staff agree to and believe in so that the data have credibility. The teacher center staff have committed themselves to actively engaging teachers on a multiple contact basis. The data will provide clear feedback about the effectiveness of the program. The key point is that if staff are unwilling or unable to interpret data and set expectancy levels before the evaluation, there is no reason to believe they can do so after the evaluation. In addition, going through this process ahead of time alerts participants to additional data they need in order to make sense of the evaluation; clearly one table on frequency of visits is only a starting place. Involving staff or other decisionmakers in such a process helps clarify the evaluation criteria that are being used. Finally, if decisionmakers are involved in establishing these criteria themselves, the evaluative process may increase their commitment to use the data for program improvement. *Once the evaluation question is formulated in accordance with the basic interests of decision makers, those same decisionmakers ought to be involved in establishing explicit criteria for interpreting the data. Decisionmakers thereby commit themselves to taking the process seriously.*

Many of the most serious conflicts in evaluation research are rooted in the failure to clearly specify standards of desirability in advance of data collection. This can lead both to collection of the wrong data and to intense disagreement about the standards for interpreting data that have already been collected. Without explicit criteria, data can be interpreted to mean almost anything about the program—or to mean nothing at all.

Standards of desirability can be useful in guiding data analysis and interpretation, but such guidance is only useful if the data being analyzed are believable. Our discussion will therefore turn to measurement and design issues related to data credibility because these issues relate to the processes of data analysis and interpretation.

The Believability of Data:
Face Validity in Utilization-Focused Measurement

Involving identified decisionmakers and information users in measurement and design decisions is based on the assumption that utilization is enhanced if users believe in and have a stake in the data. Belief in the data is increased by understanding it; understanding is enhanced by involvement in the painstaking process of making decisions about what data to collect, how to collect it, and how to analyze it. Decisionmakers who acquiesce to the expertise of the evaluator may later find that they neither understand nor believe in the evaluation data. By the same token, evaluators can expect low utilization if they rely on the mysticism of their scientific priesthood to establish the credibility of data rather than on the understanding of decisionmakers directly involved with it.

One of the best ways to facilitate decisionmaker understanding of and belief in evaluation data is to place a high value on the "face validity" of research instruments. Face validity concerns "the extent to which an instrument looks as if it measures what it is intended to measure" (Nunnally, 1970: 149). An instrument has face validity if decisionmakers and information users can look at the items and understand what is being measured. Face validity, however, is generally held in low regard by measurement experts. Predictive validity, concurrent validity, construct validity—these technical approaches are much preferred by psychometricians. Nunnally (1970: 149) considered face validity to have occasional public relations value when data are gathered for the general public: "less logical is the reluctance of some administrators in applied settings, e.g., industry, to permit the use of predictor instruments which lack face validity." Yet from a utilization perspective, it is perfectly logical for decisionmakers to want to understand and believe in data which they are expected to use. Nunnally (1970: 150) disagreed: "although one could make a case for the involvement of face validity in the measurement of constructs, to do so would probably serve only to confuse the issues." It is little wonder that evaluators, most of whom cut their measurement teeth on Nunnally's textbooks, have little sympathy for the face validity needs of decisionmakers. Nor is it surprising that such evaluators complain that their findings are not used. Consider the following case.

The board of directors of a major industrial firm decided to decentralize organizational decisionmaking in hopes of raising work morale. The president of the company hired an organizational consultant to monitor and evaluate the decentralization program and its effects. From the literature on the sociology of organizations, the evaluator selected a set of research instruments designed to measure decentralization, worker autonomy, communication rates and patterns, worker satisfaction, and related organizational dimensions. The scales selected had been generated empirically and used by sociologists to measure organizational change in a number of different settings. The factorial composition of the scales had been established. The instruments had high predictive validity and construct validity, but they had low face validity.

The evaluator selected a simple pretest and posttest design with nine months separating pre- and postadministration of the instruments. Data analysis showed no statistically significant changes between pretest and posttest. The evaluator reported that the decentralization program had not been successfully implemented and that worker morale remained low. These negative findings were reported for the first time at a meeting of the board. The president of the company had a considerable stake in the success of the program; he did not have a stake in the evaluation data. He did what decisionmakers frequently do in such cases—he began to attack the data.

> *President:* "How can you be so sure that the program has not been implemented? How did you determine that the program is ineffective?"
> *Evaluator:* "We collected data using the best instruments available. I won't go into all the technical and statistical details of factor analysis and Cronbach's Alpha. Let me just say that these scales have been shown to be highly valid and reliable."
> Take this scale on "individual autonomy." It's made up of ten items. Each item is an indicator of "autonomy." For example, the best predictor item in this particular scale asks respondents: (a) "Do you take coffee breaks on a fixed schedule?" or (b) "Do you go to get coffee whenever you want to?"
> *President:* (visibly reddening and speaking in an angry tone): "Am I to understand that your entire evaluation is based on some kind of questionnaire that asks people how often they get coffee, that you never personally talked to any workers or managers, that you never even visited our operations?
> "Am I to understand that we paid you $20,000 to find out how people get their coffee?"
> *Evaluator:* "Well, there's a lot more to it than that, you see . . ."
> *President:* "That's it! We don't have any more time for this nonsense. Our lawyers will be in touch with you about whether we want to press fraud and malpractice charges!"

Clearly the president was predisposed to dismiss any negative findings. But suppose the evaluator had gone over the measurement and design decisions with the president before gathering data. Suppose the evaluator had shown him the items, explained what they were suposed to indicate, and then asked: "now, if we administer these questionnaires with these items measuring these factors, *will that tell you what you want to know*? Does this kind of evaluation make sense to you? Are you prepared to act on this kind of data? Would you believe the results if they came out negative?"

Such an exchange might not have made a difference. It is not easy to get decisionmakers to look carefully at instrumentation in advance, nor do evaluators want to waste time explaining their trade. Decisionmakers are just as happy not being bothered with technical decisions—after all, that is why they hired an evaluator in the first place, to design and conduct the evaluation! But the costs of such attitudes to utilization can be quite

high. Utilization-focused evaluation makes the face validity of instrumentation—determined before data are collected—a major criterion in
evaluation measurement. Data analysis, data interpretation, and data
utilization are all facilitated by attention to face validity criteria.

The Credibility of Evaluation Designs

Face validity criteria can also be applied to design questions. Does
the design make sense? Is the decisionmaker interested in a comparison
of group A against group B? Is the sample size sufficiently large to be
believable? The evaluator can be sure that decisionmakers will have
opinions about these issues after the data are collected, particularly if
findings are negative. By engaging the information users in consideration
of these issues before data are collected, the data are likely to be more
credible and more useful. Consider the following case.

At a recent evaluation workshop for human service agencies, the
marketing director for a major retail merchandising company had come
to find out how to get more mileage out of his marketing research department. He told the following story.

Two years earlier (1975), he had spent a considerable sum researching
the potential for new products for his company's local retail distribution
chain. A carefully selected sample of 285 respondents had been interviewed
in the Minneapolis-Saint Paul Greater Metropolitan Area. The results
indicated one very promising new line of products for which there
appeared to be growing demand. He took this finding to the board of
directors with a recommendation that the company make a major capital
investment in the new product line. The board, controlled by the veiws
of its aging chairman, vetoed ihe recommendation. The reason: "if you
had presented us with opinions from at least a thousand people we might
be able to move on this item. But we can't make a major capital commitment on the basis of a couple of hundred interviews."

The marketing director tactfully tried to explain that increased
sample size would have made only a marginal reduction in possible sampling error. The chairman remained unconvinced, the findings of an
expensive research project were ignored, and the company missed out on
a major opportunity: the item they rejected was citizen band radios, the
hottest selling new retail item in the country less than a year after the
survey results were rejected by the board!

It is easy to laugh at the board's mistake, but the marketing director
was not laughing. He wanted to know what to do. I suggested that next

time he check out the research design with the board before collecting data, going to them and saying: "our statisticians estimate that a sample of 285 respondents in the Twin Cities area will give us an accurate picture of market potential. Here are the reasons they recommend this sample size. . . . Does that make sense to you? If we come in withe recommendations based on 285 respondents will you believe the data? Can you confidently act on the basis of this research design?"

If the Board responds positively then utilization potential is enhanced. Of course, there are no guarantees. But at least the evaluator has done all that can be done. If the Board says the sample is too small then the survey might as well include more respondents—or be cancelled. There is little point in implementing a design that is known in advance to lack credibility.

The Relevance of Definitions to Data Interpretation

Definitions and classification systems are necessary for simplifying reality. The usefulness of evaluation data frequently rests on the usefulness of the definitions employed to organize the data collected. Of particular importance in this regard are operational definitions of the program's target population. Sampling schemes, determination of comparison or control groups, and specification of targets for observation or interviews— any of these design decisions can undermine the usefulness of evaluation findings if the target population is not meaningfully defined. Meaningfulness is an arbitrary criterion dependent upon the needs, perceptions, and definitions of relevant decisionmakers and information users.

Consider the issue of how to define and classify the target population in a program that is supposed to serve "poor" people. The government offers an official definition of poverty, but is it meaningful to the program at hand? Who will decide what definition prevails? Is poverty the same as being poor? Ideally, such issues would be determined by legislation or explicit program policy, but in practice definitions and classifications of client populations become quite complex.

On more than one occasion a definition or unit of analysis has predetermined evaluation findings. For example, a sociologist in a major city conducted a survey on parent participation for an innovative school. The evaluator decided that relative rates of father and mother participation should be studied, so he only sampled families with two parents. The survey found, among other things, that the school served a relatively wealthy population, which made the front page of the local newspaper. The local school teachers were furious: 60 percent of their children came from single parent, female head of household families (all of whom had been excluded from the evaluation by the sampling design), almost none of whom could be classified as "relatively wealthy." The evaluator had never discussed sampling with the school staff, clearly feeling that sample selection was a technical issue to be decided by the methodologist.

Another example is that early in the evaluation of a "family service" program, decisionmakers were asked to define their target population as part of the goals clarification process. What is a family? Who has to be doing what with whom under what conditions before we call a group a family? That turns out to be a complicated question in this last quarter of the twentieth century in North America. In this case, the program staff decided that families were no longer the relevant unit of analysis. During a century of service, the program had shifted from serving families to serving individuals, which made a big difference in the evaluation design.

In our study of the utilization of federal health evaluations, one decisionmaker described being "horrified when we got back the data and saw that it was all family aggregate data" (DM51: 17). The purpose of the evaluation was to determine if mental health centers were effectively reaching their target populations. The decisionmaker remarked throughout his interview that the family aggregate data was useless; what he wanted was highly specific, individual data. From his perspective the centers served individuals, not families. He commented at length about practical measurement and design problems that diminished the study's utility because, being familiar with program details, he could easily identify shortcomings in the data. He was most concerned with what he considered to be inappropriate definitions and units of analysis. The evaluator, on the other hand, was quite unaware of the decisionmaker's concerns; the evaluation had been well received in academic circles and was considered of high quality. When asked directly about the methodological quality of the study in question, the evaluator responded with selfcongratulatory enthusiasm:

> Super. It ought to have been, we spent enough money. No, I think, really, I think it really was good, and you know, we had severe critics from everywhere reviewing it as we went along to maintain the technical quality of the research, because, you know, one of the reasons that the thing was sort of pedantic and pedestrian was that we really attempted to maintain a quality stance. Because of that I think it was highly regarded by those who were prepared to be our critics.

If the methodological quality had not been as high, it would have been very easy to damn the entire thing. If you can pick out flaws in certain logic about the study design, it's very easy to make the transition to say the whole study was no good, and to pooh-pooh results which may have been perfectly valid, *given whatever the set of assumptions was that the researchers were working on.* But we were certainly aware of this, and aware of this potential pitfall, and really worked very hard at overcoming any potential problems. And I mean long hours. This is one thing that the project director was especially supportive in, because he was a very bright person, he knew research design, he knew study design inside and out, and he knew the pitfalls that we were going to run into if we weren't careful. He just kept us on our toes the whole time (EV51: 18-19).

Contrast the evaluator's perspective to that of the decisionmaker for this same study. The decisionmaker, who was head of an upper level division and quite knowledgeable about research, was asked to rate the quality of the same evaluation.

Obviously not high, I would say probably average for many evaluation studies of that generation. Low quality in terms of what we would have preferred. From a program standpoint, or from the program evaluation standpoint. . . . In terms of usefulness of data, I don't give any high marks at all.

It was just not useable for follow up analysis. Very limited, limited analysis has been done on it. This is what happens to most surveys. It's creamed at 5 percent of the data, and nothing else is taken out of it. The basic thing was the interview schedule itself, just not well done at all. The major deficiency being the aggregation of utilization data by family. The field health services and health survey research have known, and we had known generations before that, that family utilization data is not useful. That is without the ability to disaggregate by individuals (DM51: 11).

The evaluators had worked hard to conduct an evaluation project of high quality—given the assumptions with which they began. What they failed to do was check out their assumptions about the appropriate unit of analysis with relevant decisionmakers who would be directly using the results.

Interpreting Data Over Time

Another important reason for paying close attention to operationaliza-tion and definition of key concepts, unit of analysis, and client descriptions is that decisionmakers may have to live with those definitions for a long time. As evaluation research becomes an integral part of program development, the need for longitudinal data becomes more pronounced. Long-term monitoring of program effectiveness can produce large information dividends, but longitudinal comparisons depend upon the collection of the initial data base in categories that are meaningful and useful over time. Changes in definition produce changes in the meaning of the data. While such changes are inevitable over long periods of time (as new conditions and needs arise), they can be reduced by careful attention to initial conceptualizations and operationalizations.

Such a definitional change occurred at the national level in February, 1978, when the Federal Bureau of Labor Statistics began issuing a new Consumer Price Index. The index was first compiled in 1913, and had been most recently revised in 1968. Since 1968, it had covered only the buying habits of blue collar and clerical workers. The new index will include the very rich and the very poor—professionals and businesspersons at one end of the income ladder, welfare recipients and the unemployed at the other. The new sample includes more poor than rich (in proportion to their incidence in the population). Thus, this definitional change away from a sample made up exclusively of wage earners will lower the average annual income of those counted from $12,200 to $11,700. The new Consumer Price Index also samples different items. Instead of limiting its survey to 400 specific items, the new index will be based on monthly checks of several thousand items on a scale adjusted to their frequency of purchase in each retail unit. The sample of stores will also be broadened from 18,000 units to 21,000.

The broader coverage of the new index is both its strength and its weakness. So much money for so many groups rides on the ups and downs of the index that there is considerable demand for creating a whole series of scales, with separate breakdowns for the elderly, the poor, farmers, and urban consumers as well as for wage earners. Julius Shiskin, commissioner of labor statistics and chief architect of the new index, has estimated that the incomes of fully half the population are now automatically escalated when the overall index goes up. Besides the 31.2 million Social Security recipients, that total includes 8.5 million workers covered by cost-of-living clauses in labor-management contracts and 2.4 million pensioners under federal Civil Service and military retirement systems. The index is also a guide to allowances for 19.6 million food stamp recipients and 25.2 million children in school lunch programs; to establishment of the poverty thresholds and "low income" standards that trigger release of federal manpower training and welfare funds; and to escalator payments under scores of private arrangements, from alimony agreements to industrial leases (Raskin, 1977).

While definitional changes in most programs will have considerably less national impact than the change in the Consumer Price Index, the impact on a particular program can be substantial. Research quality is to a large extent a function of careful definition and operationalization. Focusing on the immediate information needs of decisionmakers does not mean that long-range evaluation possibilities are to be ignored.

Research Quality and Utilization of Findings: Leaping From Limited Data to Incremental Action

Although it is well to emphasize the power of research and evaluation to aid decisionmaking and improve program effectiveness, not all evaluation research studies are of sufficiently high quality to accomplish these ends. Mushkin (1973), for example, advises decisionmakers to use extreme caution when applying the findings of evaluation research. From his point of view, most evaluations are of such poor methodological quality that they do not deserve to be used.

As this book goes to press, the Senate Committee on Appropriations is studying the poor quality and high costs of government funded research. In reporting the committee investigation, the New York Times Service related the following story:

> The U.S. Department of Agriculture (USDA) hired a prestigious management consulting firm, Booz, Allen & Hamilton, to find out how to cut the cost of meat and poultry inspections. It was told that the industry could do more selfpolicing and that the chickens, which pass federal inspectors at a rate of 25 a minute, could be speeded up.
>
> This report so outraged consumers and poultry packers that the department asked another consultant to study the study.
>
> "Awful," concluded Rodney E. Leonard, executive director of the Community Nutrition Institute. The USDA, he said last week, "could have done it better in-house for less than a tenth the cost."
>
> The price of the first study was $320,000; the second, $8,000 (Thomas, 1977).

Studies of poor methodological quality ought not be funded in the first place, and if funded, they ought not be used. While this assertion is difficult to disagree with, it turns out on closer inspection to be overly simplistic. In this section on research quality four points will be made. (1) Research quality never arises as an issue in the utilization of many evaluations; in the search for information, decisionmakers use whatever is available to help reduce uncertainty. (2) Research "quality" means different things to different people. (3) There are no methodologically perfect studies. (4) Given the preceeding three points, the best way to make sure that decisionmakers and information users understand the methodological limitations of studies, and take those limitations into consideration in funding evaluations and using evaluation findings, is to actively involve them in making methods decisions, i.e., to have them participate in deciding which methodological imperfections they are willing to live with in making the eventual interpretive leaps from limited data to incremental action.

The first question is how much weight decisionmakers give to research quality when interpreting evaluation findings. In our own study of utilization, respondents placed little emphasis on methodological quality as a factor explaining utilization. Of the 15 decisionmakers who rated the methodological quality of the study about which they were interviewed, one third rated it as "high," 53 percent said it was "medium," and only 13 percent gave the study a "low" rating. Of 17 responding evaluators, there were 41 percent high, 35 percent medium, and 24 percent low ratings. No decisionmaker and only one evaluator felt that the methodology used was inappropriate for researching the question at issue.

More to the point, only four decisionmakers felt that methodological quality was "very important' in explaining the study's utilization. *In no case was methodological quality identified as the most important factor explaining either utilization or nonutilization.*

The effects of methodological quality on utilization must be understood in the full context of a study, its political environment, the degree of uncertainty with which the decisionmaker is faced, and thus his or her relative need for any and all clarifying information. If information is scarce, then new information, even if of dubious quality, may be somewhat helpful. For example, one administrator admitted that the evaluation's methodological rigor could be seriously questioned, but said the study was highly useful in policy discussions.

> The quality and methodology was not even considered. All that was considered was that management didn't know what was going on, the terms, the procedures, the program was foreign to their background. And they did not have expertise in it, so they were relying on somebody else who had the expertise to translate to them what was going on in terms that they would understand (DM312: 17).

Social scientists may lament this situation and may well feel that the methodology of evaluation research ought to be of high quality for value reasons, i.e., because poor quality studies ought not be used (cf. Rutman, 1977). *But there is little in our data to suggest that improving methodological quality in and of itself will have much effect on increasing the utilization of evaluation research.* No matter how rigorous the methodology and no matter how sophisticated the statistical manipulations, evaluation research will only be useful in proportion to its relevance to decisionmakers' questions.

Moreover, the relative unimportance of methodological quality as a factor explaining utilization is tempered by the nature of the utilization we found. Were evaluations being used as the major piece of information in making critical one-time decisions, methodological rigor might be paramount. But where evaluation research is one part in a larger whole, decisionmakers displayed less than burning interest in methodological quality. Rather, decisionmakers were more concerned that findings be at least sufficiently relevant that the data could be used to give some direction to pending action. One evaluator tied the research quality issue to the nature of uncertainty in organizational decisionmaking. This evaluator fully recognized the inadequacies in the data he had collected, but he had still worked with the decisionmaker to apply the findings, fully recognizing their problematic nature:

> You have to make the leap here from very limited data. I mean, that's what a decision's like. You make it from a limited data base; and damn it, when you're trying to use quantitative data and it's inadequate, you supposedly can't make a decision. Only you're not troubled by that. You can use impressionistic stuff. Yeah, your intuition is a lot better. I get a gestalt out of this thing on every program.
>
> This may come as a great shock to you, but that is what you use to make decisions. In Chester Barnard's definition, for example, the function of the executive is to make a decision in the absence of adequate information (EV148: 11).

It is in this context that research substance and relevance become more important to decisionmakers than research quality. Thus, the evaluator quoted above felt that the payoff from his evaluation was quite exemplary—despite admitted methods inadequacies.

> Well it was a pretty small investment on the part of the government—$47,000 bucks. In the evaluation business that's not a pile of money. The questions I had to ask were pretty narrow and the answers were equally narrow and relatively decisive, and the findings were put to use immediately and in the long term. So can you beat that? (EV148: 8).

Another evaluator echoed quite similar sentiments. In this case the evaluation had to be completed in only three months.

There are a million things I'd do differently. We should have probably spent more time. . . . I personally could not be satisfied with it. At the time, that was probably the best study we could do, but now it isn't, and that's why I couldn't be satisfied with it. . . . I'm satisfied in the sense that some people found that useful. It really was not just kept on a shelf. There were people who paid attention to that study and it had an impact. Now, I've done other studies that I thought were methodologically really much more elegant that were kind of ignored. Sitting on somebody's shelf.

My opinion is that this really modest kind of study probably has had impact all out of proportion to the quality of the research, and that's my feeling. It happened to be at a certain place at a certain time, where it at least talked about some of the things that people were interested in talking about, so it got some attention. And many other studies that I know of that have been done, not just for ASPE, but in HEW, that I would consider of higher quality, haven't really gotten used (EV145: 34).

To fully understand why issues of research quality are not more critical in affecting utilization, it is helpful to keep in mind that many decision-makers and information users are not highly sophisticated about method-ological questions. But what they have learned and what they do know (almost intuitively) is that the *methods and measurements used in any study are open to question.* McTavish et al. (1975: 63) have provided empirical support for this assertion. In using eminent social scientists to judge and rate the research quality of 126 federal studies, they found that "there appear to be important and meaningful differences between raters in their professional judgments about a project's methodology." Such differences are the basis for paradigm debates (Chapter 10) as well as for disputes about the details of research practice within a particular paradigm. One has only to read the debates over studies of student achievement and educational inequality (e.g., between Coleman and Cain in Rossi, 1972), or the recent "White Flight Debate" (Pettigrew and Green, 1977; Coleman, 1977), to know that there is no absolutely correct way to conduct research or interpret findings. As a result, experienced decisionmakers know that methods are always vulnerable. Knowing this, most program people are more interested in discussing the substance of findings than in the methods used to get the findings. One decisionmaker we interviewed explained his experience with research quality on a com-munity mental health evaluation as follows:

Well, let me put it in another context. If it were negative findings program-matically we would have hit very hard on the methodology and tried to discredit it. You know, from the program standpoint. But since it was kind of positive findings, we said, "Okay, here it is." If anybody asked us about the methodological deficiencies we were never reluctant to tell them what we thought they were. *Not many people asked* (DM51: 10).

In addition to feeling that research methods are always open to debate, many decisionmakers may simply be skeptical about large-scale, elabor-ately designed, carefully controlled studies. The experience to date is not promising. Cohen and Weiss (1977) reviewed 20 years of policy research on race and schools, and found progressive improvement in research methods, with use of increasingly rigorous designs and ever more sophis-ticated analytical techniques. Sample sizes increased, computer technology was introduced, multiple regression and path analytic techniques were employed, and more data gathering instruments were developed. After reviewing the findings of studies produced with these more rigorous methods as well as the uses made of findings from these studies, Cohen and Weiss (1977: 78) concluded that "these changes have led to more studies that disagree, to more qualified conclusions, more arguments, and more arcane reports and unintelligible results." This comes close to positing a clear negative relationship between methodological sophis-tication and utilization of research for policy formulation: the greater the improvement of research on a policy question, the greater the confusion about what the findings mean.

High quality research methods and sophisticated analytical techniques are not the ends of evaluation research, they are means to an end. In utilization-focused evaluation, the question of research quality is tied to questions of methodological appropriateness and research relevance. The concern with relevance does not mean that research quality is unim-portant. It simply means that quality is not the major factor in determining utilization of findings. Decisionmakers cannot wait forever for the perfect study. As one put it:

You can get so busy protecting yourself against criticism that you develop such an elaborate methodology that by the time your findings come out, who cares? So I mean, you get a balance—the validity of the data against its relevance. And that's pretty tough stuff. I mean, that's hard business (DM111: 26).

Utilization-focused evaluation tries to combine a concern for research quality with a concern for relevance by involving decisionmakers in the making of critical methods and measurement decisions. Since no study is ever methodologically perfect, it is important for decisionmakers to know firsthand what imperfections exist—and to be included in deciding which imperfections they will have to live with in making the inevitable leaps from limited data to incremental action.

The Dynamics of Measurement and Design Decisions

Research quality and relevance are not set in stone once a research proposal has been accepted. A variety of factors emerge throughout the life of a research project that require new decisions about methods. Face validity of instruments, the credibility of the research design, and the relevance of research definitions and units of analysis are all factors that affect the credibility and usefulness of evaluation data. Actively involving information users in making decisions about these issues means more than a one-point-in-time acquiescence to a research proposal. It is important that decisionmakers understand and approve initial evaluation research proposals. It is also important that decisionmakers and information users be involved in research decisions that affect what the final design will look like. In every one of the 20 federal health studies we investigated, there were significant methods differences between the original proposal and the project as executed. While little attention has been devoted in the evaluation literature to this phenomenon of slippage between methods as originally proposed and methods as actually implemented, the problem is quite similar to that of program implementation (see Chapter 8).

McTavish et al. (1975) studied the research implementation problem in 126 solicited research projects funded across seven HEW agencies. All 126 projects were rated by independent judges along seven descriptive methodological scales. Both original proposals and final reports were rated; the results showed substantial instability between the two. The researchers concluded:

> Our primary conclusion from the Predictability Study is that the quality of final report methodology is essentially not predictable from proposal or interim report documentation. This appears to be due to a number of factors. First, research is characterized by significant change as it develops over time. Second, unanticipated events force shifts in direction. Third, the character and quality of information available early in a piece of research makes assessment of some features of methodology difficult or impossible. Finally, there appear to be important and meaningful differences between

raters in their professional judgments about the project's methodology (McTavish et al., 1975: 62-63).

Earlier in the report, they had pointed out that

> Among the more salient reasons for the low predictability from early to late documentation is the basic change which occurs during the course of most research. It is, after all, a risky pursuit rather than a pre-programmed product. Initial plans usually have to be altered once the realities of data or opportunities and limitations become known. Typically, detailed plans for analysis and reporting are postponed and revised. External events also seem to have taken an expected toll in the studies we examined. . . . Both the context of research and the phenomena being researched are typically subject to great change (McTavish et al., 1975: 56).

If decisionmakers are involved only at the stage of approving research proposals, they are likely to be surprised when they see a final report. Even interim reports bear only moderate resemblance to final reports. Thus, the making of decisions about research methods is a continuous process that involves checking out changes as they are made. Changes in the details of research design and measurement can have important consequences when the data are analyzed and interpreted. While it is impractical to have evaluator-decisionmaker discussions about every minor change in methods, utilization-focused evaluators prefer to err in the direction of consultative rather than unilateral decisionmaking, when there is a choice. Decisionmakers also carry a responsibility to make sure they are commited to the evaluation. One internal evaluator interviewed in our federal utilization study, still smarting from critiques of his evaluation as methodologically weak, offered the following advice to decisionmakers:

> I'm not going to throw too many rocks at myself, but let me say something on that point. Very, very often those of us who are doing evaluation studies are criticized for poor methodology, and the people who levy the criticism sometimes are the people that pay for the study. You know, they'll do this more often when the study is either late or it doesn't come up with the answers that they were looking for. But I think that a large share of the blame or responsibility goes on the project monitor from the sponsor for not maintaining enough control, direct hands-on contact with the evaluation as it's ongoing.
> I don't think that it's fair to blame a contractor, even those of us within the government who are contractors in a sense to the other government agencies, you can't blame a contractor for developing a poor study approach,

a poor methodology, and absolve yourself, if you're the sponsor, of any, you know, association with that. Because it's your role as a project monitor, project officer, whatever you call yourself, to be aware of what those people that you're paying, you know, what they're doing all the time, and to guide them.

We let contracts out and we keep our hands on these contractors all the time. And when we see them going down a road that we don't think is right, we pull them back and we say, "Hey, you know, we disagree." We don't let them go down the road all the way and then say, "Hey fella, you went down the wrong road" (EV32: 15).

Data Analysis, Interpretation, and Presentation

Thus far this chapter has emphasized the importance of building utilization potential into the evaluation from the very beginning by having decisionmakers and evaluators share in making methods, measurement, and data analysis decisions. Utilization is affected only partially by research quality. Methodological relevance, appropriateness, and clarity— as judged by identified decisionmakers—are major factors in establishing the credibility and validity of evaluation findings, and in establishing standards of desirability before data collection can facilitate the utilization process. Finally, we come to the actual analysis and interpretation of collected data.

The data analysis and interpretation phases are critical in utilization-focused evaluation. This is where the evaluators and decisionmakers look at the data and try to make sense out of it. It is important to separate analysis and interpretation: analysis involves organizing the data, constructing appropriate statistical tables, and arranging for the data to be displayed in an orderly, usable format; interpretation involves making judgments about what the data mean, establishing the implications of the findings, and linking evaluation results to future action. By separating analysis from interpretation, it is possible for users to look at the data analysis alone, draw conclusions, and make interpretations unencumbered by the judgments of the evaluator.

Scriven (1967) has strongly advocated the evaluator's responsibility to draw conclusions from data and make judgments about the evaluation results. Others have argued that the evaluator's job is only to supply the data, that the decisionmaker must make the judgments (e.g. Rosen, 1973). Utilization-focused evaluation incorporates both of these views. The evaluator's job includes making judgments and recommendations, but decisionmakers and information users are first given an opportunity to

TABLE 11.3: Composition of the Group Home Treatment Environment Scale

The items which follow are the 19 juvenile interview items which are highly inter-related statistically in such a way that they can be assumed to measure the same environmental factor. The items are listed in rank order by factor loading (from .76 to .45 for a six-factor ALPHA solution). This means that when the scores were combined to create a single numerical scale the items higher on the list received more weight in the scale (based on factor score coefficients). What underlying factor or theme is represented by the combination of these 22 questions?

(1) The [group home parent name]'s went out of their way to help us.
almost always	30.9%
a lot of times	10.9%
just sometimes	34.5%
almost never	23.6% Factor loading = .76

(2) At ..... 's personal problems were openly talked about.
almost always	20.0%
a lot of time	9.1%
just sometimes	32.7%
almost never	38.2% Factor loading = .76

(3) Did you feel like the group home parents tried to help you understand yourself?
almost always	23.6%
a lot of time	29.1%
just sometimes	23.6%
almost never	23.6% Factor loading = .74

(4) How often did .... 's take time to encourage you in what you did?
almost always	27.3%
a lot of time	20.0%
just sometimes	30.9%
almost never	21.8% Factor loading = .73

(5) At ..... 's house, how much were you each encouraged to make your own decisions about things? Would you say that you were . . .
almost always	18.9%
a lot of times	30.2%
just sometimes	30.2%
almost never	20.8% Factor loading = .68

(6) How often did the .... 's let you take responsibility for making your own decisions?
almost always	23.6%
a lot of times	20.0%
just sometimes	25.5%
almost never	30.9% Factor loading = .67

(7) We really got along well with each other at .... 's.
almost always	23.6%
a lot of times	29.1%
just sometimes	32.7%
almost never	14.5% Factor loading = .66

(8) Would the group home parents tell you when you were doing well?
   almost always   30.9%
   a lot of times   30.9%
   just sometimes   29.1%
   almost never   9.1%   Factor loading = .64

(9) How often were you allowed to openly criticize the group home parents?
   almost always   14.8%
   a lot of times   7.4%
   just sometimes   24.1%
   almost never   53.7%   Factor loading = .59

(10) How much of the time would you say there was a feeling of "togetherness" at
    .... 's?
   almost always   27.3%
   a lot of times   23.6%
   just sometimes   32.7%
   almost never   16.4%   Factor loading = .59

(11) How much did ..... 's help you make plans for leaving the group home and
    returning to your real home?
   almost always   9.1%
   a lot of times   21.8%
   just sometimes   21.8%
   almost never   47.3%   Factor loading = .58

(12) How often would .... 's talk with you about what you'd be doing after you
    left the group home?
   almost always   7.3%
   a lot of times   18.2%
   just sometimes   36.4%
   almost never   38.2%   Factor loading = .58

(13) How much of the time did the kids have a say about what went on at . 's?
   almost always   13.0%
   a lot of times   29.6%
   just sometimes   27.8%
   almost never   29.6%   Factor loading = .56

(14) How much were decisions about what you all had to do at the group home made
    only by the .... 's without involving the rest of you?
   almost always   30.9%
   a lot of times   18.2%
   just sometimes   32.7%
   almost never   18.2%   Factor loading = .56

(15) How much of the time were discussions at .... 's aimed at helping you
    understand your personal problems?
   almost always   23.6%
   a lot of times   23.6%
   just sometimes   18.2%
   almost never   34.5%   Factor loading = .56

(16) How often would the group home parents take time to really find out what the rest of your wanted?

almost always   10.9%
a lot of times   21.8%
just sometimes   38.2%
almost never   29.1%   Factor loading = .54

(17) At ...... 's how much were you all encouraged to plan for the future?

almost always   21.8%
a lot of times   16.4%
just sometimes   30.9%
almost never   30.9%   Factor loading = .53

(18) Eould you say that at ...... 's house, "everyone pretty much kep their feelings to themselves"?

almost always   20.0%
a lot of times   18.2%
just sometimes   36.4%
almost never   25.5%   Factor loading = .51

(19) At .... 's how much would you say "people were ordered around"?

almost always   30.9%
a lot of times   16.4%
just sometimes   40.0%
almost never   12.7%   Factor loading = .49

study the data analysis without the intrusion of the evaluator's interpretations. An example of how this can work in practice follows.

In the Minnesota Center for Social Research evaluation of Ramsey County foster group homes for juvenile offenders, we collected data from natural parents, foster parents, juveniles, and community corrections staff. The identified and organized decisionmakers and information users were the Community Corrections Advisory Board. We worked closely with members of this board in problem identification, research design, and instrumentation. Once the data were collected, we employed a variety of statistical techniques, including alpha factor analysis and stepwise forward regression analysis. We then reduced these findings to some ten pages of data and presented it in simple form in a very readable format. The 19 items with the highest loadings on the factor analysis were presented with frequency distributions (Table 11-3); descriptive statistics for major dependent and independent variables were included; a series of simple two-by-two tables showing the relationships among major variables were constructed; and finally, a correlation matrix and regression equation predicting recidivism were shown. These materials, with no accompanying narrative, were sent to the decisionmakers. A week later we met with them and discussed their interpretations of the data. At that time they decided to seek broad involvement in the data interpretation, so a half day meeting was arranged for community corrections staff, welfare department staff, court services staff, and members of the county board. That meeting brought together some 40 of the most powerful elected and appointed officials in the county to interpret the evaluation data.

A major purpose of the evaluation was to describe and conceptualize the group home treatment environment. Variations in recidivism, runaway rates, and juvenile attitudes would then be related to variations in environments. The factor analysis of 56 items designed to measure variations in the group home environment did uncover a single major factor. The first factor explained 54 percent of the variance, with 19 items loading above .45 on that factor. *The first task in data interpretation was to label that factor in such a way that its relationship to dependent variables would represent something meaningful to identified information users.* For this purpose we used the group of 40 county officials.

The meeting began with a brief description of the methods and data, which were then distributed. Participants were divided randomly into groups of four people. Each group was asked to look at the 19 items in Table 11-3 and to label the factor or theme represented by those items in their own words. After 15 minutes, each of the ten groups reported a label; discussion followed. Consensus emerged around the terms "participation and support" as representing one end of the continuum and "authoritarian and nonsupportive" for the other end. We also asked the groups to describe the salient elements in the factor. These descriptions were combined with the labels chosen by the group; the resulting conceptualization—as it appeared in the final evaluation report—is shown in Table 11-4.

The groups then studied accompanying tables showing the relationships between this treatment environment factor and program outcome variables. The relationships were statistically significant and quite transparent. Juveniles who reported experiencing more supportive-participatory corrections environments had lower recidivism rates, lower runaway rates, and more positive attitudes. Having established the direction of the data, we discussed the limitations of the findings, methodological weaknesses, and the impossibility of making causal interpretations. Key decisionmakers were already well aware of these problems. Then, given those constraints, the group was asked for recommendations. The basic thrust of the discussion concerned ways to increase the supportive-participatory experiences of juvenile offenders. *The people carrying on*

TABLE 11.4: Group Home Treatment Environment Continuum

Descriptions of Ideal Types

Supportive-Participatory	Nonsupportive-Authoritarian
In group homes nearer this end of the continuum juveniles perceive group home parents as helpful, caring, and interested in them. Juveniles are encouraged and receive positive reinforcements. Juveniles are involved in decisions about what goes on in the home. Kids are encouraged to make their own decisions about the things they do personally. There is a feeling of togetherness, of being interested in each other, of caring about what happens now and in the future. Group home parents discuss the future with the kids and help them plan. There is a feeling of mutual support and kids feel that they can openly express their feelings, thoughts, problems, and concerns.	In group homes nearer this end of the continuum juveniles report that group home parents are less helpful, less open with them and less interested in them personally. Juveniles are seldom encouraged to make their own decisions and the parents tend to make decisions without asking their opinions about things. There isn't much planning things together or talking about the future. Kids are careful about what they say, are guarded about expressing their thoughts and feelings. Kids get little positive reinforcement. There is Not much feeling of togetherness, support, and mutual caring; group home parents kept things well under control.

Relationship Between Different Home Environments and Recidivism

	No Recidivism	Recidivism	Total
Supportive-Participatory Homes	76% (N=19z)	24% (N=6)	100% N=25)
Nonsupportive-Authoritarian Homes	44% (N=11)	56% (N=14)	100% (N=25)

Correlation r = .33
Significant at .009 level

that discussion were the people who fund, operate, and control juvenile offender programs. The final written evaluation report included the recommendations that emerged from that meeting as well as the evaluators' own conclusions and recommendations. But the final, written report took another four weeks to prepare and print; *the utilization process was already well underway before the final report was disseminated.*

Three main points are illustrated here about utilization-focused data analysis and interpretation. First, decisionmakers and information users can understand and interpret data when presented with clear, readable, and simplified statistical tables; sophisticated analyses can be reworked and presented in more simplified, tabular form. Second, as experienced data analysts know, the only way to really understand a data set is to live with it, to spend some time getting inside it; busy decisionmakers are unwilling or unable to spend days at such a task, but a couple of hours of structured time spend in directed data analysis can pay off in greater understanding of and commitment to the evaluation data. Third, evaluators can learn a great deal from decisionmaker interpretations of data if they are open and listen to what people knowledgeable about the program have to say. Just as decisionmakers do not spend as much time in data analysis as evaluators do, so evaluators do not spend as much time in program analysis, operations, and planning as do decisionmakers. Each can learn from the other in the overall effort to make sense out of the data and the situation.

Surprise Attacks

Actively working on data analysis and interpretation with decisionmakers means that evaluators cannot wait until they have a highly polished final report prepared to show the results to decisionmakers. Utilization does not center around the final report. The final report is part of a total utilization process, but in many cases it is a minor part. Evaluators who prefer to work diligently in the solitude of their offices until they can spring a final report on a waiting world may find that the world has passed them by. The reason is that evaluation feedback is most useful as part of a process of thinking about a program, rather than as a one-shot information input. Thus, evlauation surprises born of the sudden release of final reports are not likely to be particularly well received. Such surprises are more likely to increase than to reduce uncertainty.

In our study of the utilization of federal health evaluations, we asked about the relationship between surprise findings and utilization. The question was asked as follows:

> Some writers suggest that the degree to which the findings of a study were expected can affect the study's impact. Arguments on this go both ways. Some of them say that surprise findings have the greatest impact because they bring to light new information. Others say that surprises will usually

be rejected because they don't fit in with general expectations. What was your reaction to the findings of this study: were you surprised by the findings or were they about what you expected?

What we found was that evaluation research seldom produces major surprises. There are often minor surprises on peripheral questions, but major surprises on central questions are rare. This relates to the nature of the utilization we found: inasmuch as utilization is a gradual process, key decisionmakers who want information are not sitting back waiting on a single set of evaluation findings. Instead, they are collecting information from multiple sources all the time. Evaluation is one piece of information that feeds into the whole picture. Evaluation findings clarify, illuminate, and provide direction, but they do not determine the whole picture. Active decisionmakers of the information using variety thus work to stay in touch with program developments and to avoid the uncertainty of sudden surprises. One decisionmaker we interviewed made the point that a "good" evaluation process should build in feedback mechanisms that guarantee the relative predictability of the content of the final report.

> If you're a good evaluator you don't want surprises. The last thing in the world you want to do is surprise people, because the chances are surprises are not going to be well received. . . . It isn't a birthday party, and people aren't really looking for surprises. So that if you're coming up with data that is different than the conventional wisdom, you ought, a good evaluation effort I would suggest, would get those ideas floated during the evaluation process so that when the final report comes out, they aren't a surprise.
>
> So my reaction is that if you were dealing in the world of surprises you aren't doing a very good evaluation. Now you could come up with findings contrary to the conventional wisdom, but you ought to be sharing those ideas, if you will, with the people being evaluated during the evaluation process to be sure that those surprises don't have any relationship to reality and again working during that process on the acceptance that maybe . . . but if you present a surprise, it will tend to get rejected. See, we don't want surprises. We don't like surprises around here (DM346: 30-31).

The evaluator for this project expressed the same opinion: "good managers are rarely surprised by the findings. If there's a surprising finding it should be rare. I mean, *everybody's missed this insight except this great evaluator? Nonsense!*" (EV364: 13). Surprise attacks may make for good war strategy, but in evaluation the surprise attack does little to add credence to a study.

Writing Final Reports

The theme running throughout this book is that what happens before the final report is written will usually determine utilization. For that reason relatively little space need be devoted to the actual writing of the final evaluation report. Certainly evaluation reports should be understandable and intelligible. Brief executive summaries are more likely to be read than are full reports. But most important, as with all other aspects of utilization-focused evaluation, the actual format, purpose, and organization of the final report should be discussed and negotiated with identified decisionmakers and information users. There are many ways to write a final report. (For an excellent review of alternatives see Datta, 1977.) Recommendations may come at the beginning of the report or at the end; methods sections may be put in the body of the report or in an appendix; and the style of the report can be written as more or less an academic treatise. What matters is that the style and organization of the report make sense to identified users of the evaluation findings.

One evaluator in our federal utilization study described quite lucidly the difference between writing a report according to what he thought had been specified in a project officer's request-for-proposal (RFP) and writing the same report based on personal conversations with the decisionmaker for whom the study was actually conducted. As the evaluator recalled the situation, the RFP was highly misleading:

If I had done exactly what the RFP asked for and turned in a report that was responsive to the RFP but not to what I was very clear were the kinds of questions they wanted answered, they would have gotten a different report. As a matter of fact, let me just tell you the essence of the thing. I had almost no direction from the government, as I've said, except that the guy kept saying, well here on point 8, you've got to do 8 on the contract.

So when I turned in the draft of the report, I did points 1 through 9 and put that in the final report. Then I essentially wrote another report after that and made that the last half of the report. It was a detailed description of the activities of the program, it came to very specific kinds of conclusions. It wasn't what was asked for in the RFP, but it was what they needed to answer their questions. [The decisionmaker] read it and the comment back was, "It's a good report, except for all that crap in the front."

Okay, so I turned it around then in the final draft, and put all that crap in the front into an appendix. And if you look at the report it has a big, several appendices. All of that, if you compare that carefully to the contract, all that crap in the appendix is what I was asked to get. All the stuff that constitutes the body of the report was above and beyond the call (EV367: 12).

What emerges here is a picture of a decisionmaker who knew what information he wanted, an evaluator committed to answering the decisionmaker's question, and a decisionmaker committed to using that information. The result was a high level of utilization in making a decision contrary to the decisionmaker's initial personal hopes. And in the words of the evaluator, the major factor explaining utilization was

> that the guy who's going to be making the decision is aware of and interested in the findings of the study and has some hand in designing the questions to be answered, that's a very important point (EV367: 20).

The decisionmaker concurred.

> Evaluation research. Well I guess I would affirm that in many cases it has no impact for many of the reasons that the literature has suggested. But if I were to pick out factors that made a positive contribution to its use, one would be that the decisionmakers themselves wanted the evaluation study results. I've said that several times. If that is not present, it is not surprising that the results aren't used (DM367: 17).

The Power of Positive versus Negative Thinking

There is a general cynicism that permeates much of the writing on evaluation research, a cynicism based on the belief that most evaluations have negative findings. Freeman (1977: 30), in his review of the "Present Status of Evaluation Research," expressed the opinion that the preponderance of negative impact findings has diminished evaluation research utilization potential. He recommended that "in view of the experience of the failure of most evaluations to come up with positive impact findings, evaluation researchers probably would do well to encourage the 'biasing' of evaluations in the direction of obtaining positive results." He went on to explain that evaluators ought to play a more active role in helping to design programs that have some hope of demonstrating positive impact, based on treatments that are highly specific and carefully targeted.

The problem with Freeman's perspective is that he reflects the tendency among many evaluators and decisionmakers to think of evaluation findings in monolithic, absolute, and purely summative terms. In reality, evaluation findings are seldom either completely positive or completely negative. Moreover, as our federal health utilization interviews pointed out, whether findings are interpreted as "positive" or "negative" depends on who is using and interpreting the findings. In our twenty federal health evaluation case studies respondents described findings as follows:

Basically positive findings	5
Basically negative findings	2
Mixed positive-negative findings	7
Evaluator-decisionmaker disagreement on nature of findings	6
Total	20

In only one case did any respondents feel that the positive or negative nature of findings explained very much about utilization. Evaluation data, given that they were seldom surprising, were used to help decisionmakers reduce uncertainty about programmatic activity. Because we encountered few summative decisions, the overall positive or negative nature of the evaluation was not an important factor in explaining utilization. The positive or negative findings of a particular study constitute only one piece of information that feeds into a larger process; they are thus interpreted in the larger context of other available information. Absolute statements about positive or negative findings are less useful than specific, detailed statements about levels of impact, the nature of relationships, and variations in implementation and effectiveness. The issue is not whether findings are negative or positive, but whether evaluation results contain useful information that can reduce uncertainty and thereby provide direction for programmatic action.

Finally, there is a real sense in which the positive or negative nature of evaluation findings can never be established with any absolute certainty. As Mulla Nasrudin advises, a heavy dose of humility is helpful when making interpretations about the meaning of something. This advice emerged from a teahouse discussion. A monk entered and said:

"My Master taught me to spread the word that mankind will never be fulfilled until the man who has *not* been wronged is as indignant about a wrong as the man who actually *has* been wronged."

The assembly is momentarily impressed. Then Nasrudin spoke: "My Master taught *me* that nobody at all should become indignant about anything until he is sure that what he thinks is a wrong is in fact a wrong— and not a blessing in disguise" (Shah, 1964: 58-59).

Dissemination of Findings

Dissemination of findings to audiences beyond identified and organized decisionmakers and information users is a quite different issue from the kind of utilization that has been the focus of this book. Studies can impact on all kinds of audiences in all kinds of ways. As a social scientist, I value and want to encourage the full and free dissemination of evaluation findings. Each of us ought to be permitted to indulge in the fantasy that our evaluation reports will impact across the land and through the years. But only a handful of studies will ever enjoy (or suffer) such widespread dissemination!

Dissemination efforts will vary greatly from study to study. The nature of dissemination is a matter for negotiation between evaluators and decisionmakers. However, there are a few principles relevant to dissemination that can be extracted from utilization-focused evaluation.

Different individuals and audiences are interested in a given evaluation for different reasons. The questions addressed in an evaluation will have different meanings for people who were not directly involved in the painstaking process of focusing the evaluation. Those who become engaged in dissemination efforts must be highly skilled at adapting the evaluation specifics of a particular study to the program specifics of information users in a different setting. One highly experienced federal decisionmaker in our federal utilization study commented at length on the complex nature of disseminating evaluation at the federal level.

> I think all too frequently evaluation studies come in through a channel of the program or evaluation official responsible for the evaluation study, and the report gets passed up through the hierarchy to the upper echelon and people are too busy to read—particularly to read undigested material. I think the character of the presentation is critical. . . . Presentations can sometimes be overly superficial, sometimes may suffer from glibness, sometimes may be characterized as snow jobs, but, if they're really good they'll come out as solid, straightforward presentations. This means that the people making the presentations have to be able to translate their idioms into the language that's most understandable to different audiences (DM152: 25-26).

Translating evaluation findings into the idioms of particular audiences may be more of a task than the evaluator alone can easily undertake.

Several writers have commented on the need for training professionals in the specialized role of translating research results for practitioners (e.g., Guba, 1968; Havelock, 1968; Kirk, 1977). "An effective research utilization system requires linkers to act as an intermediary between researchers and practitioners. Linkers are the bridges that make research results available to practitioners" (Agarwala-Rogers, 1977: 331).

On a more limited basis, I prefer to make evaluation presentations to larger audiences a joint venture with one or more of the key decisionmakers with whom I have worked. Such presentations can provide fresh insights to both evaluator and decisionmakers, while permitting a balanced view of the project to the newly targeted audience. Joint efforts can also increase the relevance of any given presentation by combining evaluator-decision-maker experiences. Achieving relevance is no easy task when multiple agencies are targeted for dissemination.

> A presentation, for example, to a small group at NIH can address itself essentially and solely to NIH concerns. A presentation to the heads of the various health agencies, will have to be above the level of individual concerns to cross-agency concerns. The presentation that's made up at the secretary's level, or the assistant secretary for planning and evaluation, has got to take into account the perspectives of the department, the responsibilities of the department, the extent to which the department identifies itself with administration positions, the extent to which the department has expressed options, expressed alternatives to administration positions.
>
> The point is you're talking to people who perceive their roles differently. A person at the HEW level who looks at an activity that has been evaluated at an NIH institute level has a very difficult time relating to the issues involved, generally. The closest he comes to NIH is thinking of NIH in the aggregate. It is hard (DM152: 26).

The difficulty of making evaluations relevant to multiple audiences, each conceptualized in vague and general terms, is what led us to identification and organization of relevant decisionmakers and information users as the first and most critical step in utilization-focused evaluation. This is also the reason we have focused on utilization as a personal, specific, and interactive process rather than as a general dissemination problem. Dissemination can broaden and enlarge the impact of a study in important ways, but the nature of those long-term impacts are largely beyond the control of the evaluator. What the evaluator can control is the degree to which the information gathered addresses the identifiable concerns of specific decisionmakers and information users. Thus, evaluators must cease to think of dissemination as the separate and only utilization component of a project. Utilization considerations enter into the evaluation at the very beginning and at every step along the way. In utilization-focused evaluation, dissemination efforts, far from being the whole cake of utilization, are little more than frosting on the cake.

Personalizing Evaluation Reporting

This section is devoted to personal lamentations about the impersonal way in which much research is disseminated, i.e., the publication of anonymous reports from public agencies. State and federal agencies regularly issue reports under the title of the agency, with an introductory message from the agency director but no mention of the staff who conducted the research and wrote the report. The National Technical Information Service provides only the names of research organizations on their abstracts; individuals are not identified. There are several not very convincing explanations for this phenomenon: directors taking credit for the work of subordinates, staff trying to evade responsibility, the tradition of a neutral civil service, the greater authority of offices versus individuals, and institutional norms. Whatever the origins of this practice, there is no reason to believe that anonymity does anything but reduce the utilization potential of disseminated reports.

It makes a difference who conducts a study, just as it makes a difference who the identified users of the study are. Several respondents in our utilization interviews remarked that the identity of the evaluator was an important factor in establishing the credibility of the evaluation. The credibility of a report is in no way enhanced by anonymous authorship. (The national weekly news magazines have apparently recognized this inasmuch as they now include bylines on news articles as well as opinion articles.) Moreover, it is most annoying to call an agency or research organization to get additional information about a study, only to find that no one is quite sure exactly who was responsible for it. In our federal health evaluation utilization study, we had enormous difficulty establishing the identity of evaluators and decisionmakers from published research reports.

Utilization of information is, in the end, a personal process. Individual people absorb data in terms of their own needs and perceptions. *The generation of information is also a personal process.* Evaluators differ in terms of any variable one would care to name. The personal utilization process is enhanced by matching evaluator perspectives to decisionmaker perspectives. In the larger dissemination process, it can make a difference to potential users of evaluation findings to know the identities of all those involved in the process—evaluators and specific decisionmakers. The available evidence clearly indicates that personalizing the evaluation process, including the reporting of findings, can only serve to enhance research utilization. In addition, it would be interesting to observe how commitments to utilization were affected if final reports named not only evaluators but also the specific decisionmakers for whom they were prepared!

Overview

This chapter began by comparing efforts to establish the meaning of evaluation data to the Zen search for enlightenment. Evaluation research is ultimately a personal, perceptual, and interpretive approach to establishing the effectiveness of human service activities. Utilization-focused evaluation attempts to diminish uncertainty by actively involving decisionmakers and information users in methods, measurement, and design decisions that affect data analysis and interpretation. Several suggestions were made in this chapter:

(1) Standards of desirability can be established before data are collected to guide later data interpretation and to examine the need for additional information through a simulated-interpretation session.

(2) Face validity can be used as a measurement criterion to increase the believability of data to decisionmakers.

(3) The credibility of research designs to information users can be established.

(4) The relevance of definitions and units of analysis can be carefully assessed.

(5) Definition and operationalization of key concepts can be considered in terms of their potential for longitudinal comparisons and long-range relevance.

(6) Research quality can be established and negotiated taking into account both decisionmaker and evaluator criteria.

(7) The dynamics of measurement and design decisions are acknowledged by sharing methods decisions on a continual basis, not just at the initial proposal stage.

(8) Decisionmakers and information users can be induced to study the data in some depth so as to personally understand what findings mean.

(9) Data can be presented in such a way that decisionmakers can decipher and interpret findings for themselves.

(10) Surprises can be avoided by sharing data and initial findings with decisionmakers as they become available.

(11) Evaluators and decisionmakers can avoid thinking about findings in monolithic, absolute, and purely summative terms; the issue is not

whether evaluation results are negative or positive, but whether they contain useful information.

(12) The format, style, and organization of final reports can be discussed and negotiated with those who will be the primary users of each report.

(13) Dissemination efforts are also a matter for negotiation and cooperation between decisionmakers and evaluators as they work together to make study findings relevant and meaningful to various larger audiences.

(14) Reporting evaluation research can be personalized by identifying both evaluators who write reports and decisionmakers for whom reports are written.

The analysis and interpretation of evaluation data are exciting processes. Many nights have turned into morning before evaluators have finished trying new computer runs to tease out the nuances in some data set. The work of months, sometimes years, finally comes to fruition as data are analyzed and interpreted, conclusions drawn, and alternative courses of action and recommendations considered. Data analysis and interpretation need not be the sole perogative of evaluation researchers. Decisionmakers can become involved in struggling with data too, increasing both their commitment to and understanding of the findings.

In the spring of 1977, two evaluators from the Minnesota Center for Social Research were on the phone two or three times a day during data analysis of an educational project that was being evaluated to determine whether it was a valid model for dissemination funding. Program staff shared with evaluators the anxiety and excitement of watching the findings take final shape. Preliminary analyses on initial data appeared to have quite negative implications; as the sample became more complete, the findings began to look quite positive; finally, a mixed picture of positive and negative conclusions were drawn. Because the primary information users were intimately involved in the conceptualization and analysis of the evaluation, there were no last minute attacks on methods to explain away negative findings. The program staff understood the data, whence it came, where it went, and what would remain to be used for program development and improvement. A utilization-focused approach to data analysis engenders such commitments to use evaluation findings.

Finally, in utilization-focused evaluation the underlying and constantly recurring data analysis or interpretation issue is how to translate the findings into action. *What do the findings tell decisionmakers about what to do?* Chapter 3 made a distinction between knowledge as potential power and knowledge that is actually used. Utilization-focused evaluation is aimed at producing knowledge that makes a difference, that is actually used. Lazarfeld and Reitz identify the gap between knowledge and action as the most important translation step in the utilization process. Bridging that gap is a creative process that generates power: "although systematic knowledge can contribute to decision, there is always a gap between knowledge and recommendation. This gap can only be filled by creative thinking which responds with guesses of varying degrees of risk" (Lazarfeld and Reitz, 1975: 98).

Creative thinking is a critical element in utilization-focused evaluation—creativity in design, in analysis, in interpretation, and in application of findings. Creatively bridging the gap between knowledge and action is an active-reactive-adaptive process for both evaluators and decision-makers. Creatively bridging the gap between knowledge and action *is* utilization.

Chapter 12

UTILIZATION-FOCUSED EVALUATION

A Setting

The views expressed herein have been heavily influenced by discussions with program staffs, decisionmakers, and evaluators who have experienced frustration in their attempts to engage in useful evaluation research. One such decisionmaker is Wayne Jennings, Principal of the Saint Paul Open School in Minnesota. In the fall of 1975 I asked Dr. Jennings to permit me to interview him in my evaluation research seminar to help provide students with a decisionmaker perspective on the utilization of evaluation research.

Patton: I know that federal legislation requires Title III programs to be evaluated. Were there any other reasons why this evaluation was undertaken?

Jennings: It was our hope that there would be some added benefit to the school, that is to say, the school staff itself would obtain knowledge about its own program, so we could use it to improve this program.

Patton: At any time during the evaluation process was there ever an expectation that the findings would be used in the making of any specific decisions?

Jennings: Initially, we were interested in a process kind of evaluation, one that might address some of the basic issues of education. The school operates on the assumption that students learn from experience, and the more varied experiences they have, the more they learn—learn from a standpoint of the larger and perhaps vague and ambiguous goals of education: learning initiative, learning to work and cooperate together, interest in the world, concern about it, that sort of thing. And we hoped to learn what parts of the program made a contribution in this area and what parts maybe detracted from that.

We hoped to learn whether the program affected different groups of students differently; for instance, whether the program was highly effective for younger children or older children as a whole, whether it worked especially well for kids who already had a lot of initiative and drive and were selfmotivated learners, or whether it was effective for those who do not have this kind of attitude, and so we were interested in determining what aspects of the program we should concentrate on more, or continue or discontinue. But I don't think we got information to make those kind of basic decisions about education.

We asked the research firm for an evaluation design that would help us with those kinds of information. They came up with a design that seemed far off target from what we had asked. It takes a little imagination to do an evaluation. But, if I'd asked totally different questions, we'd have gotten the same design. It's as though they had a recipe or a pattern book, and whether they were evaluating us or evaluating vocational education or whether they were evaluating anything—a hospital or a prison—it would have been the same evaluation design.

Patton: You seem to be saying that the only way an evaluation would be important to you would have been if the evaluators took seriously, as given, your own conceptions of what the school was about, your own objectives, and then went ahead and designed their evaluation and asked the questions in terms of these objectives. What really is happening in the school? But they failed to do that. Okay, to what extent was this failure caused by a lack of explicitness on your part, or perhaps even a hasty decision to accept an evaluation design that you thought would be educationally useless, from your viewpoint?

Jennings: That's a good question. Perhaps I can answer that by saying a little about our experiences with evaluation firms the preceding two years. The first year we worked with an out of state firm. The president came for the initial discussion in September, when we were first getting started. He said he'd like to go to the school and look around. I found him about ten minutes later sitting in the front hall in a state of what appeared to be absolute shock. He simply was not prepared for this program. He had accepted the evaluation by mail and all that sort of thing. He came there and he found kids were running around, the place was noisy, they weren't in straight rows, it didn't resemble school in any way, apparently. He was just not prepared to do it. That was the last we saw of him. He sent out a new researcher who didn't walk around the school—we simply met in the office and hashed it out. These people were not prepared to analyze a nonstandard school operation.

I think schools have operated pretty much in the same way for so long that all of us have a mind set of what school is. So to see something different from that tends to give one a sense of shock or culture shock. We saw that in the minds of all our evaluators we've had in here. Now, I don't know how to prepare somebody for that unless it's a participant observer, an anthropological approach, where you come in and live there for a while and find out what the hell's going on. We did have, somewhere along the line, an evaluation proposal from an out of state firm which does have experience with these kinds of schools. They were going to give us the kind of evaluation we were very much interested in. We accepted that evaluation and the State Department of Education said, "no, that won't provide us with enough concrete data."

Patton: When the State Department of Education did approve the design of the evaluation for the third year, did that design provide some "concrete data?" What were the findings of that study?

Jennings: We knew politically that we had to achieve a certain degree of respectability with regard to standardized testing. So we looked at the testing results, the reading scores and all that sort of thing, and they seemed satisfactory. We didn't discover anything particularly startling to cause any serious problems with the Board of Education or the State Department of Education.

Patton: In what form did you receive the findings of the evaluation?

Jennings: In a final report. I think it would have been helpful for their staff to meet with our staff and talk us through the report, elaborate a little on it, but that didn't happen. Partly because the report came, I think, either during the summer or the following fall.

Patton: We are interested in any ways in which this evaluation may have had an impact on program operation and planning, on funding, on policymaking and decisions, and so forth. From your point of view, what would you say was the impact of this evaluation?

Jennings: It served to legitimize us. The Board of Education, the district administration, and the State Department of Education were all interested in seeing an evaluation undertaken, but I don't think a single member of the board or the administration read it. They may have glanced at the summary and the summary says that the school is okay.

Patton: Any other impacts of this study that come to mind besides the legitimization function?

Jennings: I suppose some knowledge of how difficult it is to do evaluations. To properly do it would require a lot of resources and also a lot of time on the part of the staff. I think the staff was interested in thinking through a good evaluation. What it would have meant was that we would have all had to become thoroughly backgrounded in the subject in order to help the evaluation firm think it through and provide a proper evaluation. I think we sensed that, and I think the staff has something of a negative attitude about evaluation. I mean they are interested in evaluation reports, but then the reports seem to lack so much in terms of things that would help us on a day-to-day decisionmaking basis, or give us a good reflection or mirror image of what's going on in that school from an outsider's point of view, in terms of the growth and development of kids in all dimensions.

Patton: The staff all did receive copies of the report?

Jennings: Yes. I'm not sure how many bothered to read through it. They were looking for something worthwhile and helpful, but it's just not there. You know, I don't know what kind of evaluation would do that.

Patton: We've been focusing mainly on the study's impact on the Open School itself. Sometimes studies have a broader impact on a program, and things that go beyond immediate programs. Things like general thinking on issues that arise from the study, or position papers, or legislative authorization. Did the evaluation have an impact on any of those kinds of things?

Jennings: I'm glad you're getting into that area, because that was a major interest to me. . . . It was my hope that as the school got underway, it would become fairly clear, or would be evident to those who would be interested in finding out, that this was a highly effective educational program, and that it would make a considerable difference in the lives of most children. Well the study didn't addresss that; the study simply said, "the program's okay." That's all it said. *Given the limited resources and imagination that were put into the evaluation I'm not convinced they had enough knowledge to say anything about the effectiveness of the program!*

Our major job is to educate 500 students, but we're engaged in a much larger struggle, at least I am, and that is to show that in less formal kinds of education, experiential programs are highly effective forms of education that may bring students to the same level of achievement in a shorter time. We're concerned about that aspect of the thing, but also that it is a form of education that produces genuinely humane people for a complex changing world.

In terms not quite so global the evaluations we have do say something useful. When parents or other educators ask if the program has been evaluated and what the findings were, we say yes, the evaluation shows the program is effective. Now anyone worth their salt, I suspect, if they read the evaluations carefully, would decide they don't show much of anything, really, when you come right down to it. *We're left where we began, but we have the illusion of at least having evaluated the program here.*

Patton: I pulled some of the recommendations out of the study, and I'd just like to have you react to how those were received and used in any way by the school. The first one that's listed in the report is that objectives as they are related to the goals of the Open School should be written in performance specific language. What was the reaction to that recommendation?

Jennings: I know that's the current popular view in education today, but I'm not sure it could be done. It would require an enormous amount of energy. Many of our objectives are not very specific subject matter kinds of objectives. The general goals of the school are more philosophical in tone, and I guess we're just not willing to invest the time and energy to reduce those to the kinds of performance objectives that we're speaking of, and I don't know if the end results would be particularly helpful.

Patton: Did it seem to you that that recommendation followed in any way from the findings of the study?

Jennings: When I read that one, I thought, "where did that come from?" You know, how did they arrive at that, is that just some conventional wisdom in education today, which could be plugged into any evaluation you want?

Patton: What, then, was your overall reaction to the recommendations?

Jennings: Each was too much of a simpleminded kind of statement. They lacked depth of understanding of what the program was trying to accomplish. Each recommendation could be a report in itself rather than some surface scratching and coming up with some conclusions that we recognize as not very helpful.

Patton: Thinking about the overall utilization and impact of the evaluation study, what would you identify as its single most important effect or impact?

Jennings: Legitimization. It served that function. Just the report's existence, if it had that cover on it, and it was filled with Chinese or some other language, as long as it was filled, and it had a lot of figures in it and people thought it was an evaluation, and somewhere near the end it said that the school seemed to be doing a reasonably good job, that would be satisfactory for most people.

Patton: Is there a single factor that explains that kind of impact in your mind, that people accept it that way, that the evaluation had that legitimation impact? Some factor about the evaluation itself?

Jennings: Well, I think its thickness . . . it's got numbers and statistics in it, it's authored by some Ph.D.s—I think these things all lend credibility. It was done by an outside firm.

Patton: A factor affecting utilization that's frequently mentioned has to do with the nature of contact between the evaluators and the decision-makers. Are there any aspects of that that might be important here? Do any of these kinds of factors seem to you to have an effect on the outcome of this study and how it was used?

Jennings: Very definitely. I would say that to do the job right, we'd have to have people on our own staff who were free from most other responsibilities so that they could deal with designing the evaluation and work with the evaluators. Then I think that as the evaluation proceeded, there should probably have been regular sessions or talks in which we would have been able to adjust the evaluation. There just wasn't much attention given to that.

Patton: There's a side effect that comes out of evaluation studies that affects the way people like yourself, who are administrators and work in government and agencies and schools, feel about evaluations. What we'd like to get a feel for is whether or not it's true, as is speculated on in a lot of the literature, that people in administrative positions have a rather poor opinion of evaluation research in general. How would you describe your general opinion of evaluation research—positive, negative, favorable, unfavorable?

Jennings: We want careful evaluation. We want to know what we're doing and to get it from data that will help us make the decisions for improving the program. We want that. We want the best that's available and we want it to be accurate and we want the conclusions to be justified, and so on. *We just desperately want and need that information, to know if we're on the right track.* By and large my opinion is not very good. Most reports look like they were written the last week before they're published, with hastily drawn conclusions and sometimes conclusions from data that's manipulated for a given end.

Patton: Did this study affect those opinions or did you already hold those before?

Jennings: Before. I guess the reason hope springs eternal is that I have read carefully done evaluation reports, that seemed that way to me, and they've been helpful in guiding my thinking about education and brought me to my present state of beliefs. Ninety-nine percent of evaluation is done on a model of education that I think is obsolete—a presentation, subject matter and mastery kind of mode, so it's like a factory trying to perfect its way of making wagon wheels. We went out of business making wagon wheels, and all of the evaluation and all of the research that will be done in that area isn't of much value.

Contrasting Evaluation Approaches

Shortly after this interview,* Jennings formed an evaluation task force made up of teachers, parents, students, community people, and graduate students in evaluation research from the Minnesota Center for Social Research. With very limited resources, they conducted an intensive evaluation study of Saint Paul Open School processes and outcomes. They used a variety of methods, both quantitative and qualitative. That report (Harvey and Townsend, 1976) provided useful information for incremental program development and decisionmaking. The contrasts between the Open School Task Force evaluation and the earlier, required, Title III evaluations highlight the critical elements of utilization-focused evaluation (see Table 12-1).

The actual money spent on the three years of original Title III evaluations at the Saint Paul Open School was under $40,000, which is not a great deal of money as research goes. But the Saint Paul Open School is one small program out of the hundreds that receive federal funding; in the aggregate, evaluations on those hundreds of programs represent millions of dollars. There are relatively few truly national evaluations compared to the thousands of small-scale evaluations done on single health, education, criminal justice, welfare, and other human service programs. There is no reason to write off such small-scale evaluations as meaningless: they constitute the major proportion of all evaluation research conducted in the country. The fourth Saint Paul Open School evaluation cost less than $1,000 in real money because the labor was all volunteer and release time. Due to the success of the internal task force effort, the school has continued to use the approach outlined above. They are now in their fourth year of doing utilization-focused evaluation using their own program funds and resources—because they find such evaluations useful.

---

*The evaluators were also interviewed, but when they read Jenning's comments they asked that their interviews not be used and that they not be named, because their business might be hurt.

TABLE 12.1: Contrasting Evaluation Approaches

Open School Utilization-Focused Evaluation	Original Title III Evaluations done for Open School
1. A task force was formed of identified and organized decisionmakers and information users to focus evaluation questions. This group worked together to determine what information would be useful to collect both for program improvement and to maintain public accountability.	1. No clear decisionmakers and information users for the evaluation were identified. The evaluation was aimed vaguely at multiple audiences: federal funders, school board, State Department of Education, general public, and Open School staff. Because specific people were not identified and organized as decisionmakers and information users, the evaluators unilaterally determined the focus of the research based on what they thought could be done, not on what would be useful.
2. Evaluation questions focused on needed information derived from decisions of basic program direction and areas in which it would be desirable to reduce uncertainty about program operations and effects.	2. Evaluators collected data on presumed operational goals (i.e., normal scores on standardized achievement tests), framing their questions in terms of formal goals based on a rational model that fit the evaluators' but not program assumptions.
3. Evaluation collected both implementation (process) data and outcomes data (followup of achievements and activities of Open School graduates).	3. Evaluation was largely a pure outcomes evaluation, emphasizing operational goals important to evaluators and public officials.
4. The task force based their evaluation upon an explicit statement of educational philosophy (a theory of action).	4. Evaluators ignored the program's philosophy and conceptualized the evaluation in terms of their own implicit educational theory of action.

Table 12.1 (Continued)

5. A variety of methods were used to investigate a variety of questions. Methods were selected jointly by evaluators and decisionmakers using multiple criteria: (a) methodological appropriateness; (b) face validity of instrumentation; (c) believability, credibility, and relevance of the design and measuring instruments to information users and decisionmakers; (d) scientific rigor of design as judged by the likelihood of obtaining valid, reliable, interpretable, and replicable results; and (e) available resources. The task force was involved on a continual basis in making methods and measurement decisions as circumstances changed.

6. Task force members worked together to analyze and interpret data as they were gathered. Data were discussed in rough form over a period of time before the evaluators wrote the final report. Findings and conclusions were known and being used before the final report was ready for dissemination.

7. When the final report was made public both decisionmakers (Jennings) and evaluators (Harvey and Townsend) made presentations to parents, staff, and school officials.

8. The evaluation was used by Open School staff and administrators for program development, program improvement, and public accountability.

5. The major measurement technique was use of standardized tests which had low face validity, low credibility, and low relevance to program staff; other audiences, especially federal funders, appeared to want such instruments, but it was unclear who the evaluation was supposed to serve. Methods were determined largely by evaluators, based on available resources, with only initial review by program staff and federal and state officials.

6. Evaluators analyzed and interpreted data by themselves. A final report was the only form in which findings were presented. No interpretation sessions with program staff or any audience were ever held.

7. The final report was mailed to responsible offices. No verbal presentations were made. No discussions of findings took place.

8. There was no specific utilization of the evaluation for actual decisionmaking or program planning, though the evaluation may have helped legitimize the program by giving the "illusion" of outcomes evaluation.

Utilization-Focused Evaluation:
A Flexible Approach

Utilization-focused evaluation is not a formal model or recipe for how to conduct evaluative research. Rather, it is an approach, an orientation, and a set of options. The active-reactive-adaptive evaluator chooses from among these options as he or she works with decisionmakers and information users throughout the evaluation process. There is no formula guaranteeing success in this approach—indeed the criteria for success are variable. Utilization means different things to different people in different settings, and is an issue subject to negotiation between evaluators and decisionmakers.

The outline that follows pulls together and organizes some of the critical elements and considerations in utilization-focused evaluation. This outline is not meant as a recipe, but only as a brief overview of some of the major points made above.

There are only two fundamental requirements in this approach: everything else is a matter for negotiation, adaptation, selection, and matching. First, relevant decisionmakers and information users must be identified and organized—real, visible, specific, and caring human beings, not ephemeral, general, and abstract "audiences," organizations, or agencies. Second, evaluators must work actively, reactively, and adaptively with these identified decisionmakers and information users to make all other decisions about the evaluation—decisions about research focus, design, methods, analysis, interpretation, and dissemination.

An Outline of the
Utilization-Focused Approach to Evaluation

I. IDENTIFICATION AND ORGANIZATION OF RELEVANT DECISION-MAKERS AND INFORMATION USERS

   A. Criteria for Identification: the Personal Factor

      1. People who can use information;
      2. People to whom information makes a difference;
      3. People who have questions they want to have answered; and
      4. People who care about and are willing to share responsibility for the evaluation and its utilization.

   B. Criteria for Organization

      1. Provision can be made for continuous direct contact between evaluators and decisionmakers or information users;

2. The organized group is small enough to be active, hard working, and decision-oriented (my own preference is for a task force of fewer than five, and certainly fewer than ten, people);

3. The members of the group are willing to make a heavy time commitment to the evaluation (the actual amount of time depends on the size of the group, the size and scope of the evaluation, and the members' ability to work together).

II. THE RELEVANT EVALUATION QUESTIONS ARE IDENTIFIED AND FOCUSED

A. Criteria for Identification of Questions

1. The members of the evaluation task force (i.e., identified and organized decisionmakers, information users, and evaluators) agree on the purpose(s) and emphasis of the evaluation. Options include:

    a. information for program improvement (formative evaluation);

    b. information about continuation of the program (summative evaluation); or

    c. both formative and summative evaluation but with emphasis on one or the other (equality of emphasis is not likely in practice when a a single evaluation is involved).

2. The members of the task force agree on which components and basic activities of the program will be the subject of the evaluation (the point here is simply to delineate what aspects of the program are to be discussed in detail as specific evaluation questions are focused).

B. Alternative Approaches for Focusing Evaluation Questions

1. The evaluation question can be framed in terms of the program's mission statement, goals, and objectives.

    a. evaluators must be active-reactive-adaptive in goals clarification exercises, realizing that the appropriateness of generating clear, specific, measurable goals varies depending upon the nature of the organization and the purpose of the evaluation;

    b. goals clarification provides direction in determining what information is needed and wanted—goals do not automatically determine the content and focus of the evaluation, which depend on what task force members want to know;

    c. goals are prioritized using the criterion of information need, not just that of relative importance to program.

2. The evaluation question can be framed in terms of program implementation. Options here include:

    a. effort evaluation;

    b. process evaluation; and the

    c. treatment identification approach.

3. The evaluation question can be framed in terms of the program's theory of action:

    a. a hierarchy of objectives can be constructed to delineate the program's theory of action, wherein attainment of each lower level objective is assumed necessary for attainment of each higher level objective;

    b. the evaluation might focus on any two or more causal connections in a theory of action;

    c. the theories or causal linkages tested in the evaluation are those believed relevant by evaluation task force members; and

    d. the evaluation question links program implementation to program outcomes, i.e., determines the extent to which observed outcomes are attributable to program activities.

4. The evaluation question can be framed in terms of the point in the life of the program when the evaluation takes place. Different questions are relevant at different stages of program development.

5. The evaluation question is framed in the context of the organizational dynamics of a program. Different types of organizations use different types of information and need different types of evaluation. Programs vary in organizational terms along the following dimensions:

    a. the degree to which the environment is certain and stable versus uncertain and dynamic;

    b. the degree to which the program can be characterized as an open or closed system; and

    c. the degree to which a rational goal maximization model, an optimizing systems model, or an incremental, satisficing model best describes decision making processes.

6. The active-reactive-adaptive evaluator works with decisionmakers and information users to find the right evaluation question(s). The right question from a utilization point of view has several characteristics:

    a. it is possible to bring data to bear on the question;

    b. there is more than one possible answer to the question, i.e., the answer is not predetermined or "loaded" by the phrasing of the question;

    c. the identified decisionmakers want information to help answer the question;

    d. the identified decisionmakers feel they need information to help them answer the question;

    e. the identified and organized decisionmakers and information users want to answer the question for themselves, not just for someone else;

    f. the decisionmakers can indicate how they would use the answer to the question, i.e., they can specify the relevance of an answer for their program.

7. As the evaluation question is focused the *fundamental, ever-present question that underlies all other issues is: what difference would it make to have this information? How would the information be used and how would it be useful?*

III. EVALUATION METHODS ARE SELECTED THAT GENERATE USE-FUL INFORMATION FOR IDENTIFIED AND ORGANIZED DECISION-MAKERS AND INFORMATION USERS

A. Strengths and weaknesses of alternative methodological paradigms are considered in the search for methods that are appropriate to the nature of the evaluation question. Options include consideration of:

1. Quantitative and qualitative methods;
2. Hypothetico-deductive objectivity or subjectivity versus holistic-inductive objectivity or subjectivity;
3. Distance from versus closeness to the data;
4. Fixed versus dynamic designs;
5. Relative emphases on reliability or validity;
6. Holistic or component units of analysis; and
7. Inductive versus deductive procedures.

B. Design and measurement decisions are shared by evaluators and decision-makers to increase information users' understanding of, belief in, and commitment to evaluation data.

1. Variables are operationalized in ways that make sense to those who will use the data; face validity, as judged by decisionmakers and information users, is an important instrumentation criterion in evaluation measurement.
2. Evaluation designs are selected that are credible to decisionmakers, information users, and evaluators.
3. Major concepts and units of analysis are defined so as to be relevant to decisionmakers and information users; the long-term relevance of definitions and units of analysis are considered to increase the potential for continuous, longitudinal evaluation (where appropriate).
4. Multiple methods are used and multiple measures employed as much as possible to increase the believability of findings.
5. Decisionmakers and information users are involved in continuous methods, design, measurement, and basic data gathering decisions as changed circumstances, resources, and time lines force changes in methods. Recognizing that initial proposals are poor predictors of final designs, active-reactive-adaptive evaluators seek involvement of relevant decisionmakers in design and measurement questions as they arise.
6. Decisionmakers weigh with evaluators the methodological constraints introduced by limited resources, time deadlines, and data accessibility problems. All task force members must be highly knowledgeable about the strengths and weaknesses of data collection procedures.
7. The utilization assumption guiding methods discussions is that it is better to have an approximate and highly probabilistic answer to the right question than a solid and relatively certain answer to the wrong question.

IV. DECISIONMAKERS AND INFORMATION USERS PARTICIPATE
WITH EVALUATORS IN DATA ANALYSIS AND DATA INTERPRE-
TATION

A. Data analysis is separated from data intrepretation so that decisionmakers
can work with the data without biases introduced by the evaluator's conclusions.

B. Standards of desirability are established before data analysis to guide data
interpretation; the nature of the standards of desirability will vary along a
continuum from highly crystalized to highly ambiguous.

C. Data analysis is presented in a form that makes sense to decisionmakers
and information users. Decisionmakers are given an opportunity to struggle
with the data as they become available, so that surprises are avoided.

D. Evaluators work with decisionmakers and information users to make full use
of the data.

1. Realizing that "positive" and "negative" are perceptual labels, the responsive evaluator avoids characterizing results in such monolithic terms.
Most studies include both somewhat positive and somewhat negative
findings, depending upon one's point of view. Analysis and interpretation
focus on specific results, relationships, and implications rather than
general characterizations of the program.

2. Both strengths and weaknesses of the data are made clear and explicit.

E. Evaluators work with decisionmakers and information users to develop
specific plans for action and utilization based upon evaluation findings and
interpretation.

1. Evaluation ultimately necessitates making leaps from data to judgment,
from analysis to action.

2. Utilization-focused data analysis and interpretation includes the judgments, conclusions, and recommendations of both evaluators and
decisionmakers.

V. EVALUATORS AND DECISIONMAKERS NEGOTIATE AND CO-
OPERATE IN DISSEMINATION EFFORTS.

A. Dissemination of findings is only one aspect of evaluation utilization, and a
minor aspect in many cases. The primary utilization target consists of
relevant decisionmakers and information users identified and organized
during the first step in the evaluation process.

B. Dissemination takes a variety of forms for different audiences and different
purposes.

C. Throughout dissemination efforts both evaluators and decisionmakers
take responsibility for the evaluation from initial conceptualization to final
data analysis and interpretation. Options include:

1. Both evaluators and decisionmakers are present at dissemination presentations; and

2. Both evaluators and those for whom the evaluation was conducted are identified in all reports and presentations.

Evaluation and Change

In an important article on the utilization of evaluation, Davis and Salasin (1975: 652) asserted that any change model should . . . generally *accommodate* rather than *manipulate* the views of persons involved." Utilization-focused evaluation does just that. The evaluator does not attempt to mold and manipulate decisionmakers and information users to accept the evaluator's preconceived notions about what constitutes useful or high quality research, but neither is the evaluator a mere technician who does whatever decisionmakers want. Utilization-focused evaluation brings together evaluators, decisionmakers, and information users in an active-reactive-adaptive process where all participants share responsibility for creatively shaping and rigorously implementing an evaluation that is both useful and of high quality. Egon Guba (1977: 1) has described in powerful language the archetypical evaluator, who is the antithesis of the active-reactive-adaptive researcher in utilization-focused evaluation:

> It is my experience that evaluators sometimes adopt a very supercilious attitude with respect to their clients; their presumptuousness and arrogance are sometimes overwhelming. We treat the client as a "child-like" person who needs to be taken in hand; as an ignoramus who cannot possibly understand the tactics and strategies that we will bring to bear; as someone who doesn't appreciate the questions he *ought* to ask until we tell him—and what we tell him often reflects our own biases and interests rather than the problems with which the client is actually beset. The phrase "Ugly American" has emerged in international settings to describe the person who enters into a new culture, immediately knows what is wrong with it, and proceeds to foist his own solutions onto the locals. In some ways I have come to think of evaluators as "Ugly Americans." And if what we are looking for are ways to manipulate clients so that they will fall in with *our* wishes and cease to resist our blandishments, I for one will have none of it.

For others who "will have none of it" there is the alternative of undertaking an active-reactive-adaptive evaluator role based on mutual respect between evaluators and decisionmakers. Part of this active-reactive-adaptive process involves defining and working toward utilization in a way that is meaningful and rewarding to both evaluators and decisionmakers. Reduction of decisionmaker uncertainty through evaluation research may or may not always lead to concrete behavioral change, the indicator of utilization specified by

Davis and Salasin (1975). Rather than narrowly constructing utilization as equivalent to behavioral change, the decisionmakers interviewed in our federal utilization study reported that information capable of reducing uncertainty was meaningful, important, and in scarce supply. The nature of utilization will depend on the nature of evaluation, the needs of identified decisionmakers and information users, and the circumstances in which the evaluation is conducted.

At the same time, the hope expressed by Davis and Salasin (1975) that evaluators can be expected to play a "change consultant role" is entirely compatible with utilization-focused evaluation. The change consultant role begins in the very first step, with identification and organization of relevant evaluators and decisionmakers. Both the change process (behavioral or otherwise) and the utilization process begin at step one and carry through as the evaluation takes shape and finally reaches its culmination in data analysis and interpretation. Bringing together a group of people who actively engage in discussions about what a program is doing, where it is going, how it could be improved, and what information is needed to reduce uncertainty about program implementation and effects—these processes are in themselves change producing. In my experience, the people who engage in utilization-focused evaluation come out of those processes with more penetrating perspectives, increased capabilities, and greater commitments to action than they had before the evaluation began. It is a deeply involving process for both evaluators and decisionmakers. Ultimately, the generation and utilization of information is a personal process. Therein lies the power of evaluation—*in the mobilization of individual energies for action.* As the barrier of uncertainty is attacked and as systematic information emerges to increase decisionmaker discretion for improving programmatic activity and effectiveness, evaluation research is used.

A Final Note

Utilization-focused evaluation is an approach that combines style and substance, activism and science, personal perspective and systematic information. I have used a variety of approaches in trying to describe utilization-focused evaluation: scenarios, case examples, quotations from our federal utilization study, Sufi parables, and children's stories. In the end, this approach to evaluation must also be judged by its usefulness.

At the same time, there are no guarantees that the utilization-focused approach will always work. Just as decisionmakers live in a world of uncertainty, so too evaluators are faced with the ever-present possibility that despite their best efforts, their work will be ignored. The challenge of producing good evaluation studies that are actually used is enormous. In many ways the odds are all against utilization, and it is quite possible to become skeptical about the futility of trying to have impact in a world where situation after situation seems impervious to change. Active-reactive-adaptive evaluators may be told that they are wasting their time. A final Sufi story perhaps provides a reply to skeptics.

> Yogurt is made by adding a small quantity of old yogurt to a larger measure of milk. The action of the bacillus bulgaricus in the seeding portion of yogurt will in time convert the whole into a mass of new yogurt.
> One day some friends saw Nasrudin down on his knees beside a pond. He was adding a little yogurt to the water. One of the men said, "what are you trying to do, Nasrudin?"
> "I am trying to make yogurt."
> "But you can't make yogurt in that way!"
> "Yes, I know; but just *supposing* it takes!" (Shah, 1964: 90).

The effort involved in being active, reactive, and adaptive is considerable. Utilization-focused evaluation may, indeed, be a long shot, but the potential payoff is worth the risk. At stake is improving the effectiveness of human services programs that express and embody the highest ideals of humankind. Utilization-focused evaluation may, indeed, be a long shot, "but just supposing it works!"

REFERENCES

Ackerman, Bruce A. 1977. "Illusions About New Cars, Clean Air." Minneapolis *Tribune* (August 29):4A.

Adelson, Marvin, Marvin Alkin, Charles Carey and Olaf Helmer. 1967. "Planning Education for the Future." *American Behavioral Scientist* 10, 7 (March): 1-29.

Agarwala-Rogers, Rehka. 1977. "Why is Evaluation Research Not Utilized?" pp. 327-333 in Marcia Guttentag (ed.), *Evaluation Studies, Review Annual, Volume 2*. Beverly Hills, Cal.: Sage.

Alkin, Marvin C. 1975a. "Evaluation: Who Needs It? Who Cares?" *Studies in Educational Evaluation* 1, 3 (Winter): 201-212.

——— 1975b. "Framing the Decision Context." *AERA Cassette Series in Evaluation*. Washington, D.C.: American Educational Research Association.

——— 1972. "Wider Context Goals and Goal-Based Evaluators." *Evaluation Comment: The Journal of Educational Evaluation* (Center for the Study of Evaluation, UCLA) 3, 4 (December): 10-11.

——— 1970. "A Review of the Evaluation of the Follow Through Program." An individual report written as a member of the USOE Review Team, May 14-15, 1970, Washington, D.C. Center for the Study of Evaluation, Working Paper No. 10. Los Angeles: Center for the Study of Evaluation, UCLA.

Alkin, Marvin C., Jacqueline Kosecoff, Carol Fitz Gibbon and Richard Seligman. 1974. *Evaluation and Decision-Making: The Title VII Experience*. Los Angeles: Center for the Study of Evaluation, UCLA.

Allison, Graham T. 1971. *Essence of Decision: Explaining the Cuban Missile Crisis*. Boston: Little-Brown.

American Institutes for Research. 1970. *Evaluative Research Strategies and Methods*. Pittsburgh: American Institutes for Research.

Anastasi, Anne. 1973. "Preface." *Assessment in a Pluralistic Society*. Proceedings of the 1972 Invitational Conference on Testing Problems. Princeton, N.J.: Educational Testing Service.

Anderson, Gary and Herbert Walberg. 1968. "Classroom Climate and Group Learning." *International Journal of the Educational Sciences* (September): 175-180.

Anderson, Richard B. 1977. "The Effectiveness of Follow Through: What Have We Learned?" Paper presented at the Annual Meeting of the American Educational Research Association at New York, April 5.

Anderson, Scarvia B., Samuel Bell, Richard T. Murphy, and Associates, 1976. *Encyclopedia of Educational Evaluation*. San Francisco: Jossey-Bass.

Archibald, Kathleen. 1970. "Alternative Orientations to Social Science Utilization." *Social Science Information* 9, 2: 7-34.

Asai, Kiyoji, Hideo Tanaka, and Tetsuji Okuda. 1975. "Decison-Making and Its Goal in a Fuzzy Environment," pp. 257-277 in Lofti A. Zadeh, King-Sun Fu, Kokichi Tanaka and Masamichi Shimura (eds.), *Fuzzy Sets and Their Applications to Cognitive and Decision Processes*. New York: Academic Press.

Azumi, Koya and Jerald Hage (eds.) 1972. *Organizational Systems*. Lexington, Mass.: D.C. Heath.

Baizerman, Michael. 1974. "Evaluation Research and Evaluation: Scientific Social Reform Movement and Ideology." *Journal of Sociology and Social Welfare* (Winter): 277-288.

Becker, Howard. 1970. "Whose Side Are We On?" pp. 15-26 in William J. Filstead (ed.) *Qualitative Methodology.* Chicago: Markham.

Becker, Selwyn W. and Duncan Neuhauser. 1975. *The Efficient Organization.* New York: Elsevier.

Bennett, Carl A. and Arthur A. Lumsdaine (eds.) 1975. *Evaluation and Experiment: Some Critical Issues in Assessing Social Programs.* New York: Academic Press.

Bennis, Warren G., Kenneth Benne, Robert Chen, and Kenneth Corey (eds.) 1976. *The Planning of Change.* New York: Holt, Rinehart and Winston.

Bernstein, Ilene and Howard E. Freeman. 1975. *Academic and Entrepreneurial Research: Consequences of Diversity in Federal Evaluation Studies.* New York: Russell Sage.

Blalock, Jr., Hubert M. 1964. *Causal Inferences in Nonexperimental Research.* Chapel Hill, N.C.: University of North Carolina Press.

Blau, Peter. 1967. "Formal Organizations: Dimensions of Analysis," pp. 336-350 in Walter A. Hill and Douglas Egan (eds.), *Readings in Organizations: A Behavioral Approach.* Boston: Allyn and Bacon.

Blau, Peter and Otis D. Duncan. 1967. *The American Occupational Structure.* New York: John Wiley.

Blau, Peter and William R. Scott. 1962. *Formal Organizations.* San Francisco: Chandler.

Blumer, Herbert. 1969. *Symbolic Interactionism.* Englewood Cliffs, N.J.: Prentice-Hall.

Bracht, Glenn H. and Gene V. Glass 1968. "The External Validity of Experiments." *American Educational Research Journal* 5: 437-474.

Braybrooke, David and C. E. Lindblom. 1963. *A Strategy of Decision.* Glencoe, Ill.: Free Press.

Bruyn, Severyn. 1966. *The Human Perspective in Sociology: The Methodology of Participant Observation.* Englewood Cliffs, N.J.: Prentice-Hall.

——— 1963. "The Methodology of Participant Observation." *Human Organization* 21: 224-235.

Bunge, Mario. 1959. *Causality.* Cambridge, Mass.: Harvard University Press.

Burns, Tom and G. M. Stalker. 1961. *The Management of Innovations.* London: Tavistock.

Bussis, Anne, Edward A. Chittenden, and Marianne Amarel. 1973. "Methodology in Educational Evaluation and Research." Unpublished mimeograph. Princeton, N.J.: Educational Testing Service.

Campbell, Donald T. and Robert F. Boruch. 1975. "Making the Case for Randomized Assignment to Treatments by Considering the Alternatives: Six Ways in Which Quasi-Experimental Evaluations in Compensatory Education Tend to Underestimate Effects," pp. 195-296 in Carol A. Bennett and Arthur A. Lumsdaine (eds.), *Evaluation and Experiment.* New York: Academic Press.

Campbell, Donald T. and Julian C. Stanley. 1963. *Experimental and Quasi-Experimental Designs for Research.* Chicago: Rand McNally.

Caplan, Nathan. 1977. "A Minimal Set of Conditions Necessary for the Utilization of Social Science Knowledge in Policy Formulation at the National Level," pp. 183-198 in Carol H. Weiss (ed.), *Using Social Research in Public Policy Making.* Lexington, Mass.: Lexington Books/D.C. Heath.

Caplan, Nathan, Andrea Morrison and Russell J. Stambough. 1975. "The Use of Social Science Knowledge in Policy Decisions at the National Level." Ann Arbor, Mich.: Center for Research on Utilization of Scientific Knowledge, Institute for Social Research, University of Michigan.

Carini, Patricia F. 1975. *Observation and Description: An Alternative Methodology for the Investigation of Human Phenomena.* North Dakota Study Group on Evaluation monograph series. Grand Forks, N.D.: University of North Dakota.

Caro, Francis G. (ed.) 1971. *Readings in Evaluation Research.* New York: Russell Sage.

Champion, Dean J. 1975. *The Sociology of Organizations.* New York: McGraw-Hill.

Chang, C. L. 1976. "Interpretation and Execution of Fuzzy Programs," pp. 191-218 in Lofti A. Zadeh, King-Sun Fu, Kokichi Tanaka and Masamichi Shimura (eds.), *Fuzzy Sets and Their Applications to Cognitive and Decision Processes.* New York: Academic Press.

Cherney, Paul R. (ed.) 1971. *Making Evaluation Research Useful.* Columbia, Md: American City Corporation.

Cicarelli, Victor. 1971. "The Impact of Head Start: Executive Summary," pp. 397-401 in Francis G. Caro (ed.), *Readings in Evaluation Research.* New York: Russell Sage.

Cohen, David K. 1970. "Politics and Research: Evaluation of Social Action Programs in Education." *Educational Evaluation.* American Educational Research Association, *Review of Educational Research* (April): 213-238.

Cohen, David K. and Michael S. Garet. 1975. "Reforming Educational Policy with Applied Social Research." *Harvard Educational Review* 45 (February): 17-41.

Cohen, David K. and Janet A. Weiss. 1977. "Social Science and Social Policy: Schools and Race," pp. 67-84 in Carol H. Weiss (ed.), *Using Social Research in Public Policy Making.* Lexington, Mass.: Lexington Books/D.C. Heath.

Coleman, James C. 1972. "Policy Research in the Social Sciences." Morristown, N.J.: General Learning Press.

Coleman, James F. 1977. "Response to Professors Pettigrew and Green," pp. 417-424 in Marcia Guttentag (ed.), *Evaluation Studies, Annual Review, Volume 2.* Beverly Hills, Cal.: Sage.

Corwin, Ronald G. 1973. *Reform and Organizational Survival.* New York: Wiley-Inter-science.

Coser, Lewis. 1964. *The Functions of Social Conflict.* Glencoe, Ill.: Free Press.

Cronbach, Lee. 1966. "The Logic of Experiments on Discovery," pp. 77-92 in Less S. Shulman and Evan R. Keislar (eds.), *Learning by Discovery.* Chicago: Rand McNally.

——— 1964. "Evaluation for Course Improvement," pp. 231-248 in R. Heath (ed.), *New Curricula.* New York: Harper and Row.

Crozier, Michel. 1964. *The Bureaucratic Phenomenon.* Chicago: University of Chicago Press.

Cyert, Richard and James G. March. 1963. *A Behavioral Theory of the Firm.* Englewood Cliffs, N.J.: Prentice-Hall.

Dahl, Robert. 1957. "The Concept of Power." *Behavioral Science* II (July): 201-215.

Dalkey, N. C. 1969. *The Delphi Method: An Experimental Study of Group Opinion.* Santa Monica, Cal. Rand Corporation.

Datta, Lois-Ellen. 1977. "Does It Work When It Has Been Tried? And Half Full or Half Empty?" pp. 301-319 in Marcia Guttentag (ed.), *Evaluation Studies, Annual Review, Volume 2.* Beverly Hills, Cal.: Sage.

Davis, Howard R. and Susan E. Salasin. 1975. "The Utilization of Evaluation," pp. 621-666 in Elmer L. Struening and Marcia Guttentag (eds.), *Handbook of Evaluation Research, Volume I.* Beverly Hills, Cal.: Sage.

Deitchman, Seymour. 1976. *The Best-Laid Schemes: A Tale of Social Research and Bureaucracy.* Cambridge, Mass.: MIT Press.

Deutscher, Irwin. 1970. "Words and Deeds: Social Science and Social Policy," pp. 27-51 in William J. Filstead (ed.), *Qualitative Methodology.* Chicago: Markham.

Devaney, Kathleen. 1977. "Surveying Teachers' Centers." *Teachers' Centers Exchange,* Occasional Paper No. 1, National Institute of Education (April): 7.

Dewey, John. 1956a. *The Child and the Curriculum.* Chicago: University of Chicago Press.

——— 1956b. *The School and Society.* Chicago: University of Chicago Press.

deWilde, John C. 1967. *Experiences with agricultural Development in Tropical Africa, Volumes I and II.* Baltimore: Johns Hopkins University Press.

Dornbush, Sanford and Richard Scott. 1975. *Evaluation and the Exercise of Authority.* San Francisco: Jossey-Bass.

Dunagin, Ralph. 1977. *Dunagin's People.* Sentinel Star, Field Newspaper Syndicate (August 30).

Dunkel, Harold B. 1972. "Wanted: New Paradigms and a Normative Base for Research," pp. 77-93 in Lawrence G. Thomas (ed.), *Philosophical Redirection of Educational Research: The Seventy-First Yearbook of the National Society for the Study of Education.* Chicago: University of Chicago Press.

Edwards, Ward and Marcia Guttentag. 1975. "Experiments and Evaluations: A Re-examination," pp. 409-463 in Carl Bennett and Arthur Lumsdaine (eds.), *Evaluation and Experiment: Some Critical Issues in Assessing Social Programs.* New York: Academic Press.

Edwards, Ward, Marcia Guttentag and Kurt Snapper. 1975. "A Decision-Theoretic Approach to Evaluation Research," pp. 139-182 in Elmer L. Struening and Marcia Guttentag (eds.), *Handbook of Evaluation Research, Volume 1.* Beverly Hills, Cal.: Sage.

Eidell, Terry L. and Joanne M. Kitchel (eds.) 1968. *Knowledge Production and Utilization in Educational Administration.* University Council for Educational Administration (Columbus, Ohio) and Center for the Advanced Study of Educational Administration (Eugene, Oregon) Career Development Seminar, October, 1967. Eugene, Oregon: University of Oregon Press.

Eisenstadt, S. N. 1966. *Modernization: Protest and Change.* Englewood Cliffs, N. J.: Prentice-Hall.

Elmore, Richard F. 1976. "Follow Through Planned Variation," pp. 101-123 in Walter Williams and Richard Elmore (eds.), *Social Program Implementation.* New York: Academic Press.

Emery, F. W. and E. L. Trist. 1965. "The Causal Texture of Organizational Environment." *Human Relations,* 18 (February): 21-31.

Engstrom, George A. "Research Utilization: The Challenge of Applying SRS Research." *Welfare in Review* 8, 5 (September/October): 1-7.

Etzioni, Amitai. 1968. *The Active Society: A Theory of Societal and Political Processes.* New York: Free Press.

———— 1964. *Modern Organizations.* Englewood Cliffs, N.J.: Prentice-Hall.

———— 1961. *A Comparative Analysis of Complex Organizations.* New York: Free Press.

Etzioni, Amitai and Michael Patton. 1976. "Update on Policy Research." Videotape interview with Michael Patton, April 22, 1976. Minneapolis, Minn.: Program Evaluation Resource Center.

Evans, John W. 1971. "Head Start: Comments on Criticisms," pp. 401-407 in Francis G. Caro (ed.), *Readings in Evaluation Research.* New York: Russell Sage.

Fairweather, George W. 1967. *Methods for Experimental Social Innovation.* New York: John Wiley.

Feiman, Sharon. 1977. "Evaluating Teacher Centers." *Social Review* 8 (May): 395-411.

———— 1975. *Teacher Curriculum Work Center: A Descriptive Study.* North Dakota Study Group on Evaluation monograph. Grand Forks, North Dakota: University of North Dakota.

Filstead, William J. (ed.) 1970. *Qualitative Methodology.* Chicago: Markham.

Freeman, Howard E. 1977. "The Present Status of Evaluation Research," pp. 17-51 in Marcia Guttentag (ed.), *Evaluation Studies: Review Annual, Volume 2.* Beverly Hills, California: Sage.

Gardiner, Peter C. and Ward Edwards. 1975. "Public Values: Multi-attribute-Utility Measurement for Social Decision Making," pp. 1-38 in Martin F. Kaplan and Steven Schwartz (eds.), *Human Judgment and Decision Processes.* New York: Academic Press.

GCCPC (Governor's Commission on Crime Prevention and Control). 1976. "Residential Community Corrections Programs in Minnesota: An Evaluation Report." Saint Paul, Minn.: State of Minnesota.

Glaser, Edward M. 1967. "Utilization of Applicable Research and Demonstration Results." Final Report to Vocational Rehabilitation Administration, HEW. Los Angeles: Human Interaction Research Institute.

Glaser, Edward M. and Samuel H. Taylor. 1969. "Factors Influencing the Success of Applied Research: A Study of Ten NIMH Funded Projects." Los Angeles: Human Interaction Research Institute.

Glass, Gene V. (ed.). 1976. *Evaluation Studies: Review Annual, Volume 1.* Beverly Hills, Cal.: Sage.

Gouldner, Alvin. 1970. *The Coming Crisis of Western Sociology.* New York: Basic Books.

Gross, B. M. 1969. "The Definition of Organizational Goals." *British Journal of Sociology* 20: 227-297.

Guba, Egon G. 1977. "Overcoming Resistance to Evaluation." Paper presented at the Second Annual Conference on Evaluation, University of North Dakota, Bismarck, N.D. (November 2).

——— 1968. "Development, Diffusion and Evaluation," pp. 37-63 in Terry L. Eidell and Joanne M. Kitchel (eds.), *Knowledge Production and Utilization in Educational Adminis- tration.* University Council for Educational Administration (Columbus, Ohio) and Center for the Advanced Study of Educational Administration (Eugene, Oregon) Career Development Seminar, October, 1967. Eugene, Oregon: University of Oregon Press.

Guttentag, Marcia and Elmer L. Struening. 1975a. *Handbook of Evaluation Research, Volumes 1 and 2.* Beverly Hills, Cal.: Sage.

——— 1975b. "The Handbook: Its Purpose and Organization," pp. 3-10 in Marcia Guttentag and Elmer L. Struening (eds.), *Handbook of Evaluation Research, Volume 2.* Beverly Hills, Cal.: Sage.

Hage, Jerald. 1977. "Generalizing Particularities and Particularizing Generalities: Tech- niques for Constructing Multi-variate Hypotheses." Paper presented at the 72nd Annual Meeting of the American Sociological Association, Chicago, Illinois.

——— 1972. *Techniques and Problems of Theory Construction in Sociology.* New York: Wiley-Interscience.

——— 1965. "An Axiomatic Theory of Organizations." *Administrative Science Quarterly* 10 (December): 289-321.

Hage, Jerald and Michael Aiken. 1970. *Social Change in Complex Organizations.* New York: Random House.

——— 1969. "Routine, Technology, Social Structure, and Organizational Goals." *Adminis- trative Science Quarterly* 12: 72-92.

Halpert, Harold P. 1969. "Communications as a Basic Tool in Promoting Utilization of Research Findings," pp. 203-225 in Herbert C. Schulberg, Alan Sheldon, Frank Baker (eds.), *Program Evaluation in the Mental Health Fields.* New York: Behavioral Publica- tions.

Hammond, Kenneth R., Thomas R. Stewart, Berndt Brehmer, and Derick O. Steinmann. 1975. "Social-Judgment Theory," pp. 271-307 in Martin Kaplan and Steven Schwartz (eds.), *Human Judgment and Decision Processes.* New York: Academic Press.

Harvey, Leah and John Townsend, Co-Chairpersons, Saint Paul Open School Evaluation Task Force. 1976. *Evaluation of the Saint Paul Open School.* Saint Paul, Minn.: Saint Paul Open School.

Havelock, Ronald G. 1973. *The Change Agent's Guide to Innovation in Education.* Engle- wood Cliffs, N.J.: Educational Technology Publications.

——— 1968. "Dissemination and Translation Roles," pp. 64-119 in Terry L. Eidell and

Joanne M. Kitchel (eds.), *Knowledge Production and Utilization in Educational Adminis-tration (Columbus, Ohio) and Center for the Advanced Study of Educational Administra-tion (Eugene, Oregon) Career Development Seminar, October, 1967.* Eugene, Oregon: *University of Oregon Press.*

Hayman, John L., Jr. and Rodney N. Napier. 1975. Evaluation in the Schools: A Human *Renewal Process.* Monterey, Cal.: Brooks/Cole.

Helmer, Olaf. 1966. *Social Technology.* New York: Basic Books.

Hirschman, Albert O. and Charles E. Lindblom. 1962. "Economic Development, Research and Development, Policy Making: Some Converging Views." *Behavioral Sciences* 7: 211-222.

Hoffman, Yoel. 1975. *The Sound of One Hand.* New York: Basic Books.

Homans, George. 1949. "The Strategy of Industrial Sociology." *American Journal of Sociology* 54: 330-337.

House, Ernest. 1974. *The Politics of Educational Innovation.* Berkeley, Cal.: McCutchan.

———— (ed.) 1973. *School Evaluation: The Politics and Process.* Berkeley, Cal.: McCutchan.

———— 1972. "The Conscience of Educational Evaluation." *Teachers College Record* 73, 3: 405-414.

Jain, Nemi C. 1970. "Communication Patterns and Effectiveness of Linkers in a Formal Organization." Paper presented at the Speech Communication Association Convention, New Orleans, Louisiana (December 27-30).

Kagan, Jerome. 1966. "Learning, Attention and the Issue of Discovery," pp. 151-161 in Lee S. Shulman and Evan R. Keislar (eds.), *Learning by Discovery: A Critical Appraisal.* Chicago: Rand McNally.

Kirk, Stuart A. 1977. "Understanding the Utilization of Reserach in Social Work and Other Applied Professions." University of Wisconsin-Milwaukee. Paper presented at the Conference on Reserach Utilization in Social Work Education, New Orleans, Louisiana (October).

Kneller, George F. 1972. "Goal-Free Evaluation." *Evaluation Comment: The Journal of Educational Evaluation* (Center for the Study of Evaluation, UCLA) 3, 4 (December): 13-15.

Kochen, Manfred. 1975. "Applications of Fuzzy Sets in Psychology," pp. 395-407 in Lofti A. Zadeh, King-Sun Fu, Kokichi Tanaka and Masamichi Shimura (eds.), *Fuzzy Sets and Their Applications to Cognitive and Decision Processes.* New York: Academic Press.

Kourilsky, Marilyn. 1974. "An Adversary Model for Educational Evaluation." *Evaluation Comment* 4, 2.

Kuhn, Thomas. 1970. *The Structure of Scientific Revolutions.* Chicago: University of Chicago Press.

Lawrence, Paul R. and Jay W. Lorsch. 1972. "Differentiation and Integration in Complex Organizations," pp. 334-358 in Koya Azumi and Jerald Hage (eds.), *Organizational Systems.* Lexington, Mass.: D. C. Heath.

———— 1967. *Organization and Environment.* Boston: Graduate School of Business Adminis-tration, Harvard University.

Lazarsfeld, Paul F. and Jeffrey G. Reitz. 1975. *An Introduction to Applied Sociology.* New York: Elsevier.

Levine, Adeline and Murray Levine. 1977. "The Social Context of Evaluative Research." *Evaluation Quarterly* 1, 4 (November): 515-542.

Levine, Murray. 1974. "Scientific Method and the Adversary." *American Psychologist* (September): 666-677.

———— 1965. *The Intelligence of Democracy.* New York: Free Press.

Lindbolm, Charles E. 1965. *The Intelligence of Democracy.* New York: Free Press.
——— 1959. "The Science of Muddling Through." *Public Administration Review* 19: 79-99.
Lofland, John. 1971. *Analyzing Social Settings.* Belmont, Cal.: Wadsworth.
Lynne, Jr., Lawrence E. and Susan Salasin. 1974. "Human Services: Should We, Can We Make Them Available to Everyone?" *Evaluation* (Spring Special Issue): 4-5.
MacRae, Jr., Duncan. 1976. *The Social Function of Social Science.* New Haven, Conn.: Yale University Press.
Mann, Floyd C. and F. W. Neff. 1961. *Managing Major Change in Organizations.* Ann Arbor, Mich.: Foundation for Research on Human Behavior.
March, James G. (ed.) 1965. *Handbook of Organizations.* Chicago: Rand McNally.
March, James G. and Herbert Simon. 1958. *Organizations.* New York: John Wiley.
Maurer, John (ed.) 1971. *Open-System Approaches in Organizational Theory.* New York: Random House.
Mayntz, Renate. 1977. "Sociology, Value Freedom, and the Problems of Political Counseling," pp. 55-66 in Carol H. Weiss (ed.), *Using Social Research in Public Policy Making.* Lexington, Mass.: Lexington Books/D.C. Heath.
McIntyre, Ken. 1976. "Evaluating Educational Programs." *Review,* The University Council for Educational Administration 18, 1 (September): 39.
McLaughlin, Milbrey. 1976. "Implementation as Mutual Adaptation," pp. 167-180 in Walter Williams and Richard F. Elmore (eds.), *Social Program Implementation.* New York: Academic Press.
McTavish, Donald, E. Brent, J. Cleary, and K. R. Knudsen. 1975. "The Systematic Assessment and Prediction of Research Methodology, Volume 1, Advisory Report." Final Report on Grant OEO 005-P-20-2-74, Minnesota Continuing Program for the Assessment and Improvement of Research. Minneapolis, Minn.: University of Minnesota, Sociology.
Merton, Robert K. 1957. *Social Theory and Social Structure.* Glencoe, Ill.: Free Press.
Mills, C. Wright. 1959. *The Sociological Imagination.* New York: Oxford University Press.
Moos, Rudolf. 1975. *Evaluating Correctional and Community Settings.* New York: Wiley-Interscience.
——— 1974. *Evaluating Treatment Environments.* New York: Wiley-Interscience.
Murphy, Jerome T. 1976. "Title V of ESEA: The Impact of Discretionary Funds on State Education Bureaucracies," pp. 77-100 in Walter Williams and Richard Elmore (eds.), *Social Program Implementation.* New York: Academic Press.
Mushkin, S. 1973. "Evaluations: Use With Caution." *Evaluation* 1, 2: 31-35.
Nagel, Ernest. 1961. *The Structure of Science.* New York: Harcourt, Brace, and World.
National Academy of Sciences. 1968. *The Behavioral Sciences and the Federal Government.* Washington, D.C.: U.S. Government Printing Office.
Nunnally, Jr., Jim C. 1970. *Introduction to Psychological Measurement.* New York: McGraw-Hill.
NWREL (Northwest Regional Educational Laboratory). 1977. *3-on-2 Evaluation Report, 1976-1977, Volumes I, II and III.* Portland, Ore.: NWREL.
Office of Program Analysis, General Accounting Office. 1976. *Federal Program Evaluations: A Directory for the Congress.* Washington, D.C.: U.S. Government Printing Office.
Owens, Thomas. 1973. "Education Evaluation by Adversary Proceeding," in Ernest R. House (ed.), *School Evaluation: The Politics and Process.* Berkeley, CAl.: McCutchan.
Parlett, Malcolm and David Hamilton. 1976. "Evaluation as Illumination: A New Approach to the Study of Innovatory Programs," pp. 140-157 in Gene V. Glass (ed.), *Evaluation Studies: Review Annual, Volume 1.* Beverly Hills, Cal.: Sage.

———— 1972. "Evaluation as Illumination: A New Approach to the Study of Innovatory Programs." Occasional Paper No. 9, Center for Research in the Educational Sciences University of Edinburgh.

Parsons, Talcott. 1960. *Structure and Process in Modern Society.* Glencoe, Ill.: Free Press.

Patton, Michael Q. 1975a. *Alternative Evaluation Research Paradigm.* North Dakota Study Group on Evaluation Monograph Series. Grand Forks, North Dakota: University of North Dakota.

———— 1975b. "Understanding the Gobble-dy-gook: A People's Guide to Standardized Test Results and Statistics." *Testing and Evaluation: New Views.* Washington, D.C.: Association for Childhood Education International.

———— 1973. *Structure and Diffusion of Open Education.* Report on the Trainers of Teacher Trainer Program, New School of Behavioral Studies in Education, Grand Forks, N.D.: University of North Dakota.

Patton, Michael Q., Patricia S. Grimes, Kathryn M. Guthrie, Nancy J. Brennan, Barbard D. French, and Dale A. Blyth. 1977. "In Search of Impact: An Analysis of the Utilization of Federal Health Evaluation Research," pp. 141-164 in Carol Weiss (ed.), *Using Social Research in Public Policy Making.* Lexington, Mass.: Lexington Books/D.C. Heath.

Patton, Michael Q., Kathy Guthrie, Steven Gray, Carl Hearle, Rich Wiseman, and Neala Yount. 1977. *Environments That Make a Difference: An Evaluation of Ramsey County Corrections Foster Group Homes.* Minneapolis, Minn.: Minnesota Center for Social Research, University of Minnesota.

Pederson, Clara A. (ed.) 1977. *Informal Education: Evaluation and Record Keeping.* Grand Forks, N.D.: Center for Teaching and Learning, University of North Dakota.

Perrone, Vito. 1977. *The Abuses of Standardized Testing.* Bloomington, Ind.: Phi Delta Kappa Educational Foundation.

Perrone, Vito, Michael Q. Patton and Barbara French. 1976. *Does Accountability Count Without Teacher Support?* Minneapolis, Minn.: Minnesota Center for Social Research, University of Minnesota.

Perrow, Charles. 1970. *Organizational Analysis: A Sociological View.* Belmont, Cal.: Wadsworth.

———— 1968. "Organizational Goals," pp. 305-311 in *International Encyclopedia of Social Sciences.* New York: Macmillan.

———— 1961. "The Analysis of Goals in Complex Organizations." *American Sociological Review* 6 (December): 854-866.

Petrie, Hugh G. 1972. "Theories Are Tested By Observing the Facts: Or Are They?" pp. 47-73 in Lawrence G. Thomas (ed.), *Philosophical Redirection of Educational Research: The Seventy-First Yearbook of the National Society for the Study of Education.* Chicago: University of Chicago Press.

Pettigrew, Thomas F. and Robert L. Green. 1977. "School Desegregation in Large Cities: A Critique of the Coleman 'White Flight' Thesis," pp. 363-416 in Marcia Guttentag (ed.) *Evaluation Studies, Annual Review, Volume 2.* Beverly Hills, Cal.: Sage.

Popham, James W. 1972. "Results Rather Than Rhetoric." *Evaluation Comment: The Journal of Educational Evaluation* (Center for the Study of Evaluation, UCLA) 3, 4 (December): 12-13.

———— 1969. *Instructional Objectives.* Chicago: Rand McNally.

Popham, James W. and Dale Carlson. 1977. "Deep Dark Deficits of the Adversary Evaluation Model." *Educational Researcher* (June): 3-6.

Price, James. 1967. *Organizational Effectiveness.* Homewood, Ill.: Irwin.

Provus, Malcolm. 1971. *Discrepancy Evaluation for Educational Program Improvement and Assessment.* Berkeley, Cal.: McCutchan.

Raskin, A. H. 1977. "Major Impact of the New Consumer Price Index." New York Times Service. Minneapolis *Tribune* (July 21): 11A.

Reicken, Henry W. and Robert F. Boruch. 1974. *Social Experimentation: A Method for Planning and Evaluating Social Intervention.* New York: Academic Press.

Rogers, Everett. 1962. *Diffusion of Innovations.* New York: Free Press.

Rogers, Everett M. and Lynne Svenning. 1969. *Managing Change.* San Mateo, Cal.: Operation PEP.

Rogers, Everett M. with Floyd F. Shoemaker. 1971. *Communication of Innovations.* New York: Free Press.

Rosen, David. 1973. "New Evaluation for New Schools." *Changing Schools: Special Issue on Evaluation for Alternative Schools.* Bloomington, Ind.: National Consortium for Options in Public Education.

Rosenthal, Elsa J. 1976. "Delphi Technique," pp. 121-122 in S. Anderson, S. Ball, R. T. Murphy and Associates (eds.), *Encyclopedia of Educational Evaluation.* San Francisco: Jossey-Bass.

Rosenthal, Elsa J. and Ann Z. Smith. 1976. "Goals and Objectives," pp. 179-184 in Scarvia B. Anderson, Samuel Ball, Richard T. Murphy and Associates, *Encyclopedia of Educational Evaluation.* San Francisco: Jossey-Bass.

Rossi, Peter H. 1972. "Testing for Success and Failure in Social Action," pp. 11-65 in Peter H. Rossi and Walter Williams (eds.), *Evaluating Social Programs.* New York: Seminar Press.

Rossi, Peter H. and Walter Williams (eds.). 1972. *Evaluating Social Programs: Theory, Practice, and Politics.* New York: Seminar Press.

Rutman, Leonard. 1977. "Barriers to the Utilization of Evaluation Research." Panel presentation at the 27th Annual Meeting of the Society for the Study of Social Problems, Chicago, 4 September.

——— 1976. *Planning an Evaluation Study.* Evaluation Research Training Institute monograph. Ottawa, Canada: Centre for Social Welfare Studies, Carleton University.

Salasin, Susan (ed.). 1974. "The Human Services Shortfall." Special Issue of *Evaluation: A Forum for Human Service Decision-Makers* (Spring). Minneapolis, Minn.: Minneapolis Medical Research Foundation.

Sax, Gilbert. 1974. "The Use of Standardized Tests in Evaluation," pp. 243-307 in W. James Popham (ed.), *Evaluation in Education: Current Applications.* Berkeley, Cal.: McCutchan.

Scriven, Michael. 1972a. "Objectivity and Subjectivity in Educational Research," pp. 94-142 in Lawrence G. Thomas (ed.), Philosophical Redirection of Educational Research: The *Seventy-First Yearbook of the National Society for the Study of Education.* Chicago: University of Chicago Press.

——— 1972b. "Prose and Cons About Goal-Free Evaluation," *Evaluation Comment: The Journal of Educational Evaluation* (Center for the Study of Evaluation, UCLA) 3, 4 (December): 1-7.

——— 1967. "The Methodology of Evaluation," pp. 39-83 in Ralph W. Tyler, Robert M. Gagne, and Michael Scriven (eds.), *Perspectives of Curriculum Evaluation.* AERA Monograph Series on Curriculum Evaluation, No. 1. Chicago: Rand McNally.

Scriven, Michael and Michael Patton. 1976. "A Perspective on Evaluation." Videotape interview. Minneapolis, Minn.: Program Evaluation Resource Center.

Shackle, G.L.S. 1961. *Decision, Order, and Time in Human Affairs.* Cambridge, Mass.: Harvard University Press.

Shah, I. 1964. *The Sufis.* New York: Doubleday.

Shapiro, Edna. 1973. "Educational Evaluation: Rethinking the Criteria of Competence." *School Review* (November): 523-549.

Sharpe, L. J. 1977. "The Social Scientist and Policymaking: Some Cautionary Thoughts and Transatlantic Reflections," pp. 37-54 in Carol Weiss (ed.), *Using Social Research In Public Policy Making.* Lexington, Mass.: Lexington Books/D.C. Heath.

Silberman, Charles E. 1970. *Crisis in the Classroom: The Remaking of American Education.* New York: Random House.

Silverman, David. 1971. *The Theory of Organizations.* New York: Basic Books.

Simon, Herbert A. 1957. *Administrative Behavior.* New York: Macmillan.

Sjoberg, Gideon. 1975. "Politics, Ethics and Evaluation Research," pp. 29-51 in Marcia Guttentag and Elmer L. Struening (eds.), *Handbook of Evaluation Research, Volume 2.* Beverly Hills, Cal.: Sage.

Sjoberg, Gideon and R. Nett. 1968. *A Methodology for Social Research.* New York: Harper and Row.

Skager, Rodney, 1971. "The System for Objectives-Based Evaluation." *Evaluation Comment: The Journal of Educational Evaluation* (Center for the Study of Evaluation, UCLA) 3, 1 (September): 6-11.

Smelser, Neil. 1959. *Social Change in the Industrial Revolution.* Chicago: University of Chicago Press.

Social Science Research Council, National Academy of Sciences. 1969. *The Behavioral and Social Sciences: Outlook and Need.* Englewood Cliffs, N.J.: Prentice-Hall.

Special Commission on the Social Sciences, National Science Foundation. 1968. *Knowledge Into Action: Improving the Nation's Use of the Social Sciences.* Washington, D.C.: U.S. Government Printing Office.

Stake, Robert E. 1975. *Evaluating the Arts in Education: A Responsive Approach.* Columbus, Ohio: Charles E. Merrill.

——— 1973. "Evaluation Design, Instrumentation, Data Collection, and Analysis of Data." pp. 303-316 in Blaine R. Worthen and James R. Sanders (eds.), *Educational Evaluation: Theory and Practice.* Worthington, Ohio: Charles A. Jones.

——— 1967. "The Countenance of Educational Evaluation." *Teachers College Record* 68 (April): 523-540.

Statewide Study of Education. 1967. *Educational Development for North Dakota, 1967-1975.* Grand Forks, N.D.: University of North Dakota.

Stephens, John. 1967. *The Process of Schooling.* New York: Holt, Rinehart, and Winston.

Stinchcombe, Arthur. 1965. "Social Structure and Organizations," pp. 142-193 in James G. March (ed.), *Handbook of Organizations.* Chicago: Rand McNally.

Stolurow, Lawrence M. 1965. "Model the Master Teacher or Master the Teaching Model," pp. 223-247 in John D. Krumboltz (ed.), *Learning and the Educational Process.* Chicago: Rand McNally.

Strike, Kenneth. 1972. "Explaining and Understanding: The Impact of Science on Our Concept of Man," pp. 26-46 in Lawrence G. Thomas (ed.), *Philosophical Redirection of Educational Research: The Seventy-First Yearbook of the National Society for the Study of Education.* Chicago: University of Chicago Press.

Stufflebeam, Daniel L. 1972. "Should or Can Evaluation Be Goal-Free?" *Evaluation Com-*

ment: The Journal of Educational Evaluation (Center for the Study of Evaluation, UCLA) 3, 4 (December): 7-9.

Stufflebeam, Daniel L. and Egon Guba. 1970. "Strategies for the Institutionalization of the CIPP Evaluation Model." An address delivered at the Eleventh Annual PDK Symposium on Education Research, Columbus, Ohio (June 24).

Stufflebeam, Daniel L., W. J. Foley, W. J. Gephart, E. G. Guba, L. R. Hammond, H. O. Merriman, and M. M. Provus. 1971. *Educational Evaluation and Decision-Making in Education.* Itasca, Ill.: F. E. Peacock.

Suchman, Edward A. 1972. "Action for What? A Critique of Evaluative Research," pp. 42-84 in Carol H. Weiss (ed.), *Evaluating Action Programs.* Boston: Allyn and Bacon.

——— 1967. *Evaluative Research: Principles and Practice in Public Service and Social Action Programs.* New York: Russell Sage.

Taylor, Donald W. 1965. "Decision Making and Problem Solving," pp. 48-86 in James G. March (ed.), *Handbook of Organizations.* Chicago: Rand McNally.

Terreberry, Shirley. 1971. "The Evaluation of Organizational Environments," pp. 58-73 in John G. Maurer (ed.), *Open-System Approaches in Organization Theory.* New York: Random House. Reprinted from *Administrative Science Quarterly* 12, 4 (March, 1968): 590-613.

Thomas, Jo. 1977. "Consultant Costs Concern Carter, Congress." New York Times Service. Minneapolis *Tribune* (December 12): 17A.

Thompson, James D. 1967. *Organizations in Action.* New York: McGraw-Hill.

Thompson, Mark. 1975. *Evaluation for Decision in Social Programmes.* Lexington, Mass.: Lexington Books/D.C. Heath.

Tolman, E. and E. Brunswik. 1935. "The Organism and the Causal Texture of the Environment." *Psychological Review* 42: 43-47.

Tripodi, Tony, Phillip Fellin, and Irwin Epstein. 1971. *Social Program Evaluation: Guidelines for Health, Education, and Welfare Administration.* Itasca, Ill.: F. E. Peacock.

Tucker, Eugene. 1977. "The Follow Through Planned Variation Experiment: What is the Pay-Off? Paper presented at the Annual Meeting of the American Educational Research Association, April 5.

United States House of Representatives Committee on Government Operations, Research and Technical Programs Subcommittee. 1967. *The Use of Social Research in Federal Domestic Programs.* Washington, D.C.: U.S. Government Printing Office.

Ward, David, Gene Kassebaum and Daniel Wilner. 1971. *Prison Treatment and Parole Survival: An Empirical Assessment.* New York: John Wiley.

Weber, Max. 1947. *The Theory of Social and Economic Organization.* New York: Oxford University Press.

Weidman, Donald R., Pamela Horst, Grace Mr. Taher, and Joseph S. Wholey. 1973. "Design of an Evaluation System for NIMH." *Contract Report 962-7.* Washington, D.C.: The Urban Institute.

Weiss, Carol H. 1977. "Introduction," pp. 1-22 in Carol H. Weiss (ed.), *Using Social Research in Public Policy Making.* Lexington, Mass.: Lexington Books/D. C. Heath.

——— 1975. "Evaluation Research in the Political Context," pp. 13-26 in Marcia Guttentag and Elmer L. Struening (eds.), *Handbook of Evaluation Research, Volume 1.* Beverly Hills, Cal.: Sage.

——— (ed.) 1972a. *Evaluating Action Programs.* Boston: Allyn and Bacon.

——— 1972b. *Evaluation Research: Methods of Assessing Program Effectiveness.* Englewood Cliffs, N.J.: Prentice-Hall.

—— 1972c. "Evaluating Educational and Social Action Programs: A Treeful of Owls," pp. 3-27 in Carol H. Weiss (ed.), *Evaluating Action Programs*. Boston: Allyn and Bacon.

—— 1972d. "Utilization of Evaluation," pp. 318-326 in Carol H. Weiss (ed.), *Evaluating Action Programs*. Boston: Allyn and Bacon.

—— 1970. "The Politicization of Evaluation Research." *Journal of Social Issues* 26, 4: 57-68.

Westinghouse Learning Corporation. 1969. *The Impact of Head Start: An Evaluation of the Effects of Head Start on Children's Cognitive and Affective Development*. Bladensburg, Md.: Westinghouse Learning Corporation.

Wholey, Joseph S., John W. Scanlon, Hugh G. Duffy, James S. Fukumotu, and Leona M. Vogt. 1970. *Federal Evaluation Policy: Analyzing the Effects of Public Programs*. Washington, D.C.: The Urban Institute.

Williams, Jay. 1976. *Everyone Knows What a Dragon Looks Like*. New York: Four Winds Press.

Williams, Walter. 1976. "Implementation Analysis and Assessment," pp. 267-292 in Williams and Elmore (eds.), *Social Program Implementation*. New York: Academic Press.

Williams, Walter and John W. Evans. 1969. "The Politics of Evaluation: The Case of Head Start." *Annals of the American Academy of Political and Social Science* 385 (September): 118-132.

Williams, Walter and Richard F. Elmore. 1976. *Social Program Implementation*. New York: Academic Press.

Windle, Charles. n.d. "Factors in the Success of NIMH's Community Mental Health Centers Program Evaluation Studies." Unpublished mimeograph.

Wirth, Louis. 1949. "Preface," pp. x-xxii in Karl Mannheim, *Ideology and Utopia*. New York: Harcourt Brace Jovanovich.

Wolf, Robert L. 1975. "Trial by Jury: A New Evaluation Method." *Phi Delta Kappan* (November).

Worley, D. R. 1960. "Amount and Generality of Information-Seeking Behavior in Sequential Decision Making As Dependent on Level of Incentive," pp. 1-11 in D. W. Taylor (ed.), *Experiments on Decision Making*. Technical Report 6. New Haven, Conn.: Yale University, Dept. of Industrial Administration and Psychology.

Worthen, Blaine R. and James R. Sanders (eds.) 1973. *Educational Evaluation: Theory and Practice*. Worthington, Ohio: Charles A. Jones.

Zadeh, Lofti A. 1965. "Fuzzy Sets." *Inform and Control* 8: 338-353.

Zadeh, Lofti, King-sun Fu, Kokichi Tanaka and Masamichi Shimura (eds.) 1975. *Fuzzy Sets and Their Applications to Cognitive and Decision Processes*. New York: Academic Press.

ABOUT THE AUTHOR

MICHAEL QUINN PATTON is director of the Minnesota Center for Social Research and adjunct professor of the School of Public Affairs, both at the University of Minnesota, where he was named outstanding teacher of the year in 1976. He holds M.S. and Ph.D. degrees in sociology from the University of Wisconsin, and is the author of numerous articles, reports, and conference papers in the field of evaluation research. Dr. Patton has also served as an evaluation consultant to many educational and human services projects in the United States and abroad.